Frommer's

PORTABLE

Los Cabos
& Baja

3rd Edition

by Lynne Bairstow

Here's what critics say about Frommer's:

"Amazingly easy to use. Very portable, very complete."
—*Booklist*

"Detailed, accurate, and easy-to-read information for all price ranges."
—*Glamour Magazine*

Wiley Publishing, Inc.

Published by:

WILEY PUBLISHING, INC.
111 River St.
Hoboken, NJ 07030

ISBN: 0-7645-3820-9
ISSN: 1521-5059

Editor: Marie Morris
Production Editor: Bethany André
Photo Editor: Richard Fox
Cartographer: Roberta Stockwell
Production by Wiley Indianapolis Composition Services

For information on our other products and services or to obtain technical
support, please contact our Customer Care Department within the U.S. at
800-762-2974, outside the U.S. at 317-572-3993 or fax 317-572-4002.

Wiley also publishes its books in a variety of electronic formats. Some content that appears in print may not be available in electronic formats.

Manufactured in the United States of America

5   4   3

Contents

List of Maps

ACKNOWLEDGMENTS

Many thanks to all of the many people who helped me gather the information, tips, and treasures that have made their way into this book. I am especially grateful for the assistance of Claudia Velo, whose tireless work helped to ensure the information in this book is correct, and for her valuable ideas and contributions.

—*Lynne Bairstow*

ABOUT THE AUTHOR

For **Lynne Bairstow,** Mexico has become more home than her native United States. After living in Puerto Vallarta for most of the past 11 years, she's developed an appreciation and a true love of this country and its complex, colorful culture. Her travel articles on Mexico have appeared in the *New York Times,* the *San Francisco Chronicle,* the *Los Angeles Times, Frommer's Budget Travel* magazine, and *Alaska Airlines Magazine.* In 2000, Lynne was awarded the Pluma de Plata, a top honor granted by the Mexican government to foreign writers, for her work in the Frommer's guidebook to Puerto Vallarta.

AN INVITATION TO THE READER

In researching this book, we discovered many wonderful places—hotels, restaurants, shops, and more. We're sure you'll find others. Please tell us about them, so we can share the information with your fellow travelers in upcoming editions. If you were disappointed with a recommendation, we'd love to know that, too. Please write to:

Frommer's Portable Los Cabos & Baja, 3rd Edition
Wiley Publishing, Inc. • 111 River St. • Hoboken, NJ 07030

AN ADDITIONAL NOTE

Please be advised that travel information is subject to change at any time, and this is especially true of prices. We therefore suggest that you write or call ahead for confirmation when making your travel plans. The authors, editors, and publishers cannot be held responsible for the experiences of readers while traveling. Your safety is important to us, however, so we encourage you to stay alert and be aware of your surroundings. Keep a close eye on cameras, purses, and wallets, all favorite targets of thieves and pickpockets.

FROMMER'S STAR RATINGS, ICONS & ABBREVIATIONS

Every hotel, restaurant, and attraction listing in this guide has been ranked for quality, value, service, amenities, and special features using a **star-rating system.** In country, state, and regional guides, we also rate towns and regions to help you narrow down your choices and budget your time accordingly. Hotels and restaurants are rated on a scale of zero (recommended) to three stars (exceptional). Attractions, shopping, nightlife, towns, and regions are rated according to the following scale: zero stars (recommended), one star (highly recommended), two stars (very highly recommended), and three stars (must-see).

In addition to the star-rating system, we also use **seven feature icons** that point you to the great deals, in-the-know advice, and unique experiences that separate travelers from tourists. Throughout the book, look for:

Finds	Special finds—those places only insiders know about
Fun Fact	Fun facts—details that make travelers more informed and their trips more fun
Kids	Best bets for kids—advice for the whole family
Moments	Special moments—those experiences that memories are made of
Overrated	Places or experiences not worth your time or money
Tips	Insider tips—some great ways to save time and money
Value	Great values—where to get the best deals

The following abbreviations are used for credit cards:

AE American Express	DISC Discover	V Visa
DC Diners Club	MC MasterCard	

FROMMERS.COM

Now that you have the guidebook to a great trip, visit our website at **www.frommers.com** for travel information on more than 3,000 destinations. With features updated regularly, we give you instant access to the most current trip-planning information available. At Frommers.com, you'll also find the best prices on airfares, accommodations, and car rentals—and you can even book travel online through our travel booking partners. At Frommers.com, you'll also find the following:

- Online updates to our most popular guidebooks
- Vacation sweepstakes and contest giveaways
- Newsletter highlighting the hottest travel trends
- Online travel message boards with featured travel discussions

Planning Your Trip to Baja California

A little planning can make the difference between a good trip and a great trip. When should you go? What's the best way to get there? How much should you plan on spending? What festivals or special events will be taking place during your visit? What safety or health precautions are advised? I'll answer these and other questions for you in this chapter.

1 Baja California at a Glance

The Baja Peninsula is part of Mexico—and yet it is not. Attached to the mainland United States and separated from the rest of Mexico by the Sea of Cortez (also called the Gulf of California), the Baja peninsula is longer than Italy, stretching 1,410km (876 miles) from Mexico's northernmost city of Tijuana to Cabo San Lucas at its southern tip. Volcanic uplifting created the craggy desertscape you see today. Whole forests of cardón cactus, spiky Joshua trees, and spindly ocotillo bushes populate the raw, untamed landscape.

Culturally and geographically, Baja is set apart from mainland Mexico, and it remained isolated for many years. Now the state of Baja California del Sur has developed into a vacation haven that offers spectacular golf, fishing, diving, and whale-watching. Great sportfishing originally centered attention on Los Cabos, and it remains a lure today, although golf has overtaken it as the principle attraction. Once accessible only by water, Baja attracted a hearty community of cruisers, fishermen, divers, and adventurers starting in the late 1940s. By the early 1980s, the Mexican government realized the growth potential of Los Cabos and invested in new highways, airport facilities, golf courses, and modern marine facilities. Expanded air traffic and the opening of Transpeninsular Highway 1 in 1973 paved the way for the area's spectacular growth.

BAJA SUR   Of the peninsula's three regions, Baja Sur has attracted the most attention and travelers, and is increasingly known as a haven for golfers. Twin towns with distinct personalities sit at the tip of the peninsula: **Cabo San Lucas** and **San José del Cabo.** The two Cabos are the center of accommodations and activities.

The road that connects Cabo San Lucas and San José del Cabo is the centerpiece of resort growth. Known as **the Corridor,** this stretch of four well-paved lanes offers cliff-top vistas but has no nighttime lighting. The area's most deluxe resorts and renowned golf courses are here, along with a collection of dramatic beaches and coves.

Although Los Cabos often feels like the southern playground of the United States' West Coast, other areas of Baja Sur can seem like the least crowded corners of Mexico. **Todos Santos,** an artistic community on the Pacific side of the coastal curve, just north of the tip, draws travelers who find that Cabo San Lucas has outgrown them. **La Paz,** the capital of Baja Sur, remains an easygoing maritime port, with an interesting assortment of small lodgings and a growing diversity of eco- and adventure tours.

MID-BAJA   Among the highlights of the mid-Baja region are the east coast towns of **Loreto, Mulegé,** and **Santa Rosalía.** Although they have a much richer historic and cultural heritage than Baja Sur's resort towns, they've been eclipsed by the growth of tourism infrastructure and services in the two Cabos. Loreto currently stands at the center of attention of the Mexican government's promotional and investment focus, so expect this quiet town to be growing soon.

This area's natural attractions have made it a center for sea kayaking, sportfishing, and hiking—including excursions to view indigenous cave paintings, which UNESCO has named a World Heritage Site. This is also the place to come if you're interested in whale-watching; many tour companies operate out of Loreto and smaller neighboring towns. For more information, see "Whale-Watching in Baja: A Primer," in chapter 4.

BAJA NORTE   **Tijuana** has the dubious distinction of being the most visited and perhaps most misunderstood town in all of Mexico. Dog racing, free-flowing tequila, and a sin-city reputation have all been hallmarks of this classic border town, a favored resort for the Hollywood elite during Prohibition. New cultural and sporting attractions, extensive shopping, and strong business growth—of the reputable kind—are helping to brighten Tijuana's image.

The Baja Peninsula

Tranquil **Rosarito Beach** is also reemerging as a resort town, given a boost after the movie *Titanic* was filmed here (the set is now a movie-themed amusement park). Farther down the Pacific coast is the lovely port town of **Ensenada,** also known for its prime surfing and spirited sportfishing. The nearby vineyards of Mexico's wine country are a new and growing attraction.

2 Visitor Information

The **Mexico Hot Line** (℗ 800/44-MEXICO) is an excellent source of general information; you can request brochures on the country and get answers to the most commonly asked questions. To receive information by fax, use the Ministry of Tourism's **Fax-Me-Mexico** service (℗ 541/385-9282). Call, key in your fax number, and select from a variety of topics.

More information is available on the Ministry of Tourism's website, **www.visitmexico.com**.

The **U.S. State Department** (℗ 202/647-5225; http://travel.state.gov/mexico.html) offers a Consular Information Sheet on Mexico, with safety, medical, driving, and general travel information gleaned from reports by official U.S. State Department offices in Mexico. You can also request the Consular Information Sheet by fax (℗ 202/647-3000). Visit **http://travel.state.gov/travel_warnings.html** for other Consular Information sheets and travel warnings, and **http://travel.state.gov/tips_mexico.html** for the State Department's "Tips for Travelers to Mexico."

MEXICAN GOVERNMENT TOURISM BOARD   Offices in North America include:

United States: Chicago (℗ 312/606-9252); Houston (℗ 713/772-2581 ext. 105); Los Angeles (℗ 213/351-2069, fax 213/351-2074); Miami (℗ 305/718-4095); and New York (℗ 800/446-3942). The Mexican Embassy is at 1911 Pennsylvania Ave. N.W., Washington, D.C. 20005 (℗ 202/728-1750).

Canada: 1 Place Ville-Marie, Suite 1931, Montréal, QUE, H3B 2C3 (℗ 514/871-1052); 2 Bloor St. W., Suite 1502, Toronto, ON, M4W 3E2 (℗ 416/925-2753); and 999 W. Hastings, Suite 1110, Vancouver, BC, V6C 2W2 (℗ 604/669-2845).

3 Entry Requirements & Customs

ENTRY REQUIREMENTS

All travelers to Mexico are required to present proof of citizenship, such as an original birth certificate with a raised seal, a valid passport, or naturalization papers. Those using a birth certificate should also have current photo identification, such as a driver's license or official ID. Those whose last name on the birth certificate is different from their current name (women using a married name, for example) should also bring a photo ID and legal proof of the name change, such as the original marriage license or certificate. This proof of citizenship may also be requested when you want to reenter either the United States or Mexico. Note that photocopies are not acceptable.

You must also carry a **Mexican Tourist Permit (FMT),** which Mexican border officials issue, free of charge, after proof of citizenship is accepted. Airlines generally provide the necessary forms on flights into Mexico. The tourist permit is more important than a passport in Mexico, so guard it carefully. If you lose it, you may not be permitted to leave the country until you can replace it— a bureaucratic hassle that can take anywhere from a few hours to a week. (If you do lose your tourist permit, get a police report from local authorities indicating that your documents were stolen; having one might lessen the hassle of exiting the country without all your identification. Also, make sure to report the loss to your embassy or consulate.)

A tourist permit can be issued for up to 180 days, although your stay may be shorter than that. Sometimes officials don't ask—they just stamp a time limit, so be sure to say "6 months" (or at least twice as long as you intend to stay). If you should decide to extend your stay, you may request that additional time be added to your permit from an official immigration office in Mexico. In Baja California, tourist visas (FMT) are allowed for a maximum period of 180 days per year, with a maximum of 30 days per visit. This is to encourage the more regular visitors, or those who spend longer periods in Mexico, to obtain immigration documents that denote partial residency.

Note: Children under age 18 traveling without parents or with only one parent must have a notarized letter from the absent parent or parents authorizing the travel.

For travelers entering Mexico by car at the border of Baja California, note that tourist permits (FMTs) for driving a car into Mexico are issued only in Tijuana, Tecate, Mexicali, Ensenada, and Guerrero Negro. If you travel anywhere beyond the frontier zone without this document, you will be fined $40. Permits for driving a car with foreign plates in Mexico are available only in Tijuana, Ensenada, Tecate, Mexicali, and La Paz.

CUSTOMS

When you enter Mexico, Customs officials will be tolerant as long as you have no illegal drugs or firearms. You're allowed to bring in two cartons of cigarettes or 50 cigars, plus a kilogram (2.2 lb.) of smoking tobacco; two 1-liter bottles of wine or hard liquor; and 12 rolls of film. A laptop computer, camera equipment, and sporting equipment that could feasibly be used during your stay are also allowed. The underlying guideline is that you shouldn't bring anything that looks as if it's meant to be resold in Mexico.

Returning **U.S. citizens** who have been away for at least 48 hours are allowed to bring back, once every 30 days, $800 worth of merchandise duty-free. You'll be charged a flat rate of 4% duty on the next $1,000 worth of purchases. On mailed gifts, the duty-free limit is $200. With some exceptions, you cannot bring fresh fruits and vegetables into the United States. For specifics on what you can bring back, download the invaluable free pamphlet *Know Before You Go Online Brochure* from **www.customs.gov**. Or contact the **U.S. Customs Service,** 1300 Pennsylvania Ave., NW, Washington, DC 20229 (© **877/287-8867**) and request the pamphlet.

For a clear summary of **Canadian** rules, check the booklet *I Declare,* issued by the **Canada Customs and Revenue Agency** (© **800/461-9999** in Canada, or 204/983-3500; www.ccra-adrc. gc.ca). Canada allows citizens a $750 exemption, and you're allowed to bring back duty-free one carton of cigarettes, one can of tobacco, 40 imperial ounces of liquor, and 50 cigars. In addition, you're allowed to mail gifts to Canada valued at less than $60 a day, provided they're unsolicited and don't contain alcohol or tobacco (write on the package "Unsolicited gift, under $60 value"). All valuables should be declared on the Y-38 form before departure from Canada, including serial numbers of valuables you already own. *Note:* The $750 exemption can only be used once a year and only after an absence of 7 days.

U.K. citizens returning from a non-EU country have a Customs allowance of: 200 cigarettes; 50 cigars; 250g of smoking tobacco; 2 liters of still table wine; 1 liter of spirits or strong liqueurs (over 22% volume); 2 liters of fortified wine, sparkling wine, or other liqueurs; 60cc (ml) of perfume; 250cc (ml) of toilet water; and £145 worth of all other goods, including gifts and souvenirs. People under 17 cannot have the tobacco or alcohol allowance. For more information, contact **HM Customs & Excise** (© **0845/010-9000** or 020/8929-0152 from outside the U.K.; www.hmce.gov.uk).

> ### (Tips A Few Words About Prices in Mexico
>
> The peso's value continues to fluctuate—at press time it was close to 10 pesos to the dollar. Prices in this book (which are always given in U.S. dollars) have been converted to U.S. dollars at 10 pesos to the dollar. Most hotels in Mexico—with the exception of places that receive little foreign tourism—quote prices in U.S. dollars. Thus, currency fluctuations are unlikely to affect the prices charged by most hotels.
>
> Mexico has a **value-added tax** of 15% (*Impuesto al Valor Agregado,* or IVA, pronounced *ee-bah*) on almost everything, including restaurant meals, bus tickets, and souvenirs. One of the exceptions is Los Cabos, where the IVA is 10%; as ports of entry, the towns receive a break on taxes. Hotels charge the usual 15% IVA, plus a locally administered bed tax of 2% (in many but not all areas), for a total of 17%. In Los Cabos, hotels charge the 10% IVA plus 2% room tax. Prices quoted by hotels and restaurants will not necessarily include IVA. You may find that upper-end properties quote prices without IVA included, while lower-priced hotels include IVA. Always ask to see a printed price sheet, and always ask if the tax is included.

The duty-free allowance in **Australia** is $400 or, for those under 18, $200. Citizens can bring in 250 cigarettes or 250 grams of loose tobacco, and 1,125ml of alcohol. If you're returning with valuables you already own, file form B263. A helpful brochure, available from Australian consulates or Customs offices, is *Know Before You Go.* For more information, contact **Australian Customs Services** (© **1300/363-263;** www.customs.gov.au).

The duty-free allowance for **New Zealand** is $700. Citizens over 17 can bring in 200 cigarettes, or 50 cigars, or 250 grams of tobacco (or a mixture if their combined weight doesn't exceed 250g); plus 4.5 liters of wine and beer, or 1.125 liters of liquor. New Zealand currency does not carry import or export restrictions. Fill out a certificate of export, listing the valuables you are taking out of the country; that way, you can bring them back without paying duty. A free pamphlet available at New Zealand consulates and Customs offices, *New*

Zealand Customs Guide for Travellers, Notice no. 4, answers most questions. For more information, contact **New Zealand Customs,** The Customhouse, 17–21 Whitmore St., Box 2218, Wellington (② **04/ 473-6099** or 0800/428-786; www.customs.govt.nz).

GOING THROUGH CUSTOMS   Mexican Customs inspection has been streamlined. At most points of entry, tourists are requested to press a button in front of what looks like a traffic signal, which alternates on touch between red and green. Green light and you go through without inspection; red light and your luggage or car may be inspected briefly or thoroughly. If you have an unusual amount of luggage or an oversized piece, you may be subject to inspection anyway.

4 Money

The currency in Mexico is the **peso.** Paper currency comes in denominations of 20, 50, 100, 200, and 500 pesos. Coins come in denominations of 1, 2, 5, and 10 pesos, and 20 and 50 *centavos* (100 centavos = 1 peso). The current exchange rate for the U.S. dollar is around 10 pesos; at that rate, an item that costs 10 pesos would be equivalent to $1.

Getting change is a problem. Small-denomination bills and coins are hard to come by, so start collecting them early in your trip. Shopkeepers seem always to be out of change and small bills; that's doubly true in markets.

Many establishments that deal with tourists, especially in coastal resort areas, quote prices in dollars. To avoid confusion, they use the abbreviations "Dlls." for dollars and "M.N." (*moneda nacional,* or national currency) for pesos. All dollar equivalencies in this book were based on an exchange rate of 10 pesos per dollar.

The rate of exchange fluctuates a tiny bit daily, so you probably are better off not exchanging too much of your currency at once. Don't forget, however, to have enough pesos to carry you over a weekend or Mexican holiday, when banks are closed. In general, avoid carrying the U.S. $100 bill, the bill most commonly counterfeited in Mexico and therefore the most difficult to exchange, especially in

---

Money Matters

The universal currency sign ($) is used to indicate pesos in Mexico. The use of this symbol in this book, however, denotes U.S. currency.

smaller towns. Because small bills and coins in pesos are hard to come by in Mexico, the U.S. $1 bill is very useful for tipping. A tip in U.S. coins, which Mexican banks do not accept, is of no value to the service provider.

The bottom line on exchanging money of all kinds: It pays to ask first and shop around. Banks pay the top rates.

Exchange houses *(casas de cambio)* are generally more convenient than banks because they have more locations and longer hours; the rate of exchange may be the same as a bank or only slightly lower. Before leaving a bank or exchange-house window, always count your change in front of the teller before the next client steps up.

Large airports have currency-exchange counters that often stay open whenever flights are arriving or departing. Though convenient, these generally do not offer the most favorable rates. The San José del Cabo and La Paz airports have exchange counters.

A hotel's exchange desk commonly pays less favorable rates than banks; however, when the currency is in a state of flux, higher-priced hotels are known to beat bank rates, in their effort to attract dollars. It pays to shop around, but in almost all cases, you receive a better exchange by changing money first, then paying for goods or services, rather than by paying with dollars directly.

BANKS & ATMs Banks in Mexico are rapidly expanding and improving services. They tend to be open weekdays from 9am until 5 or 6pm, and often for at least a half day on Saturday. In larger resorts and cities, they can generally accommodate the exchange of dollars, which used to stop at noon, anytime during business hours. Some, but not all, banks charge a service fee of about 1% to exchange traveler's checks. However, you can pay for most purchases directly with traveler's checks at the establishment's stated exchange rate. Don't even bother with personal checks drawn on a U.S. bank—the bank will wait for your check to clear, which can take weeks, before giving you your money.

Travelers to Mexico can also withdraw money from automatic teller machines (ATMs) in most major cities and resort areas. Universal bankcards (such as the Cirrus and PLUS systems) can be used. This is a convenient way to withdraw money from your bank and avoid carrying too much with you at any time. The exchange rate is generally more favorable than the one at a currency house. Most machines offer Spanish/English menus and dispense pesos, but some offer the option of withdrawing dollars. Be sure to check your daily withdrawal limit before you depart. For Cirrus locations abroad, check ℂ **800/424-7787** or **www.mastercard.com**. For PLUS usage abroad, check ℂ **800/843-7587** or **www.visa.com**. Also keep in mind that many banks impose a fee every time a card is used at a different bank's ATM, and that fee can be higher for international transactions (up to $5 or more) than for domestic ones.

TRAVELER'S CHECKS   Traveler's checks denominated in dollars are readily accepted nearly everywhere, but they can be difficult to cash on a weekend or holiday or in an out-of-the-way place. Banks and other establishments in Mexico frequently charge a small commission when traveler's checks are used. Their best value is in replacement in case of theft.

CREDIT CARDS   Visa, MasterCard, and American Express are the most accepted cards. You'll be able to charge most hotel, restaurant, and store purchases, as well as almost all airline tickets, on your credit card. You generally can't charge gasoline purchases in Mexico. You can get cash advances of several hundred dollars on your card, but there may be a wait of 20 minutes to 2 hours.

Charges will be billed in pesos, then converted into dollars by the bank issuing the credit card. Generally you receive the favorable bank rate when paying by credit card, but keep in mind that most credit card companies charge a fee of 1% to 3% for processing the foreign-currency transaction. You won't usually see the fee on your statement; it's factored into the conversion rate.

5 When to Go

Mexico has two principal travel seasons. **High season** begins around December 20 and continues through Easter, although in some places high season can begin as early as mid-November; during Christmas and New Year's, it's almost impossible to find a room. **Low season** begins the day after Easter and continues to mid-December; during low season, prices may drop 20% to 50%.

The weather in Baja, land of extremes, can be unpredictable. It can be sizzling hot in summer and cold and windy in winter—so windy that fishing and other nautical expeditions may be grounded for a few days. Though winter is often warm enough for watersports, bring a wet suit if you're a serious diver or snorkeler, as well as warmer clothes for unexpectedly chilly weather at night.

BAJA CALENDAR OF EVENTS

Note: Banks, government offices, and many stores close on national holidays.

January

New Year's Day *(Año Nuevo)*. Parades, religious observances, parties, and fireworks welcome the New Year everywhere. January 1. National holiday.

February

Day of the Constitution *(Día de la Constitución)*. The current constitution was signed in 1917 as a result of the revolutionary war of 1910. It is sometimes celebrated with parades. February 5. National holiday.

Carnaval. Carnaval takes place over the 3 days before the beginning of Lent. La Paz celebrates with special zeal, and visitors enjoy a festive atmosphere and parades. The 3 days preceding Ash Wednesday.

March

Holy Week. Celebrates the last week in the life of Christ from Palm Sunday through Easter Sunday with somber religious processions almost nightly, spoofing of Judas, and reenactments of biblical events, plus food and craft fairs. Businesses close during this traditional week of Mexican national vacations.

If you plan on traveling to or around Mexico during Holy Week, make reservations early. Seats on flights into and out of the country will be reserved months in advance. For 2004, April 4 through 9 is Holy Week, and Easter Sunday is April 11. The week following is a traditional vacation period.

May

Labor Day, celebrated nationwide. Workers' parades countrywide, and everything closes. May 1. National holiday.

Cinco de Mayo, celebrated nationwide. A national holiday that commemorates the defeat of the French at the Battle of Puebla. May 5.

La Paz Foundation. Celebrates the founding of La Paz by Cortez in 1535, and features *artesanía* exhibitions from throughout southern Baja. May 1 to 5. La Paz.

June

Navy Day *(Día de la Marina)*. Celebrated in all coastal towns, with naval parades and fireworks. June 1.

September

Independence Day. Celebrates Mexico's independence from Spain. A day of parades, picnics, and family reunions throughout the country. At 11pm on September 15, the president of Mexico gives the famous independence *grito* (shout) from the National Palace in Mexico City. At least half a million people crowd into the *zócalo* (town square), and the rest of the country watches the event on TV. September 15 and 16. September 16 is a national holiday.

October

Festival Fundador. Celebrates the founding of the town of Todos Santos in 1723. Streets around the main plaza fill with food, games, and wandering troubadours. October 10 to 14.

November

Day of the Dead. Actually 2 days: All Saints' Day—honoring saints and deceased children—and All Souls' Day, honoring deceased adults. Relatives gather at cemeteries countrywide, carrying candles and food, often spending the night beside graves of loved ones. November 1 and 2. November 1 is a national holiday.

Revolution Day. Commemorates the start of the Mexican Revolution in 1910 with parades, speeches, rodeos, and patriotic events. November 20. National holiday.

December

Feast of the Virgin of Guadalupe. Throughout the country, religious processions, street fairs, dancing, fireworks, and Masses honor the patroness of Mexico. This is one of Mexico's most moving and beautiful displays of traditional culture. The Virgin of Guadalupe appeared to a young man, Juan Diego, in December 1531, on a hill near Mexico City. He convinced the bishop that he had seen the apparition by revealing his cloak, upon which the Virgin was emblazoned. It's customary for children to dress up as Juan Diego, wearing mustaches and red bandannas. December 12.

Christmas. Mexicans extend this celebration and leave their jobs, often beginning 2 weeks before Christmas and continuing all the way through New Year's. Many businesses close, and resorts and hotels fill. On December 23 also there are significant celebrations. December 24 and 25.

New Year's Eve. As in the rest of the world, New Year's Eve in Mexico is celebrated with parties, fireworks, and plenty of noise. December 31.

6 Travel Insurance

Check your existing insurance policies and credit card coverage before you buy travel insurance. You may already be covered for cancelled tickets, medical expenses, or lost luggage. The cost of travel insurance varies widely, depending on the cost and length of your trip, your age and health, and the type of trip you're taking.

The bottom line: Always, always check the fine print before you sign; more and more policies have built-in exclusions and restrictions that may leave you out in the cold if something goes awry.

Trip-cancellation insurance helps you get your money back if you have to back out of a trip, you have to go home early, or your travel supplier goes bankrupt. In this unstable world, trip-cancellation insurance is a good buy if you're getting tickets well in advance. Policy details vary, so read the fine print—and make sure that your airline or cruise line is on the list of carriers covered in case of bankruptcy. For information, contact one of the following insurers: **Access America** (© 866/807-3982; www.accessamerica.com); **Travel Guard International** (© 800/826-4919; www.travelguard.com); **Travel Insured International** (© 800/243-3174; www.travel insured.com); and **Travelex Insurance Services** (© 888/457-4602; www.travelex-insurance.com).

Most **health insurance** policies cover you if you get sick away from home—but check, particularly if you're insured by an HMO. With the exception of certain HMOs and Medicare/Medicaid, your medical insurance should cover medical treatment overseas. However, most hospitals make you pay your bills up front, and send you a refund after you've returned home and filed the necessary paperwork. If you require additional medical insurance, try **MEDEX International** (© 800/527-0218 or 410/453-6300; www.medexassist.com) or **Travel Assistance International** (© **800/821-2828;** www.travel assistance.com; for general information on services, call the company's Worldwide Assistance Services, Inc., © **800/777-8710**).

On international flights (including U.S. portions of international trips), baggage is limited to approximately $9.07 per pound, up to approximately $635 per checked bag. If you plan to check items more valuable than the standard liability, see if your homeowner's policy covers your valuables, get baggage insurance as part of your comprehensive travel-insurance package, or buy Travel Guard's "BagTrak" product. Don't buy insurance at the airport, where it's usually overpriced. Be sure to take any valuables or irreplaceable items with you in your carry-on luggage, because airline policies don't cover many valuables.

If your luggage is lost, immediately file a lost-luggage claim at the airport, detailing the contents. For most airlines, you must report delayed, damaged, or lost baggage within 4 hours of arrival. The airlines are required to deliver luggage, once found, directly to your house or destination free of charge.

7 Health & Safety

STAYING HEALTHY

Mosquitoes and gnats are prevalent along the coast. Insect repellent *(repelente contra insectos)* is a must, and it's not always available in Mexico. Bring along a repellent that contains the active ingredient DEET. Avon's Skin So Soft also works extremely well. If you're sensitive to bites, pick up some antihistamine cream from a drugstore at home.

Most readers won't ever see a scorpion *(alacrán)*. But if you're stung by one, go immediately to a doctor.

MORE SERIOUS DISEASES   You shouldn't be overly concerned about tropical diseases if you stay on the normal tourist routes and don't eat street food. However, both dengue fever and cholera have appeared in Mexico in recent years. Talk to your doctor or to a medical specialist in tropical diseases about precautions you should take. You can also get medical bulletins from the U.S. State Department (see "Visitor Information," earlier in this chapter) and the Centers for Disease Control (© **800/311-3435** or 404/ 639-3534; www.cdc.gov). You can protect yourself by taking some simple precautions: Watch what you eat and drink; don't swim in stagnant water (ponds, slow-moving rivers, or wells); and avoid mosquito bites by covering up, using repellent, and sleeping under mosquito netting. The most dangerous areas seem to be on Mexico's west coast, away from the big resorts, which are relatively safe.

Tips Over-the-Counter Drugs in Mexico

Mexican pharmacies sell antibiotics and other drugs that you'd need a prescription to buy in the States. Pharmacies also carry common over-the-counter cold, sinus, and allergy remedies, although not the broad selection we're accustomed to.

Tips What to Do If You Get Sick

It's called "travelers' diarrhea" or *turista,* the Spanish word for "tourist": persistent diarrhea, often accompanied by fever, nausea, and vomiting, that used to attack many travelers to Mexico. (Some in the United States call this "Montezuma's revenge," but you won't hear it called that in Mexico.) Widespread improvements in infrastructure, sanitation, and education have practically eliminated this ailment, especially in well-developed resort areas. Most travelers make a habit of drinking only bottled water, which helps to protect against unfamiliar bacteria. In resort areas, and generally throughout Mexico, only purified ice is used. If you do come down with this ailment, nothing beats Pepto Bismol, readily available in Mexico. Imodium is also available in Mexico, and many travelers use it for a quick fix. A good high-potency (or "therapeutic") vitamin supplement and even extra vitamin C can help; yogurt is good for healthy digestion.

Dehydration can quickly become life threatening, so the Public Health Service advises that you be especially careful to replace fluids and electrolytes (potassium, sodium, and the like) during a bout of diarrhea. Do this by drinking Pedialyte, a rehydration solution available at most Mexican pharmacies, or glasses of natural fruit juice (high in potassium) with a pinch of salt added. Or you can try a glass of boiled pure water with a quarter teaspoon of sodium bicarbonate (baking soda) added.

How to Prevent It: The U.S. Public Health Service recommends the following measures for preventing travelers' diarrhea: **Drink only purified water** (boiled water; canned or bottled carbonated beverages, beer, wine). **Choose food carefully.** In general, avoid salads (except in first-class restaurants), uncooked vegetables, and unpasteurized milk or milk products (including cheese). Choose food that is freshly cooked and still hot. In addition, something as simple as **clean hands** can go a long way toward preventing *turista.*

EMERGENCY EVACUATION   For extreme medical emergencies, a 24-hour air-ambulance service from the United States will fly people to American hospitals. **Global Lifeline** (© **888/554-9729,**

or 01-800/305-9400 in Mexico) is a 24-hour air ambulance. Several other companies offer air-evacuation services; for a list, refer to the U.S. State Department website, http://travel.state.gov/medical.html.

STAYING SAFE

CRIME I have lived and traveled in Mexico for more than a decade, have never had any serious trouble, and rarely feel suspicious of anyone or any situation. You probably will feel physically safer in most Mexican cities and villages than in any comparable place at home.

When traveling anyplace in the world, common sense is essential. A good rule is that you can generally trust people whom you approach for help, assistance, or directions—but be wary of anyone who approaches you offering the same. The more insistent they are, the more cautious you should be. The crime rate is on the whole much lower in Mexico than in most parts of the United States, and the nature of crimes in general is less violent—most crime is motivated by robbery or jealousy. Random, violent crime or serial crime is essentially unheard of in Mexico.

BRIBES & SCAMS As is the case around the world, there are the occasional bribes and scams, targeted at people believed to be naive in the ways of the place—obvious tourists, for example. For years Mexico was known as a place where bribes—called *propinas* (tips) or *mordidas* (bites)—were expected; however, the country is rapidly changing. Frequently, offering a bribe today, especially to a police officer, is considered an insult, and can land you in deeper trouble.

Whatever you do, avoid impoliteness; under no circumstances should you insult a Latin American official. Mexico is ruled by extreme politeness, even in the face of adversity. In Mexico, gringos have a reputation for being loud and demanding. By adopting the local custom of excessive courtesy, you'll have greater success in negotiations of any kind. Stand your ground, but do it politely.

8 Specialized Travel Resources

FAMILY TRAVEL

I can't think of a better place to introduce children to the exciting adventure of exploring a different culture. Among the best destinations for children in Mexico is La Paz (see chapter 3). The larger hotels in Los Cabos can often arrange for a babysitter. Some hotels in the moderate-to-luxury range have small playgrounds and pools for children and hire caretakers with special activity programs during the day. Few budget hotels offer these amenities.

Before leaving, you should check with your doctor to get advice on medications to take along. Disposable diapers cost about the same in Mexico but are of poorer quality. You can get Huggies Supreme and Pampers identical to the ones sold in the United States, but at a higher price. Many stores sell Gerber's baby foods. Dry cereals, powdered formulas, baby bottles, and purified water are all easily available in midsize and large cities or resorts.

Cribs, however, may present a problem—only the largest and most luxurious hotels provide them. Rollaway beds are often available for children staying in the room with parents. Child seats or high chairs at restaurants are common, and most restaurants will go out of their way to accommodate your child.

Because many travelers to Baja will rent a car, it is advisable to bring your car seat. Leasing agencies in Mexico do not rent car seats.

For more resources, check the following websites: **Family Travel Network** (www.familytravelnetwork.com) and **Travel with Your Children** (www.travelwithyourkids.com).

GAY & LESBIAN TRAVELERS

Mexico is a conservative country, with deeply rooted Catholic religious traditions. Public displays of same-sex affection are rare and still considered shocking for men, especially outside of urban or resort areas. Women in Mexico frequently walk hand in hand, but anything more would cross the boundary of acceptability. However, gay and lesbian travelers are generally treated with respect and should not experience any harassment, assuming the appropriate regard is given to local culture and customs. The **International Gay & Lesbian Travel Association** (© 800/448-8550 or 954/776-2626; fax 954/776-3303; www.iglta.org) can provide helpful information and additional tips. **Arco Iris** (© 800/795-5549; www.arcoiristours.com) is a gay-owned, full-service travel agency and tour operator specializing in Mexico packages and special group travel.

TRAVELERS WITH DISABILITIES

Mexico may seem like one giant obstacle course to travelers in wheelchairs or on crutches. At airports, you may encounter steep stairs before finding a well-hidden elevator or escalator—if one exists. Airlines will often arrange wheelchair assistance for passengers to the baggage area. Porters are generally available to help with luggage at airports and large bus stations, once you've cleared baggage claim.

In addition, escalators (there aren't many in the country) are often out of operation. Few restrooms are equipped for travelers with disabilities, or when one is available, access to it may be through a narrow passage that won't accommodate someone in a wheelchair or on crutches. Many deluxe hotels (the most expensive) now have rooms with baths for people with disabilities. Those traveling on a budget should stick with one-story hotels or those with elevators. Even so, there will probably still be obstacles somewhere. Stairs without handrails abound in Mexico. Generally speaking, no matter where you are, someone will lend a hand, although you may have to ask.

SENIOR TRAVEL

Mexico is a popular country for retirees. For decades, North Americans have been living indefinitely in Mexico by returning to the border and recrossing with a new tourist permit every 6 months. Mexican immigration officials have caught on, and now limit the maximum time in the country to 6 months within any year. This is to encourage even partial residents to obtain proper documentation.

AIM, Apdo. Postal 31–70, 45050 Guadalajara, Jalisco, Mexico, is a well-written, informative newsletter on retirement in Mexico. Subscriptions are $18 to the United States and $21 to Canada. Back issues are three for $5.

Members of **AARP** (formerly the American Association of Retired Persons), 601 E. St. NW, Washington, D.C. 20049 (© **800/424-3410;** www.aarp.com), receive discounts at hotel chains such as Best Western, Holiday Inn, and Marriott, as well as car rentals from companies like Avis and Hertz.

Tips Advice for Female Travelers

As a female traveling alone, I can tell you firsthand that I feel safer traveling in Mexico than in the United States. But I use the same common-sense precautions I follow traveling anywhere else in the world and am alert to what's going on around me.

Mexicans in general, and men in particular, are nosy about single travelers, especially women. If taxi drivers or anyone else with whom you don't want to become friendly asks about your marital status, family, and so forth, my advice is to make up a set of answers (regardless of the truth): "I'm married, I'm traveling with friends, and I have three children." Saying you are single and traveling alone may send out the wrong message.

---

9 Planning Your Trip Online

The "big three" online travel agencies, **Expedia.com, Travelocity. com,** and **Orbitz.com,** sell most of the air tickets bought on the Internet. (Canadian travelers should try Expedia.ca and Travelocity.ca; U.K. residents can go for Expedia.co.uk and Opodo. co.uk.) Each has different deals with the airlines and may offer different fares on the same flights, so it's wise to shop around.

But don't fire your travel agent just yet. Although online booking sites offer tips and data to help you bargain shop, they cannot offer the experience that makes a seasoned, reliable travel agent an invaluable resource.

Of the smaller travel agency websites, **SideStep** (www.sidestep. com) has gotten the best reviews from Frommer's authors. It's a browser add-on that purports to "search 140 sites at once," but in reality only beats competitors' fares as often as other sites do.

Also remember to check **airline websites.** For a list of the major airlines that serve Mexico, see "Getting There," below. Even with major airlines, you can often shave a few bucks from a fare by booking directly through the airline and avoiding a travel agency's fee. But you'll get these discounts only by **booking online:** Most airlines now offer online-only fares that even their phone agents know nothing about. For the websites of airlines that fly to and from your destination, go to "Getting There," later in this chapter.

If you're willing to give up some control over your flight details, use an **opaque fare service** like **Priceline** (www.priceline.com or www.priceline.co.uk) or **Hotwire** (www.hotwire.com). Both offer rock-bottom prices in exchange for travel on a "mystery airline" at a mysterious time of day, often with a mysterious change of planes en route. The airlines are all major, well-known carriers. But your chances of getting a 6am or 11pm flight are pretty high. Hotwire tells you flight prices before you buy; Priceline usually has better deals than Hotwire, but you have to play their "name our price" game. If you're new at this, the helpful folks at **BiddingForTravel** (www.biddingfor travel.com) do a good job of demystifying Priceline's prices.

For much more about airfares and savvy air-travel tips and advice, pick up a copy of *Frommer's Fly Safe, Fly Smart* (Wiley Publishing, Inc.).

SURFING FOR HOTELS

Shopping online for hotels is much easier in the U.S., Canada, and certain parts of Europe than it is in the rest of the world. Of the "big three" sites, **Expedia** may be the best choice, thanks to its long list

> ## _Tips_ Frommers.com: The Complete Travel Resource
>
> For an excellent travel-planning resource, we highly recommend **Frommer's Travel Online** (www.frommers.com). You'll find the travel tips, reviews, monthly vacation giveaways, and online-booking capabilities indispensable. Among the special features are our popular **Message Boards,** where Frommer's readers post queries and share advice (sometimes we authors even show up to answer questions); **Frommers.com Newsletter,** for the latest travel bargains and insider travel secrets; and **Frommer's Destinations Section,** where you'll get expert travel tips, hotel and dining recommendations, and advice on the sights to see for more than 3,000 destinations around the globe. When your research is done, the **Online Reservations System** (www.frommers.com/book_a_trip) takes you to preferred online partners for booking your vacation at affordable prices.

of special deals. **Travelocity** runs a close second. Hotel specialist sites **hotels.com** and **hoteldiscounts.com** are also reliable. An excellent free program, **TravelAxe** (www.travelaxe.net), can help you search multiple hotel sites at once, even ones you may never have heard of.

Priceline and Hotwire are even better for hotels than for airfares; with both, you're allowed to pick the neighborhood and quality level of your hotel before offering up your money. Priceline's hotel product even covers Europe and Asia, though it's much better at getting five-star lodging for three-star prices than at finding anything at the bottom of the scale. *Note:* Hotwire overrates its hotels by one star—what Hotwire calls a four-star is a three-star anywhere else.

SURFING FOR RENTAL CARS

For booking rental cars online, the best deals are usually at rental-car company websites, although all the major online travel agencies also offer rental-car reservations services. Priceline and Hotwire work well for rental cars, too; the only "mystery" is which major rental company you get, and for most travelers the difference between Hertz, Avis, and Budget is negligible.

10 Getting There

BY PLANE

The airline situation in Mexico is changing rapidly, with many new regional carriers offering flights to areas previously not served. In addition to regularly scheduled service, charter service direct from U.S. cities to resorts is making Mexico more accessible.

THE MAJOR INTERNATIONAL AIRLINES   The main airlines operating direct or nonstop flights from the United States to points in Baja include **AeroCalifornia** (© 800/237-6225), **Aeromexico** (© 800/237-6639, www.aeromexico.com), **Alaska Airlines** (© 800/426-0333, www.alaskaair.com), **America West** (© 800/235-9292, www.americawest.com), **American Airlines** (© 800/433-7300, www.aa.com), **Continental** (© 800/231-0856, www.continental.com), **Mexicana** (© 800/531-7921, www.mexicana.com), **Northwest/KLM** (© 800/225-2525, www.nwa.com), **United** (© 800/241-6522, www.united.com), and **US Airways** (© 800/428-4322, www.usairways.com). **Southwest Airlines** (© 800/435-9792, www.iflyswa.com) serves San Diego.

The main departure points in North America for international airlines are Atlanta, Chicago, Dallas/Fort Worth, Denver, Houston, Los Angeles, Miami, New Orleans, New York, Orlando, Philadelphia, Raleigh/Durham, San Antonio, San Francisco, Seattle, Toronto, Tucson, and Washington, D.C.

BY CAR

Consider renting a car for touring around a specific region once you arrive in Mexico. Rental cars in Mexico are generally new, clean, and well maintained. Although they're pricier than in the United States, discounts are often available for rentals of a week or longer, especially when you make arrangements in advance. (See "Car Rentals" in "Getting Around," below, for more details.)

If, after reading the section that follows, you have any additional questions or you want to confirm the current rules, call your nearest Mexican consulate, Mexican Government Tourist Office, or AAA.

CAR DOCUMENTS   To drive your car into Mexico, you'll need a temporary car-importation permit, which is granted after you provide a strictly required list of documents (see below). The permit can be obtained either through Banco del Ejército (Banjercito) officials, who have a desk, booth, or office at the Mexican Customs (Aduana)

Travel in the Age of Bankruptcy

At press time, two major U.S. airlines were struggling in bankruptcy court, and most of the rest weren't doing very well either. To protect yourself, **buy your tickets with a credit card;** the Fair Credit Billing Act guarantees that you can get your money back from the credit card company if a travel supplier goes under (and if you request the refund within 60 days of the bankruptcy). **Travel insurance** can also help, but make sure it covers "carrier default" for your provider. And be aware that if a U.S. airline goes bust mid-trip, a 2001 federal law requires other carriers to take you to your destination (albeit on a space-available basis) for a fee of no more than $25, provided you rebook within 60 days of the cancellation.

building after you cross the border into Mexico. Or you can obtain the permit before you travel, through Sanborn's Insurance or the American Automobile Association (AAA), each of which maintains border offices in Texas, New Mexico, Arizona, and California. The companies may charge a fee for this service, but it will be worth it to avoid the uncertain prospect of traveling all the way to the border without proper documents for crossing. Even if you go through Sanborn's or AAA, however, your credentials may be reviewed again by Mexican officials at the border—you must take them all with you.

The following requirements for border crossing were accurate at press time:

- A **valid driver's license,** issued outside of Mexico.
- Current, original **car registration** and a copy of the **original car title.** If the registration or title is in more than one name and not all the named people are traveling with you, a notarized letter from the absent person(s) authorizing use of the vehicle for the trip is required; have it ready just in case. The car registration and your credit card (see below) must be in the same name.
- A **valid international major credit card.** With a credit card, you are required to pay only a $22.50 car-importation fee. The credit card must be in the same name as the car registration. If you do not have a major credit card (American Express, Diners Club, Visa, or MasterCard), you will have to post a bond or make a deposit equal to the value of the vehicle. Check cards are not accepted.

- **Original immigration documentation.** This is either your tourist permit (FMT), or the original immigration booklet, FM2 or FM3, if you hold this more permanent status.
- A signed declaration promising to return to your country of origin with the vehicle. This form *(Carta Promesa de Retorno)* is provided by AAA or Sanborn's before you go or by Banjercito officials at the border. There's no charge.
- **Temporary Importation Application.** By signing this form, you state that you are only temporarily importing the car for your personal use and will not sell the vehicle.

For up-to-the-minute information, a great source is the Customs office in Nuevo Laredo, or Módulo de Importación Temporal de Automóviles, Aduana Nuevo Laredo (© **867/712-2071**).

Important reminder: Someone else may drive the car, but the person (or a relative of the person) whose name appears on the car-importation permit must always be in the car at the same time. (If stopped by police, a nonregistered family member traveling in the car without the registered driver must be prepared to prove familial relationship to the registered driver—no joke.) Violation of this rule makes the car subject to impoundment and the driver to imprisonment, a fine, or both. You can only drive a car with foreign license plates if you have an international (non-Mexican) driver's license.

MEXICAN AUTO INSURANCE   Auto insurance is now legally required in Mexico. U.S. insurance is invalid in Mexico; to be

---

Tips **Carrying Car Documents**

You must carry your temporary car-importation permit, tourist permit (see "Entry Requirements," earlier in this chapter), and, if you purchased it, your proof of Mexican car insurance (see below) in the car at all times. The temporary car-importation permit papers will be issued for 6 months to a year; the tourist permit is usually issued for 30 days. It's a good idea to overestimate the time you'll spend in Mexico, so that if something unforeseen happens and you have to (or want to) stay longer, you'll avoid the hassle of getting your papers extended. Whatever you do, don't overstay either permit. Doing so invites heavy fines and confiscation of your vehicle, which will not be returned. Remember also that 6 months does not necessarily work out to be 180 days.

See Baja by Boat: Cruising the Sea of Cortez

John Steinbeck made this journey famous, recording his observations and philosophies on a 4,000-mile expedition during which he collected marine specimens in the 1951 classic *The Log from the Sea of Cortez*. These days, a few companies offer small-ship cruises from Cabo San Lucas north to the colonial town of Santa Rosalía, an ideal way to sample the best of Baja. Any travel agent can price or book Sea of Cortez cruises.

Cruise West (© 800/888-9378 or 206/441-8687 in the U.S.; fax 206/441-4757; www.cruisewest.com) offers several voyages that explore the interior Baja coast. Along the way, the ship pulls into small, pristine coves where passengers can participate in nature walks, hiking, snorkeling, and kayaking. One itinerary has stops at Loreto, Santa Rosalía, Mulegé, and La Paz, and an overland side trip to Bahía Magdalena for a day of whale-watching. There are two ships: the 65m (217-foot) *Spirit of Endeavor,* with 51 cabins, all with double accommodations and full facilities; and the 58m (192-ft.) *Spirit of '98,* with 48 double cabins with full facilities. Prices range from $2,095 to $4,695 per person (based on double occupancy) for the 7-night cruise; all meals and activities are included. This cruise is oriented toward a slightly older passenger; there's an exceptional educational orientation aimed at learning about the areas explored, especially the regional flora and fauna. Photography-themed cruises also are available.

Baja Expeditions, 2625 Garnet Ave., San Diego, CA 92109 (© 800/843-6967 or 858/581-3311; www.bajaex.com), offers natural-history cruises, whale-watching, sea kayaking, and scuba-diving trips out of La Paz.

insured in Mexico, you must purchase Mexican insurance. Any party involved in an accident who has no insurance may be sent to jail and his or her car impounded until all claims are settled. This is true even if you just drive across the border to spend the day. U.S. companies that broker Mexican insurance are commonly found at the border crossings, and several quote daily rates.

You can also buy car insurance through **Sanborn's Mexico Insurance,** P.O. Box 52840, 2009 S. 10th, McAllen, TX 78505-2840 (© **800/222-0158** or 956/686-3601; fax 956/686-0732; www. sanbornsinsurance.com). The company has offices at all U.S. border crossings. Its policies cost the same as the competition's do, but with Sanborn's you get legal coverage (attorney and bail bonds, if needed) and a detailed mile-by-mile guide for your proposed route. Most of the Sanborn's border offices are open Monday through Friday, and a few are staffed on Saturday and Sunday. The American Automobile Association (AAA) also sells insurance. Another good source is www.mexico-car-insurance.com.

RETURNING TO THE UNITED STATES WITH YOUR CAR

You must return the car papers you obtained when you entered Mexico when you cross back with your car, or at some point within 180 days. (You can cross as many times as you wish within the 180 days.) If the documents aren't returned, heavy fines are imposed ($250 for each 15 days late), and your car may be impounded and confiscated or you may be jailed if you return to Mexico. You can only return the car documents to a Banjercito official on duty at the Mexican Customs building before you cross back into the United States. Some border cities have Banjercito officials on duty 24 hours a day, but others do not; some also do not have Sunday hours.

BY SHIP

Numerous cruise lines serve Mexico, with many ships (including specialized whale-watching trips) originating in California and traveling down to the Baja Peninsula. If you don't mind taking off at the last minute, several cruise-tour specialists arrange substantial discounts on unsold cabins. One such company is **The Cruise Line,** 150 NW 168 St., North Miami Beach, Miami, FL 33169 (© **800/777-0707** or 305/521-2200).

11 Packages for the Independent Traveler

Package tours are not the same thing as escorted tours. They are simply a way of buying your airfare, accommodations, and other pieces of your trip (usually airport transfers, and sometimes meals and activities) at the same time.

For popular destinations like the Los Cabos beach resorts, package tours are often the smart way to go, because they can save you a ton of money. In many cases, a package that includes airfare, hotel, and transportation to and from the airport will cost you less than the hotel alone if you booked it yourself. You can buy a package at any time of year, but the best deals usually coincide with low season—May to early December—when room rates and airfares plunge. Packages vary widely. Some offer a better class of hotels than others. Some offer the same hotels for lower prices. Some offer flights on scheduled airlines, while others book charters. Each destination usually has some packagers that are better than the rest because they buy in even bigger bulk. Not only can that mean better prices, but it can also mean more hotels to choose from.

WHERE TO BROWSE

- For one-stop shopping, go to **www.vacationpackager.com**, an extensive search engine that'll link you with more than 30 packagers offering Mexican beach vacations—and even let you design your own package.
- Check out **www.2travel.com** and find a page with links to a number of the big-name Mexico packagers, including several of the ones listed here.
- Several big **online travel agencies**—Expedia, Travelocity, Orbitz, Site59, and Lastminute.com—also do a brisk business in packages.

RECOMMENDED PACKAGERS

- **Aeromexico Vacations** (© **800/245-8585;** www.aeromexico. com) offers Los Cabos packages year-round. Aeromexico has a large selection of resorts in a variety of price ranges. The best deals are from Houston, Dallas, San Diego, Los Angeles, Miami, and New York, in that order.
- **Alaska Airlines Vacations** (© **800/426-0333;** www. alaskair.com) sells packages to Los Cabos. Alaska flies direct to Mexico from Los Angeles, San Diego, San Jose, San Francisco, Seattle, Vancouver, Anchorage, and Fairbanks.
- **American Airlines Vacations** (© **800/321-2121;** www.aa vacations.com) has packages to Los Cabos year-round. You don't have to fly with American if you can get a better deal on another airline; land-only packages include hotel, room tax, and airport transfers. American's hubs to Mexico are Dallas/Fort Worth, Chicago, and Miami.
- **America West Vacations** (© **800/356-6611;** www.america westvacations.com) has deals to Los Cabos, mostly from its Phoenix gateway. Golfers can book golf vacations to Los Cabos through www.awagolf.com or by calling 888/AWA-GOLF.

- **Apple Vacations** (© **800/365-2775**) offers inclusive packages and has the largest choice of hotels (14 in Los Cabos). Scheduled carriers booked for the air portion include AeroCalifornia, Aeromexico, Alaska Airlines, American, Delta, Mexicana, Reno Air, United, and US Airways. Apple perks include baggage handling and the services of an Apple representative at the major hotels.
- **Continental Vacations** (© **800/634-5555** and 888/989-9255; www.continental.com) has year-round packages. The best deals are from Houston; Newark, NJ; and Cleveland. You must buy air from the carrier if you want to book a room.
- **Funjet Vacations** (book through travel agents; get information at www.funjet.com), one of the largest vacation packagers in the United States, has packages to Los Cabos. You can choose a charter or fly on Aeromexico, Alaska Air, American, Continental, Delta, United, or US Airways.
- **Mexicana Vacations,** or MexSeaSun Vacations (© **800/531-9321;** www.mexicana.com), offers getaways and daily direct flights from Los Angeles to Los Cabos.
- **Suntrips** (© **800/357-2400** or 888/888-5028 for departures within 14 days; www.suntrips.com) is one of the largest packagers for Mexico on the West Coast. It arranges regular charters to Los Cabos from San Francisco and Denver, and offers a large selection of hotels.

12 The Active Traveler

Los Cabos, where several championship tournaments are held each year, has become the preeminent golf destination in Mexico. Visitors to Baja can enjoy tennis, racquetball, squash, water-skiing, surfing, bicycling, and horseback riding. Scuba diving is excellent in the Sea of Cortez.

OUTDOORS ORGANIZATIONS & TOUR OPERATORS
AMTAVE, or Asociación Mexicana de Turismo de Aventura y Ecoturismo, A.C. (© **800/509-7678;** www.amtave.com), is an association of eco- and adventure tour operators. It publishes an annual catalog of participating firms and their offerings, all of which must meet criteria for security, quality, and training of the guides, as well as for sustainability of natural and cultural environments.

The **American Wilderness Experience** (Globe Travel), P.O. Box 1486, Boulder, CO 80306 (© **800/444-3833** or 303/444-2622), leads catered camping, kayaking, biking, and hiking trips in Baja California.

Baja Expeditions, 2625 Garnet Ave., San Diego, CA 92109 (© **800/843-6967** or 858/581-3311; www.bajaex.com), offers natural-history cruises, whale-watching, sea kayaking, camping, and scuba-diving trips out of Loreto, La Paz, and San Diego. Small groups and special itineraries are the firm's specialty.

Mountain Travel Sobek, 6420 Fairmount Ave., El Cerrito, CA 94530 (© **800/227-2384** or 510/527-8100), leads kayaking groups in the Sea of Cortez.

Natural Habitat Adventures, 2945 Center Green Court, Suite H, Boulder, CO 80301 (© **800/543-8917** or 303/449-3711; www.nathab.com), offers naturalist-led natural history and adventure travel. Expeditions focus on whale-watching in Baja.

Naturequest, 30872 South Coast Highway, Suite 185, Laguna Beach, CA 92651 (© **800/369-3033** or 949/499-9561; natureqst@aol.com), offers Baja trips that get close to nature with special permits for venturing by two-person kayak into sanctuaries for whales and birds, and slipping among mangroves and into shallow bays, estuaries, and lagoons.

North Star (© **800/258-8434** or 520/773-9917; fax 520/773-9965; www.adventuretrip.com) guides 6-day sea-kayaking trips with boat support in the Sea of Cortez from October to May. Several routes are available along the coast from San José and past the San Francisco Islands and the Sierra de la Giganta. A 10-day trip from Loreto to La Paz is also offered. No prior kayaking experience is necessary, but you have to be in good physical condition. Custom trips for groups of 10 or more can be arranged.

One World Workforce, P.O. Box 3188, La Mesa, CA 91944 (© **800/451-9564**), has weeklong "hands-on conservation trips" that offer working volunteers a chance to help with sea-turtle conservation at Bahía de Los Angeles, Baja (spring, summer, and fall).

For more than 20 years, local resident Trudi Angell has guided sea-kayaking tours in the Loreto area with **Tour Baja,** P.O. Box 827, Calistoga, CA 94515 (© **800/398-6200** or 707/942-4550; fax 707/942-8017; www.tourbaja.com). She and her guides offer first-hand knowledge of the area, its natural history, and local culture. Her company's kayaking, mountain biking, pack trips, and sailing charters combine these elements with great outdoor adventures.

By alternating sea-kayaking trips between Alaska and Baja for two decades, **Sea Trek Sea Kayaking Center** (© **415/488-1000;** fax

415/488-1707; www.seatrekkayak.com) has gained an intimate knowledge of the remote coastline of Baja. Eight-day trips depart from and return to Loreto; a 12-day expedition travels from Loreto to La Paz. An optional day excursion to Bahía Magdalena for whale-watching is also available. Full boat support is provided, and no previous paddling experience is necessary.

13 Getting Around

An important note: If your travel schedule depends on an important connection, use the telephone numbers in this book or other resources mentioned here to find out whether the connection you are depending on is still available. Although we've done our best to provide accurate information, transportation schedules can and do change.

BY PLANE

To fly from point to point within Mexico, you'll rely on Mexican airlines. Mexico has two privately owned large national carriers: **Mexicana** (© 800/366-5400) and **Aeromexico** (© 800/021-4000), in addition to several up-and-coming regional carriers. Mexicana and Aeromexico both offer extensive connections to the United States as well as within Mexico.

AIRPORT TAXES   Mexico charges an airport tax on all departures. Passengers leaving the country on an international departure pay $18 (in dollars or the peso equivalent). It has become a common practice to include this departure tax in your ticket price, but double-check to make sure so you're not caught by surprise at the airport. Taxes on each domestic departure you make within Mexico are around $12.50, unless you're on a connecting flight and have already paid at the start of the flight, in which case you shouldn't be charged again. Mexico charges an $18 "tourism tax," the proceeds of which go into a tourism promotional fund. Your ticket price may not include it, so be sure to have enough money to pay it at the airport upon departure.

BY CAR

Most Mexican roads are not up to U.S. standards of smoothness, hardness, width of curve, grade of hill, or safety marking. Driving at night is dangerous—the roads are rarely lit; trucks, carts, pedestrians, and bicycles usually have no lights; and you can hit potholes, animals, rocks, dead ends, or bridges out with no warning.

The spirited style of Mexican driving sometimes requires super vision and reflexes. Be prepared for new customs, as when a truck driver flips on his left turn signal when there's not a crossroad for miles. He's probably telling you the road's clear ahead for you to pass. Another custom that's very important to respect is how to make a left turn. Never turn left by stopping in the middle of a highway with your left signal on. Instead, pull off the highway onto the right shoulder, wait for traffic to clear, and then proceed across the road.

GASOLINE   There's one government-owned brand of gas and one gasoline station name throughout the country—**Pemex** *(Petroleras Mexicanas)*. There are two types of gas in Mexico: *magna,* 87-octane unleaded gas, and premium 93 octane. In Mexico, fuel and oil are sold by the liter, which is slightly more than a quart (40 liters equals about 10½ gal.). Many franchise Pemex stations have bathroom facilities and convenience stores—a great improvement over the old ones.

Important note: No credit cards are accepted for gas purchases.

BREAKDOWNS   If your car breaks down on the road, help might already be on the way. Radio-equipped green repair trucks operated by uniformed English-speaking officers patrol the major highways during daylight hours to aid motorists in trouble. These Green Angels *(Angeles Verdes)* will perform minor repairs and adjustments for free, but you pay for parts and materials.

To find a mechanic on the road, look for a sign that says *taller mecánico.*

Flat tires are repaired at places called *vulcanizadora* or *llantera;* it is common to find such places open 24 hours a day on the most traveled highways.

MINOR ACCIDENTS   When possible, many Mexicans drive away from minor accidents or try to make an immediate settlement to avoid involving the police. If the police arrive while the involved persons are still at the scene, everyone may be locked in jail until blame is assessed. In any case, you have to settle up immediately, or be faced with days of red tape. Foreigners who don't speak fluent Spanish are at a distinct disadvantage when trying to explain their side of the event. Three steps may help the foreigner who doesn't wish to do as the Mexicans do: If you are in your own car, notify your Mexican insurance company, whose job it is to intervene on your behalf; if you are in a rental car, notify the rental company immediately and ask how to contact the nearest adjuster (you did buy insurance with the rental, right?); finally, if all else fails, ask to contact the nearest Green Angel, who may be able to explain to officials that you are covered by insurance. See also "Mexican Auto Insurance" in "Getting There," above.

CAR RENTALS   You'll get the best price if you reserve a car a week in advance in the United States. U.S. car-rental firms include **Avis** (© 800/331-1212 in the U.S., 800/TRY-AVIS in Canada), **Budget** (© 800/527-0700 in the U.S. and Canada), **Hertz** (© 800/654-3131 in the U.S. and Canada), and **National** (© 800/CAR-RENT in the U.S. and Canada). For European travelers, **Kemwel Holiday Auto** (© 800/678-0678) and **Auto Europe** (© 800/223-5555) can arrange Mexican rentals, sometimes through other agencies. You'll find rental desks at airports, all major hotels, and many travel agencies.

Car-rental costs are high in Mexico because cars are more expensive. The condition of rental cars has improved greatly over the years, however, and clean, comfortable, new cars are the norm. At press time, the basic cost of a 1-day rental of a Volkswagen Beetle, with unlimited mileage (but before 15% tax and $15 daily insurance), was $58 in Los Cabos. Renting by the week gives you about a 15% lower daily rate. Rental prices may be considerably higher around a major holiday.

Car-rental companies usually write up a credit card charge in U.S. dollars.

Deductibles   Be careful—these vary greatly in Mexico; some are as high as $2,500, which comes out of your pocket immediately in case of car damage. Hertz's deductible is $1,000 on a VW Beetle; Avis' is $500 for the same car.

Insurance   Insurance is offered in two parts: **Collision and damage** insurance covers your car and others if the accident is your fault, and **personal accident** insurance covers you and anyone in your car. Read the fine print on the back of your rental agreement and note that insurance may be invalid if you have an accident while driving on an unpaved road.

Travel Tip

Little English is spoken at bus stations, so come prepared with your destination written down, then double-check the departure.

Damage Always inspect your car carefully and note every damaged or missing item, no matter how minute, on your rental agreement, or you may be charged.

BY TAXI

Taxis are the preferred way to get around in almost all the resort areas of Mexico, but are very expensive in the Los Cabos area. One-way travel between Cabo San Lucas and San José del Cabo averages $35. Short trips within towns are generally charged by preset zones and are quite reasonable compared with U.S. rates. For longer trips or excursions to nearby cities, taxis can generally be hired for around $10 to $15 per hour, or for a negotiated daily rate. Even drops to different destinations can be arranged. A negotiated one-way price is usually much less than the cost of a rental car for a day, and service is much faster than travel by bus. For anyone who is uncomfortable driving in Mexico, this is a convenient, comfortable alternative. A bonus is that you have a Spanish-speaking person with you in case you run into any car or road trouble. Many taxi drivers speak at least some English. Your hotel can assist you with the arrangements.

BY BUS

Bus service is not as well developed in the Baja peninsula as in other parts of the country, although it is available between principle points. Travel class is generally labeled second *(segunda)*, first *(primera)*, and deluxe *(ejecutiva)*. The deluxe buses often have fewer seats than regular buses, show movies en route, are air-conditioned, and make few stops; some have complimentary refreshments. Many run express from origin to the final destination. They are well worth the few dollars more that you'll pay. In rural areas, buses are often of the school-bus variety, with lots of local color.

 FAST FACTS: Baja California

Abbreviations Dept. (apartments); Apdo. (post office box); Av. (*Avenida;* avenue); c/ (*calle;* street); Calz. (*Calzada;* boulevard). C on faucets stands for *caliente* (hot), F for *fría* (cold). PB *(planta baja)* means ground floor; most buildings count the next floor up as the first floor (1).

Business Hours In general, businesses in larger cities are open between 9am and 7pm; in smaller towns many close between

2 and 4pm. Most close on Sunday. Bank hours are Monday through Friday from 9 or 9:30am to 3 or 5pm. Increasingly, banks open Saturday for at least a half-day (10am–2pm).

Cameras/Film Film costs about the same as in the United States.

Customs See "Entry Requirements & Customs," earlier in this chapter.

Doctors/Dentists Every embassy and consulate is prepared to recommend local doctors and dentists with good training and modern equipment; some of the doctors and dentists speak English. See the list of embassies and consulates under "Embassies & Consulates," below. Hotels with a large foreign clientele can often recommend English-speaking doctors. Almost all first-class hotels in Mexico have a doctor on call.

Drug Laws To be blunt, don't use or possess illegal drugs in Mexico. Mexican officials have no tolerance for drug users, and jail is their solution, with very little hope of getting out until the sentence (usually a long one) is completed or heavy fines or bribes are paid. Remember, in Mexico the legal system assumes you are guilty until proven innocent. *Important note:* It isn't uncommon to be befriended by a fellow user, only to be turned in by that "friend," who's collected a bounty. Bring prescription drugs in their original containers. If possible, pack a copy of the original prescription with the generic name of the drug.

U.S. Customs officials are also on the lookout for diet drugs sold in Mexico but illegal in the U.S., possession of which could land you in a U.S. jail. If you buy antibiotics over the counter (which you can do in Mexico) and still have some left, you probably won't be hassled by U.S. Customs.

Drugstores See "Pharmacies," below.

Electricity The electrical system in Mexico is 110 volts AC (60 cycles), as in the United States and Canada. In reality, however, it may cycle more slowly and overheat your appliances. To compensate, select a medium or low speed for hair dryers.

Embassies & Consulates They provide valuable lists of doctors and lawyers, as well as regulations concerning marriages in Mexico. Contrary to popular belief, your embassy cannot get you out of a Mexican jail, provide postal or banking services, or fly you home when you run out of money. Consular officers can provide you with advice on most matters and problems, however.

The **Embassy of Australia** in Mexico City is at Ruben Darío 55, Col. Polanco (© **55/5531-5225;** fax 5/531-9552); it's open Monday through Friday from 9am to 1pm.

The **Embassy of Canada** in Mexico City is at Schiller 529, in Polanco (© **55/5724-7900**); it's open Monday through Friday from 9am to 1pm and 2 to 5pm. (At other times the name of a duty officer is posted on the embassy door.) There are **consular agencies** in San José del Cabo (© **624/142-4333**) and Tijuana (© **664/684-0461**). Visit **www.canada.org.mx** for a listing of consular agencies in Mexico.

The **Embassy of New Zealand** in Mexico City is at José Luis Lagrange 103, 10th floor, Col. Los Morales Polanco (© **55/5283-9460**); it's open Monday through Thursday from 9am to 2pm and 3 to 5pm, and Friday from 9am to 2pm.

The **Embassy of the United Kingdom** in Mexico City is in Río Lerma 71, Col. Cuauhtemoc (© **55/5207-2089;** www.embajada britanica.com.mx); it's open Monday through Friday from 8:30am to 3:30pm.

The **Embassy of Ireland** in Mexico City is at Cerrada Blv. Avila Camacho 76, 3rd floor, Col. Lomas de Chapultepec (© **55/5520-5803**); it's open Monday through Friday from 9am to 3pm.

The **South African Embassy** in Mexico City is at Andres Bello 10, 9th floor, Col. Polanco (© **55/5282-9260**). Open Monday through Friday from 8am to 4pm.

The **Embassy of the United States** in Mexico City is at Paseo de la Reforma 305, next to the Hotel María Isabel Sheraton at the corner of Río Danubio (© **55/5080-2000** or 55/5209-9100). Visit **www.usembassy-mexico.gov** for a list of U.S. consulates in Mexico. There is a **U.S. Consulate General** in Tijuana, at Tapachula 96 (© **664/622-7400**), and a consular agency in Cabo San Lucas (© **624/143-3566**).

Emergencies Dial © **060** to reach police in most cities. They can usually assist in getting an ambulance or reaching the fire department, but most operators do not speak English. You should also contact the closest consular office in case of an emergency.

Internet Access In large cities and resort areas, a growing number of top hotels offer business centers with Internet access. You'll also find cybercafes in destinations that are popular with ex-pats and business travelers. Even in remote spots, Internet access is common. Note that many ISPs will automatically cut off your Internet connection after a specified period of time (say, 10 min.) because telephone lines are at a premium.

Legal Aid **International Legal Defense Counsel,** 111 S. 15th St., 24th Floor, Packard Building, Philadelphia, PA 19102 (© 215/ 977-9982), is a law firm that specializes in legal difficulties of Americans abroad. See also "Embassies & Consulates," above.

Liquor Laws The legal drinking age in Mexico is 18; asking for ID or dening purchase is extremely rare. If you look 18, you will likely be able to buy liquor easily. Authorities are beginning to target drunk drivers more aggressively.

It is not legal to drink in the street; however, many tourists do. Use your judgment—if you are getting drunk, you shouldn't drink in the street, because you are more likely to get stopped by the police. As is the custom in Mexico, it is not so much what you do, but how you do it.

Lost Documents To replace a lost passport, contact your embassy or nearest consular agent. You must establish a record of your citizenship and fill out a form requesting another Mexican tourist permit (FMT) if it, too, was lost. Without the FMT you can't leave the country, and without an affidavit affirming your passport request and citizenship, you may have problems at Customs when you get home. Mexican Customs may accept the police report of the loss of the FMT and allow you to leave.

Mail Postage for a postcard or letter is 59¢; it may arrive anywhere from 1 to 6 weeks after it's mailed. A registered letter costs $1.90. To send a package can be quite expensive—the Mexican postal service charges $8 per kilo (2.2 lbs.)—and unreliable; it takes between 2 and 6 weeks, if it arrives at all. The recommended way to send a package or important mail continues to be through DHL, Federal Express, UPS, or any other reputable international mail service.

Newspapers/Magazines In southern Baja, a number of local English-language papers are available, including *Baja Life, Baja Sun,* and the irreverent, entertaining *Gringo Gazette.*

Pharmacies *Farmacias* will sell you just about anything you want, with a prescription or without one. Most drugstores are open Monday through Saturday from 8am to 8pm. Generally, the major resort areas have one or two 24-hour pharmacies. If you are in a smaller town and need to buy medicine after normal hours, ask for the name of the nearest 24-hour pharmacy; they are becoming more common.

Police Especially in the tourist areas, most officers are very protective of international visitors.

Smoking Smoking is permitted and generally accepted in most public places, including restaurants, bars, and hotel lobbies. Nonsmoking areas and hotel rooms for nonsmokers are becoming more common in higher-end establishments, but they tend to be the exception rather than the rule.

Taxes There's a 15% IVA (*Impuesto al Valor Agregado,* or value-added tax) on goods and services in most of Mexico, and it's supposed to be included in the posted price. This tax is 10% in Los Cabos. Mexico imposes an exit tax of around $18 on every foreigner leaving the country; the price of airline tickets usually includes it.

Telephone/Fax Mexico's telephone system is slowly but surely catching up with modern times. All telephone numbers have 10 digits. Every city and town that has telephone access has a 2-digit (Mexico City, Monterrey, and Guadalajara) or 3-digit (everywhere else) area code. In Mexico City, Monterrey, and Guadalajara, local numbers have 8 digits; elsewhere, local numbers have 7 digits. To place a local call, you do not need to dial the area code. Many fax numbers are also regular telephone numbers; ask whoever answers for the fax tone *("me da tono de fax, por favor").* Cellular phones are very popular for small businesses in resort areas and smaller communities. To call a cellular number inside the same area code, dial 044 and then the number. To dial the cellular phone from anywhere else in Mexico, first dial 01, then the 3-digit area code and the 7-digit number. To dial it from the U.S., dial 011-52, plus the 3-digit area code and the 7-digit number.

The **country code** for Mexico is **52.**

To call Mexico: If you're calling Mexico from the United States:

1. Dial the international access code: 011
2. Dial the country code: 52
3. Dial the 2- or 3-digit area code, then the 8- or 7-digit number. For example, if you wanted to call the U.S. consulate in Acapulco, the whole number would be 011/52-744-469-0556. If

you wanted to dial the U.S. Embassy in Mexico City, the whole number would be 011-52-55-5209-9100.

To make international calls: To make international calls from Mexico, first dial 00, then the country code (U.S. or Canada 1, U.K. 44, Ireland 353, Australia 61, New Zealand 64). Next, dial the area code and number. For example, to call the British Embassy in Washington, you would dial 00-1-202-588-7800.

For directory assistance: Dial *©* **040** if you're looking for a number inside Mexico. *Note:* Listings usually appear under the owner's name, not the name of the business, and your chances to find an English-speaking operator are slim to none.

For operator assistance: If you need operator assistance in making a call, dial 090 to make an international call, and 020 to call a number in Mexico.

Toll-free numbers: Numbers beginning with 800 within Mexico are toll-free, but calling a U.S. toll-free number from Mexico costs the same as an overseas call. To call an 800 number in the U.S., dial 001-880 and the last 7 digits of the toll-free number. To call an 888 number in the U.S., dial 001-881 and the last 7 digits of the toll-free number.

Time Zone Central Standard Time prevails throughout most of Mexico. The state of Baja California Norte is on Pacific Standard Time, but Baja California Sur is on Mountain Standard Time. Mexico observes daylight savings time.

Tipping Most service employees in Mexico count on tips to make up the majority of their income—especially bellboys and waiters. Bellboys receive the equivalent of 50¢ to $1 per bag; waiters generally receive 10% to 20% of the bill, depending on the level of service. In Mexico, it is not customary to tip taxi drivers, unless they are hired by the hour or provide touring or other special services.

Useful Phone Numbers **Tourist Help Line,** available 24 hours (*©* 800/903-9200 toll-free inside Mexico). **Mexico Hotline** (*©* 800/44-MEXICO). **U.S. Dept. of State Travel Advisory,** staffed 24 hours (*©* 202/647-5225). **U.S. Passport Agency** (*©* 202/647-0518). **U.S. Centers for Disease Control International Traveler's Hotline** (*©* 404/332-4559).

Water Most hotels have decanters or bottles of purified water in the rooms; the better hotels have either purified water from regular taps, or special taps marked *agua purificada*. Some hotels will charge for in-room bottled water. Virtually any hotel, restaurant, or bar will bring you purified water if you specifically request it, but you'll usually be charged for it. Bottled purified water is sold at drugstores and grocery stores (popular brands include Santa María, Ciel, and Bonafont).

2

Los Cabos

The most popular destinations in Baja Sur are the twin towns at the peninsula's tip: Cabo San Lucas and San José del Cabo. Collectively they are known as Los Cabos (the Capes), although they couldn't be more different from one another. Cabo San Lucas is an extension of Southern California, with luxury accommodations, ubiquitous golf courses, endless shopping, franchise restaurants, and spirited nightlife. San José del Cabo remains rooted in the traditions of a quaint Mexican town, although it's rapidly becoming gentrified.

Thirty kilometers (18 miles) of smooth highway known as the Corridor lie between the two Cabos. Along this stretch, major new resorts and residential communities, including some of the world's finest golf courses, have been developed. And what has always been here continues to beckon: dozens of pristine coves and inlets with a wealth of marine life just offshore.

Golf has overtaken sportfishing as Los Cabos' main draw, with eight championship courses open for play. Still more activities to keep you busy are sea kayaking, whale-watching, diving, surfing, and hiking, as well as the chance to explore ancient cave paintings and to camp on isolated, wild beaches.

The Los Cabos area has earned a deserved reputation for being much more expensive than other Mexican resorts. Although there has been a boom in hotel construction, these have all been luxury resorts, only solidifying Los Cabos' higher average room prices, and not adjusting prices downward with the added supply of rooms. The other factor driving up prices is that compared to mainland Mexico, there's little agriculture in Baja; most foodstuffs and other items must be shipped in. U.S. dollars are the preferred currency here, and it's not uncommon to see price listings in dollars rather than pesos.

With more than 33km (21 miles) separating the two Cabos and numerous attractions in between, you should consider renting a car, even if only for a day. Transportation by taxi is expensive, and if you are at all interested in exploring, a rental car is your most economical option. Because of the distinctive character and attractions of the two towns and the Corridor between, they are treated separately here. It is common to stay in one and make day trips to the other two.

1 San José del Cabo (★(★(★

196km (122 miles) SE of La Paz; 35km (22 miles) NE of Cabo San Lucas; 1,771km (1,100 miles) SE of Tijuana

San José del Cabo, with its pastel cottages and flowering trees lining the narrow streets, retains the air of a provincial Mexican town. Originally founded in 1730 by Jesuit missionaries, it remains the seat of the Los Cabos government and the center of its business community. The main square, adorned with a wrought-iron bandstand and shaded benches, faces the cathedral, which was built on the site of an early mission.

San José is becoming increasingly sophisticated, with a collection of noteworthy cafes, art galleries, and intriguing small inns adding a newly refined flavor to the central downtown area. This is the best choice for those who want to enjoy the paradoxical landscape but still be aware that they're in Mexico.

ESSENTIALS
GETTING THERE & DEPARTING
BY PLANE **AeroCalifornia** (© **800/237-6225** in the U.S., 624/143-3700, or 624/143-3915), has nonstop or direct flights from Los Angeles and Phoenix. **Aeromexico** (© **800/237-6639** in the U.S., 624/146-5098, or 624/146-5097; www.aeromexico.com), flies nonstop from San Diego and Ontario, CA, and has connecting flights from Houston, Dallas, New York, Tucson, Guadalajara, and Mexico City. **Alaska Airlines** (© **800/426-0333** in the U.S., or 624/146-5101; www.alaskaair.com) flies from Los Angeles, San Diego, Seattle, and San Francisco. **America West** (© **800/235-9292** in the U.S.; 624/146-5380; www.americawestvacations.com) makes connecting flights through Phoenix. **Continental** (© **800/231-0856** in the U.S., or 624/146-5040; www.continental.com) flies from Houston. **Mexicana** (© **800/531-7921** in the U.S., 624/146-5001, 624/143-5352, or 624/143-5353; www.mexicana.com) has direct or connecting flights from Denver, Guadalajara, Los Angeles, and Mexico City.

BY CAR From La Paz, take Highway 1 south, a scenic route that winds through foothills and occasionally skirts the coast; the drive takes 3 to 4 hours. From La Paz, you can also take Highway 1 south just past the village of San Pedro, then take Highway 19 south (a less

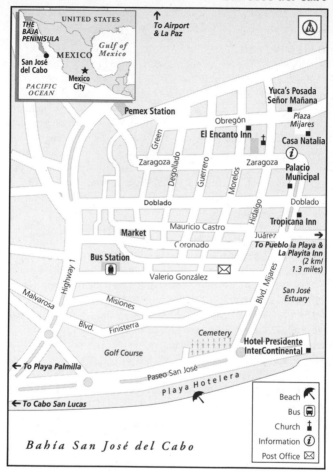

winding road than Highway 1) through Todos Santos to Cabo San Lucas, where you pick up Highway 1 east to San José del Cabo; this route takes 2 to 3 hours. From Cabo San Lucas, it's a half-hour drive.

BY BUS The bus station *(terminal de autobuses),* on Valerio González, a block east of Highway 1 (© **624/142-1100**), is open daily from 5:30am to 7pm, although buses can arrive and depart later. Buses between Cabo San Lucas and La Paz run almost hourly during the day. For points farther north you usually change buses in

La Paz. The trip to Cabo San Lucas takes 40 minutes; to La Paz, 3 hours. Buses also go to Todos Santos; the trip takes around 3 hours.

ORIENTATION

ARRIVING   The one airport (© **624/146-5111**) that serves both Cabos and the connecting Corridor is 12km (7½ miles) northwest of San José del Cabo and 35km (22 miles) northeast of Cabo San Lucas. Upon arrival at the airport, buy a ticket inside the building for a *colectivo* (minivan) or a taxi, which up to four passengers may share. Colectivo fares run about $9 for up to eight passengers and are only available from the airport. A private van for up to five passengers is $60. Taxis charge about $15 to San José. Timeshare resorts have booths in the airport's arrival/baggage area. The promoters hook visitors with a free ride to their hotel in return for listening to their sales presentation.

The major car-rental agencies all have counters at the airport, open during flight arrivals: **Avis** (© **800/331-1212** from the U.S., or 624/146-0201; avissjd@avis.com.mx; open 7am–9pm); **Budget** (© **800/527-0700** from the U.S., or 624/146-5333 at the airport, or 624/143-4190 in Cabo San Lucas; open 8am–6pm); **Hertz** (© **800/654-3131** from the U.S., or 624/146-5088 or 624/142-0375 in San José del Cabo; open 8am–8pm); and **National** (© **800/328-4567** from the U.S., 624/146-5022 at the airport, or 624/142-2424 in San José; open 8am–8pm). Advance reservations are not always necessary.

If you arrive at the bus station, it's too far from the hotels to walk with luggage. A taxi from the bus station to downtown or the hotel zone costs $2 to $4.

VISITOR INFORMATION   The **city tourist information office** (© **624/142-3310**) is in the old post office building on Zaragoza at Mijares. It offers maps, free local publications, and other basic information about the area. It's open Monday through Friday from 8am to 3pm.

CITY LAYOUT   San José del Cabo consists of two zones: downtown, where sophisticated inns as well as traditional budget hotels are located, and the hotel zone along the beach.

Zaragoza is the main street leading from the highway into town; Paseo San José runs parallel to the beach and is the principal boulevard of the hotel zone. The 1.6km (1-mile) Bulevar Mijares connects the two areas.

FAST FACTS: San José del Cabo

Area Code The local area code is **624**.

Banks Banks exchange currency during business hours, generally Monday through Friday from 8:30am to 6pm and Saturday from 10am to 2pm. There are several banks on Zaragoza between Morelos and Degollado.

Emergencies Call the local police at city hall (✆ **624/142-0361**).

Hospital **Hospital General,** Retorno Atunero s/n, Col. Chamizal (✆ **1/142-0013**).

Internet Access **Web Land,** Mijares 29, local 6 (✆ **624/142-5282;** www.webland-cabo.com), is across from the Tropicana Bar and Grill. It's open Monday to Saturday from 9am to 8pm and charges $4 for 10 minutes or $8 per hour. In addition to high-speed access, it has scanners, printers, CD burners, webcams, and joysticks. Serves coffee, too! **CaboOnline,** Malvarrosa and Gobernadora (✆ **624/142-2905**), is open Monday through Saturday 10am to 8pm and charges $7.50 per hour.

Pharmacy **Farmacia ISSTE,** Km 34 Carretera Transpeninsular, Plaza California (✆ **624/142-2645**), and **Farmacia Plaza Dorada,** Km 29 Carretera Transpeninsular, Plaza Dorada (✆ **624/142-0140**), are the two major pharmacies in the area.

Post Office The *correo,* Blv. Mijares 1924 at Valerio González (✆ **624/142-0911**), is open Monday through Friday from 8am to 4pm and Saturday from 9am to 1pm.

GETTING AROUND

There is no local bus service between downtown and the beach; **taxis** (✆ **624/142-0910** or 624/142-0580) connect the two.

For day trips to Cabo San Lucas, catch a bus (see "Getting There & Departing," above) or a cab.

BEACHES & OUTDOOR ACTIVITIES

The relaxed pace of San José del Cabo makes it an ideal place to unwind and absorb authentic Mexican flavor. Beach aficionados who want to explore the beautiful coves and beaches along the

35km (22-mile) coast between the two Cabos should consider renting a car for a day or so (from $45 per day). Frequent bus service between San José del Cabo and Cabo San Lucas makes it possible to visit both towns (see "Getting There & Departing," above).

BEACHES

The nearest beach that's safe for swimming is **Pueblo la Playa** (also called La Playita), about 3.2km (2 miles) east of town. From Bulevar Mijares, turn east at the small sign PUEBLO LA PLAYA and follow the dusty dirt road through cane fields and palms to a small village and beautiful beach where fishermen pull their *pangas* (skiffs) ashore. La Playita Resort and its adjacent restaurant (see "Where to Stay," below) offer the only formal sustenance on the beach. There are no shade *palapas.*

Estero San José, a nature reserve with at least 270 species of birds, is between Pueblo la Playa and the Hotel Presidente Inter-Continental. The estuary is a protected ecological reserve.

A fine swimming beach with beautiful rock formations, **Playa Palmilla,** 8km (5 miles) west of San José, is near the Spanish colonial–style Hotel Palmilla, which is currently under renovation. To reach Playa Palmilla, take a taxi to the road that leads to the Hotel Palmilla grounds, then take the fork to the left (without entering the hotel grounds) and follow signs to Pepe's restaurant on the beach.

For a list of other nearby beaches worth exploring if you have a rental car, see "Beaches & Outdoor Activities" under "Cabo San Lucas," later in this chapter.

CRUISES

Boats depart from Cabo San Lucas; prices and offerings vary, but cruises generally include music, open bar, and snacks for $30 to $40 per person. Daytime and sunset cruises are available. Arrange cruises through a travel agency, or call **Xplora Adventours** (✆ **624/142-9135**

(Moments Festivals & Special Events in Los Cabos

San José del Cabo celebrates the feast of its patron saint on March 19 with a fair, music, dancing, feasting, horse races, and cockfights. June 19 is the festival of the patron saint of San Bartolo, a village 100km (62 miles) north. July 25 is the festival of the patron saint of Santiago, a village 55km (34 miles) north.

Tips Swimming Safety

Although the area is ideal for watersports, predominant strong currents and undertow sometimes make swimming dangerous at Playa Hotelera, the town beach—check conditions before entering the surf. Swimming is generally safe at Pueblo la Playa (see "Beaches," above).

---

or 624/142-9000, ext. 8050; www.xploraloscabos.com). Xplora handles all tour providers in the area and can give unbiased information. It's open daily from 8am to 10pm.

LAND SPORTS

ADVENTURE TOURS   A variety of land- and water-based adventure and nature tours are available through **Tio Sports** (© 624/143-3399; www.tiosports.com), including popular ATV tours to Candelaria, and parasailing at $45 single or $75 tandem. Kayak, catamaran, snorkeling, and diving trips are also offered.

GOLF   Los Cabos is rapidly becoming a major golf destination, with several new courses open and others under construction. The most economical greens fees are at the 9-hole **Club Campo de Golf San José** (© 624/142-0900 or 624/142-0905), on Paseo Finisterra across from the Howard Johnson Hotel. The public course is open daily from 7am to 4pm (to 4:30pm in summer). Club guests can also use the swimming pool. The greens fee is $45 for 9 holes, $77 for 18 holes. Carts cost $30 for 9 holes, $45 for 18 holes. Club rentals are $16.50. For more information about playing golf in Los Cabos, see "The Lowdown on Golfing in Cabo," later in this chapter.

HORSEBACK RIDING   You can rent horses near the Presidente InterContinental, Fiesta Inn, and Palmilla hotels for $15 to $20 per hour. Most people choose to ride on the beach. You can also arrange horseback riding through **Xplora Adventours** (© 624/142-9135; www.xploraloscabos.com). It deals with a good ranch that has a stable of healthy, well-groomed horses (the horses on the beaches are often on the thin side). Xplora offers tours on the beach and down a mountain trail. One-hour rides are $30.

TENNIS   You can play tennis at the two courts of the **Club Campo de Golf San José**, Paseo Finisterra 1 (© 624/142-0905), for $12 an hour during the day, $22 an hour at night. Club guests can use the swimming pool. Tennis is also available at the **Hotel Presidente InterContinental** (two lit courts); see "Where to Stay," below.

WATERSPORTS

FISHING   The least expensive way to enjoy deep-sea fishing is to pair up with another angler and charter a *panga,* a 7m (22-foot) skiff used by local fishermen from Playa la Puebla. Several panga fleets offer 6-hour sportfishing trips, usually from 6am to noon, for $25 per hour (there's a 3-hr. minimum). Two or three people can divide the cost. For information, visit the fisherman's cooperative in Pueblo la Playa (no phone), or contact **Victor's Aquatics,** at the Hotel Posada Real (© **949/496-0960** in the U.S., or 624/142-1092; fax 624/142-1093; victor@1cabonet.com.mx), open daily from 9am to 7pm. Victor's has a full fishing fleet with both pangas ($185 for 6 hr.) and cruisers ($310–$395). Larger boats, up to 10m (33 ft.), are available for $450 to $550. Outfitters supply the boat and tackle, and the client buys the bait, drinks, and snacks.

SEA KAYAKING   Fully guided, ecologically oriented **Ocean Kayak Tours** are available through **Baja's Moto Rent** (© **624/143-2050**), **Cabo Expeditions** (© **624/143-2700**), and **Aqua Deportes** (© **624/143-0117**). Most ocean kayaking tours depart from Cabo San Lucas.

SNORKELING/DIVING   Arrange trips (from $50 per person) through **Xplora Adventours** (© **624/142-9135** or 624/142-9000, ext. 8316; www.xploraloscabos.com; open daily from 8:30am–8:30pm) or **Amigos del Mar** in Cabo San Lucas (© **624/143-0505**). Among the area's best dive sites are **Cabo Pulmo** and **Gordo Banks.** Cabo Pulmo has seven sites geared for divers of all experience levels, so it never feels crowded. It also offers the possibility to snorkel with sea lions, depending on the currents and the animals' behavior. Gordo Banks is an advanced dive site where you can see whale sharks and hammerhead sharks. It's a deep dive—between 27m and 30m (90ft.–110 ft.)—with limited visibility (9m–12m/30ft.–40 ft.). Most dives are drift dives, and wetsuits are highly recommended.

SURFING   **Playa Costa Azul,** at Km 29 on Highway 1 just south of San José, is the most popular surfing beach in the area. There are a few bungalows available for rent, or surfers can camp on the beach. The **Costa Azul Surf Shop,** Km 28, Playa Costa Azul (© **624/142-2771;** www.costa-azul.com.mx), rents surfboards by the day. It charges $5 an hour for a short or long board, leash, and rack for your rental car, but it's generally better to bring your own. Spectators can watch from the highway lookout point at the top of the hill south of Costa Azul.

Warning: Several accidents have involved visiting surfers who were not familiar with the rocky break.

When summer hurricanes spin off the southern end of the peninsula, they send huge surf northward to beaches like Zipper's, Punta Gorda, and Old Man's. Surfers have compared Zipper's (near the Brisa del Mar Trailer Park and the Costa Azul Surf Shop outside San José del Cabo) with places like Pipeline, on the north shore of Oahu. That may be a bit of an exaggeration, but there are great waves, nonetheless.

WHALE-WATCHING   From January through March, whales congregate offshore. Fishermen at Pueblo la Playa will take small groups out to see the whales; a 4-hour trip runs about $45 per person. Organized half-day tours on sportfishing boats, glass-bottom boats, and cruise catamarans depart from Plaza las Glorias in Cabo San Lucas and cost $35 to $50, depending on the type of boat. The price includes snacks and beverages. The ultimate whale excursion is a trip to **Magdalena Bay.** Tours from San José take you by plane— a 75-minute flight—to Magdalena, where you board a panga and spend 3 hours watching gray whales and humpbacks loll around the coastal lagoons. This tour is $385, including air transportation, and can be arranged through **Xplora Adventours** (© **624/142-9135;** www.xploraloscabos.com). You can also spot the whales from shore; good spots include the beach by the Solmar Suites hotel on the Pacific and the beaches and cliffs along the Corridor. For more information, see "Whale-Watching in Baja: A Primer," in chapter 4.

SHOPPING

The town has a growing selection of unique design shops, hip boutiques, and collections of fine Mexican *artesanía* (handcrafts) clustered around Bulevar Mijares and Zaragoza, the main street. The municipal market, on Mauricio Castro and Green, sells edibles and utilitarian wares. Check out some of these favorites.

ADD (Arte, Diseño y Decoración)   This shop sells creative home accessories and furnishings, mostly made of rustic wood, pewter, and Talavera ceramics. Shipping is available. Zaragoza at Hidalgo. © 624/142-2777.

Copal   Traditional and contemporary Mexican artesanía and silver jewelry are the specialties in this former residence, tastefully converted into a contemporary shop. Open weekdays from 9am to 10:30pm, weekends 10am to 2pm and 4 to 10:30pm. Plaza Mijares 10, off Av. Obregón. © 624/142-3070.

Escape This store features designer and casual sportswear and accessories, including designer jeans, leather bags, belts, and a trendy selection of sunglasses. There's also an interior decor shop by the same name next door, with a small cafe and espresso bar in the connecting courtyard. Plaza Florentine, Zaragoza, across from the cathedral. ℂ 624/142-2799.

GALLERIES

San José has a growing number of art galleries—mainly artist studios, open to the public. The most notable is **Galeria Wentworth Porter,** Av. Obregón 20 (ℂ 624/142-3141), which features a selection of original fine art, along with prints and art cards by local artists. As the name implies, locally popular artist Dennis Wentworth Porter's work figures prominently. It's open weekdays from 10am to 1pm and 4 to 7pm, Saturday from 10am to 2pm.

WHERE TO STAY

There's more demand than supply for hotel rooms in Baja Sur, so prices tend to be higher than those for equivalent accommodations in other parts of Mexico. San José has only a handful of budget hotels, so it's best to call ahead for reservations. A new trend here is toward smaller inns, or bed-and-breakfasts, offering stylish accommodations in town. The beachfront hotel zone often offers package deals that bring room rates down to the moderate range, especially during summer months. Check with your travel agent.

EXPENSIVE

Casa Natalia ★★★ *(Finds)* This acclaimed boutique hotel is exquisite. Owners Nathalie and Loic have transformed a former residence into a beautiful amalgam of palms, waterfalls, and flowers that mirrors the beauty of the land. The inn is a completely renovated historic home, which combines modern architecture with traditional Mexican touches. Each room's name reflects the decor, such as Conchas (seashells), Azul (blue), or Talavera (ceramics); all have sliding glass doors that open onto small private terraces with hammocks and chairs, shaded by bougainvillea and bamboo. The two spa suites each have a private terrace with a Jacuzzi and hammock. California palms surround the small courtyard pool; the terraces face this view. Casa Natalia offers its guests privacy, style, and romance. It's in the heart of the Bulevar Mijares action, just off the central plaza.

Blv. Mijares 4, 23400 San José del Cabo, B.C.S. ℂ **888/277-3814** in the U.S., or 624/142-5100. Fax 624/142-5110. www.casanatalia.com. 16 units. High season $220 standard, $345 spa suite; low season $180 standard, $295 spa suite. AE, MC,

V. Children under 14 not accepted. **Amenities:** Exceptional gourmet restaurant (see "Where to Dine," below); bar; heated pool with waterfall and palapa swim-up bar; spa services upon request; concierge; room service; in-room massage; laundry service. *In room:* A/C, TV, dataport, coffeemaker, hair dryer, safe-deposit boxes.

Hotel Presidente InterContinental 🗫🗫

Serenity, seclusion, and luxury are the hallmarks of the Presidente, set on a long stretch of beach next to the Estero San José. Low-rise, Mediterranean-style buildings frame the beach and San José's largest swimming pool, which has a swim-up bar. If possible, select a ground-floor ocean-front room; the lower level offers spacious terraces, but upper-level units have tiny balconies. The rooms have satellite TV and large bathrooms; suites include a separate sitting area. The all-inclusive resort is a good choice for those who principally want to stay put in one place and enjoy it; it's also popular with families.

Blv. Mijares s/n, 23400 San José del Cabo, B.C.S. ℂ 800/327-0200 in the U.S., or 624/142-0211. Fax 624/142-0232. http://loscabos.interconti.com. 395 units. High season $347–$477 standard double, $477 oceanfront double, $511–$693 double suite. Low season rates from $250 double. Rates include all meals, beverages, and many sports. AE, DC, MC, V. **Amenities:** 5 restaurants; garden cafe; 4 pools (2 heated, with swim-up bars); children's pool; golf clinics; tennis; gym; bicycles; horseback riding; tour desk; twice-daily shuttle to Cabo San Lucas (fee); room service; laundry service; safe-deposit box (in reception area). *In room:* A/C, TV, hair dryer, makeup mirror.

MODERATE

El Encanto Inn 🗫🗫 *Value*   On a quiet street in the historic downtown district, this charming small inn borders a grassy courtyard with fountain, offering a relaxing alternative to busy hotels. Rooms are attractively and uniquely decorated, with rustic wood and contemporary iron furniture. The nice-sized bathrooms have colorful tile accents. Rooms have two double beds; suites have king-size beds and an added sitting room. El Encanto's welcoming owners, Cliff and Blanca, can help arrange fishing packages and golf and diving outings. Blanca is a lifelong resident of San José, so she's a great resource for information and dining tips. It's best for couples or singles looking for a peaceful place from which to explore historic San José. The property just gained a small outdoor pool, and 12 suites and a palapa bar are scheduled to open next door to the original structure in late 2003. Room rates include continental breakfast at Jazmin's restaurant, half a block away.

Morelos 133 (between Obregón and Comonfort, ½ block from the church), 23400 San José del Cabo, B.C.S. ℂ 624/142-0388. www.elencantoinn.com. 19 units. $73 double; $85 jr. suite; $95 suite. AE (payment only), MC, V (payment and reservations). Rates include continental breakfast. Limited street parking available. **Amenities:** Small outdoor pool. *In room:* A/C, TV, coffeemaker, fan.

La Playita Inn   Removed from even the slow pace of San José, this older yet impeccably clean and friendly courtyard hotel is ideal for fishermen and those looking for something removed from a traditional hotel vacation. It's the only hotel on San José's only beach that's safe for swimming. Steps from the water and the lineup of fishing pangas, the two stories of sunlit rooms frame a patio with a pool just large enough to allow you to swim laps. Each room is spacious, with high ceilings, high-quality if basic furnishings, screened windows, and nicely tiled bathrooms, plus cable TV. Two large suites on the second floor have small refrigerators. If you catch a big one, there's a fish freezer for storage. Services include coffee every morning and golf-cart shuttle to the beach. Next door, the hotel's La Playita Restaurant is open daily from 11am to 10pm and serves a great mix of seafood and standard favorites, plus occasional live jazz or tropical music.

Pueblo la Playa, Apdo. Postal 437, 23400 San José del Cabo, B.C.S. ⓒ/fax **624/142-4166**. www.laplayitahotel.com. 26 units. $70 double. Rates include continental breakfast. MC, V. Free parking. From Blv. Mijares, follow the sign pointing to PUEBLO LA PLAYA, taking a dirt road for about 3.2km (2 miles) to the beach. The hotel is on the left, facing the water at the edge of the tiny village of Pueblo la Playa. **Amenities:** Adjoining restaurant; pool; fish freezer; morning coffee service. *In room:* A/C, TV.

Tropicana Inn 🏨   This handsome colonial-style hotel, a long-standing favorite in San José, welcomes many repeat visitors. Just behind (and adjacent to) the Tropicana Bar and Grill, it frames a plant-filled courtyard with a graceful arcade bordering the rooms and inviting swimming pool. Each nicely furnished, medium-size room in the L-shaped building (which has a two- and a three-story wing) has tile floors, two double beds, a window looking out on the courtyard, and a brightly tiled bathroom with shower. Each morning, freshly brewed coffee, delicious sweet rolls, and fresh fruit are set out for hotel guests. There's room service until 11pm from the adjacent Tropicana Bar and Grill (owned by the hotel).

Blv. Mijares 30 (1 block south of the town square), 23400 San José del Cabo, B.C.S. ⓒ **624/142-0907** or 624/142-1580. Fax 624/142-1590. 38 units. $79 double. Rates include continental breakfast. AE, MC, V. Free limited parking. **Amenities:** Restaurant/bar; small pool; tour desk; room service; laundry service. *In room:* A/C, TV, minibar, coffeemaker.

INEXPENSIVE

Posada Señor La Mañana   This comfortable two-story guesthouse, in a grove of tropical fruit trees, offers basic rooms with tile floors and funky furniture, and an abundance of hammocks strewn about the property. Guests have cooking privileges in a large, fully equipped common kitchen, set beside two palapas. Ask about discounts and weekly rates. It's next to the Casa de la Cultura, behind the main square.

Alvaro Obregón 1, 23400 San José del Cabo, B.C.S. ℂ/fax **624/142-1372**. Fax 624/142-5761. www.srmanana.com. 8 units. $42 double. No credit cards. **Amenities:** Community kitchen; pool table; half-court basketball; Ping-Pong. *In room:* Fan.

WHERE TO DINE
EXPENSIVE

Damiana ℛ SEAFOOD/MEXICAN   This casually elegant restaurant in an 18th-century hacienda is decorated in the colors of a Mexican sunset: deep-orange walls, and tables and chairs clad in bright rose, lavender, and orange cloth. The favored tables are in the tropical courtyard, where candles flicker under the trees and the bougainvillea. For an appetizer, try mushrooms diablo, a moderately zesty dish. For a main course, ranchero shrimp in cactus sauce and grilled lobster tail are flavorful choices. You can also enjoy brunch almost until the dinner hour. There is an interior dining room, but the courtyard is the most romantic dining spot in San José. Damiana is on the east side of the town plaza.

San José town plaza. ℂ **624/142-0499** or 624/142-2899. Fax 624/142-3027. damiana@1cabonet.com.mx. Reservations recommended during Christmas and Easter holidays. Lunch $9–$15; main courses $130–$50. AE, MC, V. Daily 11am–10:30pm.

Mi Cocina ℛℛℛ NOUVELLE MEXICAN/EURO CUISINE Without a doubt, this is the best dining choice in the entire Los Cabos area. From the setting to the service, a dinner at Mi Cocina is unforgettable. The plant-filled courtyard, with its towering palms and exposed brick walls, accommodates alfresco dining. But it's not just the romance of the setting—the food is creative and consistently superb. Notable starters include *chile relleno de camarones* (an ancho chile stuffed with baby shrimp and cooked with cream cheese, Brie, and cilantro). Main courses include pasta, seafood, poultry, and beef, with such favorites as Natalia-style filet, served on creamy chile sauce with mushrooms and broccoli, and jumbo shrimp sautéed with rosemary, olive oil, and sun-dried tomatoes. Save room for dessert; choices range from chocolate fondant to fresh-fruit-filled meringue discs topped with Chantilly cream. A full-service palapa bar offers an excellent selection of wines, premium tequilas, and single-malt scotches, as well as special margarita and martini menus.

In the Casa Natalia hotel, Blv. Mijares. ℂ **624/142-5100**. www.mi-cocina.com. Main courses $18–$32. AE, MC, V. Daily 6:30–10pm (to hotel guests only 7am–4pm).

Tequila ⟨⟨ MEXICAN/ASIAN   Contemporary Mexican cuisine with a light and flavorful touch is the star attraction here, although the garden setting is lovely, with rustic *equipal* furniture and lanterns scattered among palms and giant mango trees. Try the specialty, shrimp in tequila sauce. Other enjoyable options include perfectly seared tuna with cilantro and ginger, ribs topped with tamarind sauce, and baked lobster with tequila sauce. Vegetarians can enjoy bell peppers stuffed with ricotta in tomato sauce, or one of several pasta dishes. The accompanying whole-grain bread arrives fresh and hot, and attentive service complements the fine meal. Cuban cigars and an excellent selection of tequilas are available, as is an extensive wine list emphasizing California vintages.

M. Doblando s/n. ⓒ **624/142-1155.** Lunch $9–$22; main courses $15–$45. AE. Daily 11am–3pm and 6–10:30pm.

MODERATE

Tropicana Bar and Grill SEAFOOD/MEAT   The Tropicana is a popular mainstay, especially for tourists. The bar has a steady clientele day and night and often features special sporting events on satellite TV. The dining area is in a garden (candlelit in the evening) with a tiled mural at one end. Cafe-style sidewalk dining is also available, but a twirling, brightly lit dessert display makes it less romantic. The menu is too extensive to lay claim to any specialty; it aims to please everyone. All meats and cheeses are imported, and dinners include thick steaks and shrimp fajitas. Paella is the Sunday special. The restaurant is 1 block south of the Plaza Mijares.

Blv. Mijares 30. ⓒ **624/142-1580.** Breakfast $4–$6; main courses $10–$25. AE, MC, V. Daily 8am–midnight.

Zipper's ⟨ BURGERS/MEXICAN/SEAFOOD   Mike Posey and Tony Magdeleno own this popular casual hangout. Sitting at the far south end of the beach heading toward Cabo San Lucas and fronting the best surfing waters, it's become popular with gringos in search of American food and TV sports. Burgers have that back-home flavor—order one with a side of spicy curly fries. Steaks, lobster, beer-battered shrimp, deli sandwiches, and Mexican combination plates round out the menu, which is printed with dollar prices.

Playa Costa Azul just south of San José (Kilometer 28.5 on Transpeninsular Hwy.). No phone. Burgers and sandwiches $7–$10; main courses $7–$18. No credit cards. Daily 8am–10pm.

SAN JOSE AFTER DARK

San José's nightlife is nonexistent outside of the restaurant and hotel bars. Of particular note are the bars at Casa Natalia and the Tropicana—the former catering to sophisticated romantics, the latter to those in search of rowdier good times. Several of the larger hotels along the beach have Mexican fiestas and other weekly theme nights that include a buffet (usually all-you-can-eat), drinks, live music, and entertainment for $25 to $35 per person. There's also a large disco on Mijares that seems to be under different ownership each year—it was closed at press time, undergoing yet another renovation. Those intent on real nightlife will find it in Cabo San Lucas (see below).

Tropicana Bar and Grill   This is definitely the most popular place in town. Patrons hang out in leather barrel chairs in the large bar where, during the day, they tune in to American sports events on the big-screen TV. Come evening, guitarists play Mexican boleros and other traditional music from 6 to 11pm. After 9pm on some nights, a band plays Americanized rock and pop for those inclined to dance. On some weekends, there's a live Cuban band and salsa dancing. The Tropicana is open daily from 7am to 1am. Drink prices start at $3. Blv. Mijares 30. ⓒ **624/142-0907**.

2 The Corridor: Between the Two Cabos ⭐⭐

The Corridor between the towns of San José del Cabo and Cabo San Lucas contains some of Mexico's most lavish resorts. Most growth at the tip of the peninsula is occurring along the Corridor, which has already become a major locale for championship golf. The four major resort areas are **Palmilla, Querencia, Cabo Real,** and **Cabo del Sol,** each a self-contained community with golf courses, elegant hotels, and million-dollar homes (or the promise of them).

My perennial favorite along this coast, the Palmilla Resort (ⓒ **877/472-6455** or 800/637-2226; www.palmillaresort.com), has closed for major renovations and is scheduled to reopen in December 2003. Plans are to expand from 115 to 174 rooms, add an indoor/outdoor spa and fitness center to be managed by Mandara Spas, and include a restaurant owned by famed chef Charlie Trotter of Chicago.

If you plan to explore the region while staying at a Corridor hotel, you'll need a rental car for at least a day or two; cars are available at

The Two Cabos & the Corridor

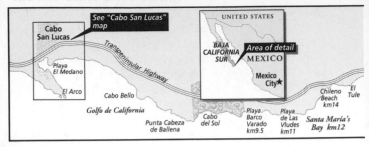

the hotels. Even if you're not staying here, the beaches and dining options are worth visiting. Hotels—all of which qualify as "very expensive"—are listed in the order in which you'll encounter them as you drive from San José to Cabo San Lucas. Rates listed are for the high season (winter); typically they're 20% lower in the summer. Most resorts offer golf and fishing packages.

WHERE TO STAY

Casa del Mar ★★ *(Finds)* A little-known treasure, this intimate resort is one of the best values along the Corridor. The hacienda-style building offers luxury accommodations in an intimate setting, as well as an on-site spa and nearby golf facilities. Located within the Cabo Real development, it's convenient to the 18-hole championship Cabo Real golf course. Gentle waterfalls lead to the adults-only pool area, and a flowered path continues to a wide, sandy stretch of beach with a clear surf break. There's even a "quiet area" on the lawn for those looking for a siesta.

Guest rooms have a bright feel, with white marble floors, light wicker furnishings, separate sitting area, and a large Jacuzzi tub, plus separate shower on the raised bathroom level. Balconies have over-sized chairs, with a view of the ocean beyond the pool. It's a romantic hotel for couples and honeymooners, known for its welcoming, personalized service.

Km 19.5 on Hwy. 1, 23410 Cabo San Lucas, B.C.S. © **800/221-8808** in the U.S., or 624/144-0030. Fax 624/144-0034. www.casadelmarresort.com. 56 units. High season $495 double, $550 suite; low season $240 double, $295 suite. AE, MC, V. **Amenities:** Restaurant; lobby bar; beach club (adults only) with pool, hot tub, pool bar, open-air restaurant; 6 other pools (2 with whirlpools and swim-up bars); 2 lighted tennis courts; privileges at Cabo Real and El Dorado golf clubs; full-service spa; small workout room; tour desk; room service; in-room massage; babysitting; laundry and dry cleaning. *In room:* A/C, TV, dataport, minibar, bathrobes, hair dryer, Jacuzzi, safe-deposit box.

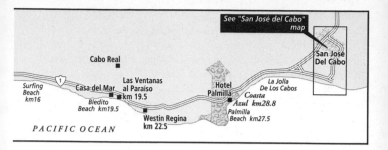

Las Ventanas al Paraíso ✶✶✶ Las Ventanas is known for its luxury accommodations and unerring attention to detail. The architecture, with adobe structures and rough-hewn wood accents, provides a soothing complement to the desert landscape. The only burst of color comes from the dazzling windows *(ventanas)* of pebbled rainbow glass—handmade by regional artisans —that reflect the changing positions of the sun. Richly furnished, Mediterranean-style rooms are large (starting at 300 sq. m/1,000 sq. ft.) and appointed with every conceivable amenity, from wood-burning fireplaces to computerized telescopes for stargazing or whale-watching. Fresh flowers and tequila setups welcome each guest, and standard features include satellite TVs with VCRs, stereos with CD players, and dual-line phones. Sizable Jacuzzi tubs overlook the room and may be closed off for privacy. Larger suites offer pampering extras like a rooftop terrace, a sunken Jacuzzi on a private patio, or a personal pool. The spa is among the best in Mexico—particularly notable is its Sea and Stars nighttime massage for two, a relaxing aromatherapy massage with two therapists that takes place on the rooftop terrace of your private suite. With a staff that outnumbers guests by four to one, this is the place for those who want (and can afford) to be seriously spoiled. The 15% service charge is not included in the prices below, which do include taxes.

Km 19.5 on Hwy. 1, 23410 San José del Cabo, B.C.S. ℂ **888/525-0483** in the U.S., or 624/144-0300. Fax 624/144-0301. www.lasventanas.com. 61 suites. $644 garden-view double; $784 oceanview double; $896 split-level oceanview suite with rooftop terrace; $1,120 split-level oceanfront suite with rooftop terrace; 1- or 3-bedroom luxury suite $2,464–$3,920. Spa and golf packages and inclusive meal plans available. AE, DC, MC, V. Rates include valet parking. **Amenities:** Oceanview gourmet restaurant with wine cellar; adjoining terrace bar with live classical music; seaside casual-dining grill; juice bar; access to adjoining championship Cabo Real golf course; deluxe European spa with complete treatment and exercise facilities; sportfishing and luxury yachts available; watersports; tour services; car rental, shuttle services; 24-hr. room service; laundry. *In room:* A/C, TV, dataport, minibar, hair dryer, iron, safe-deposit box, bathrobes.

Westin Regina 𝓡𝓡 *(Kids* Architecturally dramatic, the Westin Regina sits at the end of a long paved road atop a seaside cliff. Vivid terra-cotta, yellow, and pink walls rise against a landscape of sandstone, cacti, and palms, with fountains and gardens lining the long pathways from the lobby to the rooms. Electric carts carry guests and their luggage through the vast property. The rooms are gorgeous, with both air-conditioning and ceiling fans, private balconies, satellite TV, and walk-in showers separate from the bathtubs. This is probably the best choice among our selections for families vacationing along the Corridor, with a wealth of activities for children.

Km 22.5 on Hwy. 1, Apdo. Postal 145, 23400 San José del Cabo, B.C.S. ℰ**800/228-3000** in the U.S., or 624/142-9000. Fax 1/142-9010. 295 units. $322 double with partial ocean view; $365 double with full ocean view; $443–$925 suite. 15% low-season discount. AE, DC, MC, V. **Amenities:** 6 restaurants; 2 bars; 3 pools; 2 tennis courts; beach club, full fitness center; Xplora Adventour services; children's activities; concierge; car-rental desk; business services; salon; room service; babysitting; laundry service. *In room:* A/C, TV, minibar, hair dryer, safe.

WHERE TO DINE

Pitahayas 𝓡𝓡𝓡 PACIFIC RIM In a beachfront setting, Pitahayas offers gourmet dining under a grand palapa or on open-air terraces under a starlit sky. Master chef Volker Romeike has assembled a creative—if slightly pretentious—menu that blends Pacific Rim cuisine with Mexican herbs and seasonings. Notable sauces include mango, black bean, and curry. Rotisserie-barbecued duck is a house specialty, along with mesquite grill and wok cooking—all prepared in an impressive exhibition kitchen. A dessert pizza with fresh fruit, chocolate, and marzipan makes a fitting finish to a stunning meal. Pitahayas also boasts an extensive wine cellar, with vintages from around the world, housed in an underground *cava.* Formal resort attire is requested.

At the Hacienda del Mar resort, Km 10 on Hwy. 1, Cabo del Sol. ℰ 624/145-8010. Reservations required during high season. Main courses $12–$30. AE, MC, V. Daily 5–10:30pm.

3 Cabo San Lucas 𝓡𝓡

176km (110 miles) S of La Paz; 35km (22 miles) W of San José del Cabo; 1,803km (1,120 miles) SE of Tijuana

The hundreds of luxury hotel rooms along the corridor north of Cabo San Lucas have transformed the very essence of this formerly rustic and rowdy outpost. Although it retains boisterous nightlife, Cabo San Lucas is no longer the simple town Steinbeck wrote about

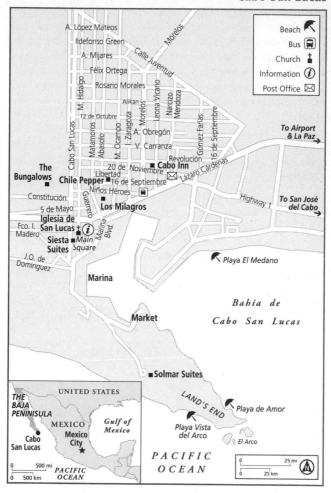

Cabo San Lucas

and enjoyed. Once legendary for the big-game fish that lurk beneath the deep blue sea, Cabo San Lucas now draws more people for its nearby fairways and greens—and the world-class golf being played on them. It caters to travelers getting away for a long weekend or indulgent stay of sport and relaxation. Cabo San Lucas has become Mexico's most elite resort destination.

Travelers enjoy a growing roster of adventure-oriented activities, and playtime doesn't end when the sun goes down. The nightlife here is as hot as the desert in July, and oddly casual, having grown up away from the higher-end hotels. It remains the raucous, playful party scene that helped put Cabo on the map. A collection of popular restaurants and bars along Cabo's main street stay open and active until the morning's first fishing charters head out to sea. Also blossoming is its array of spas—Cabo now boasts 14 resorts with luxury spas, ranging from the holistic to the hedonistic. Despite the growth in diversions, Cabo remains more or less a one-stoplight town, with almost everything along the main strip, within easy walking distance.

ESSENTIALS
GETTING THERE & DEPARTING
BY PLANE   For arrival and departure information, see "Getting There & Departing," earlier in the chapter, under "San José del Cabo." Local airline numbers are: **AeroCalifornia** (© **624/143-3700** or 624/143-3915); **Alaska Airlines** (© **624/146-5166**); and **Mexicana** (© **624/146-5001,** 624/143-5353, or 624/142-0606 at the airport).

BY CAR   From La Paz, the best route is to take Highway 1 south past the village of San Pedro, then Highway 19 south through Todos Santos to Cabo San Lucas, a 2-hour drive.

BY BUS   The bus terminal (© **624/143-5020**) is on Niños Héroes at Morelos; it is open daily from 6am to 7pm. Buses go to San José del Cabo about every hour between 6:30am and 8:30pm, and to La Paz every 90 minutes between 6am and 6pm. To and from San José, the more convenient and economical **Suburcabos** public bus service runs every 20 minutes and costs $2.50.

ORIENTATION
ARRIVING   At the airport, either buy a ticket for a colectivo from the authorized transportation booth inside the building (about $10) or arrange for a rental car, the most economical way to explore the area. Up to four people can share a private taxi; the fare to Cabo San Lucas is about $60.

The walk from the bus station to most of the budget hotels is manageable with light luggage, and taxis are readily available.

VISITOR INFORMATION   The **Secretary of Tourism** functions as the information office in Cabo. It's on Madero between Hidalgo and Guerrero (© **624/142-0446;** fax 624/142-0260). The

English-language *Los Cabos Guide, Los Cabos News, Cabo Life, Baja Sun,* and the irreverent and extremely entertaining *Gringo Gazette* are distributed free at most hotels and shops and have up-to-date information on new restaurants and clubs. On the Web, good sources include the official destination site **www.visitcabo.com**. *Note:* The many visitor-information booths along the street are actually time-share sales booths, and their staffs will pitch a visit to their resort in exchange for discounted tours, rental cars, or other giveaways.

CITY LAYOUT   The small town spreads out north and west of the harbor of Cabo San Lucas Bay, edged by foothills and desert mountains to the west and south. The main street leading into town from the airport and San José del Cabo is Lázaro Cárdenas; as it nears the harbor, Marina Boulevard branches off from it and becomes the main artery that curves around the waterfront.

GETTING AROUND

Taxis are easy to find but are expensive within Cabo, in keeping with the high cost of everything else. Expect to pay about $15 to $25 for a taxi between Cabo and the Corridor hotels.

For day trips to San José del Cabo, catch a bus (see "Getting There & Departing" under "San José del Cabo," above) or a cab. You'll see car-rental specials advertised in town, but before signing on, be sure you understand the total price, including insurance and taxes. Rates can run between $50 and $75 per day, with insurance an extra $10 per day. One of the best and most economical agencies is **Advantage Rent-A-Car** (*©* **624/143-0909;** *©*/fax 624/143-0466), on Lázaro Cárdenas between Leona Vicario and Morelos. VW sedans rent for $50 per day, and weekly renters receive one free day. Collision damage waiver will add $14 per day to the price. If you pick up the car downtown, you can return it to the airport at no extra charge.

 FAST FACTS: Cabo San Lucas

Area Code The telephone area code is **624**.

Beach Safety Before swimming in open water, it's important to check whether the conditions are safe. Undertows and large waves are common. Playa El Medano (Medano Beach), close to the marina and town, is the principal swimming beach; it has several lively beachfront restaurant-bars. It's also easy to find watersports equipment for rent here. The Hotel

Melia Cabo San Lucas, on Playa El Medano, has a roped-off swimming area to protect swimmers from jet skis and boats. Colored flags signaling swimming safety aren't generally used in Cabo, and neither are lifeguards.

Currency Exchange Banks exchange currency during normal business hours, generally Monday through Friday from 9am to 6pm and Saturday from 10am to 2pm. Currency-exchange booths, found throughout Cabo's main tourist areas, aren't as competitive but are more convenient. ATMs are widely available and even more convenient, dispensing pesos—and in some cases dollars—at bank exchange rates.

Emergencies/Hospital See "Fast Facts: San José del Cabo," earlier in this chapter.

Internet Access **Dr. Z's Internet Café & Bar,** Lázaro Cárdenas 7, edificio Posada, across from the Pemex gas station (© 624/143-5390), charges $3 for 10 minutes, $7 for 40 minutes, or $8.50 for an hour. It's open Monday to Saturday from 9am to 6pm.

Pharmacy A long-standing drugstore, with a wide selection of toiletries and medicines, is **Farmacia Aramburo,** in Plaza Aramburo, Lázaro Cárdenas at Zaragoza (© 624/143-1489); open daily from 7am to 9pm. Also try **Farmacia Faro Viejo,** Hidalgo 4, at Lázaro Cárdenas (© 624/143-3655); open daily from 9am to 9pm.

Post Office The *correo* is at Lázaro Cárdenas and Francisco Villa, on the highway to San José del Cabo, east of the bar El Squid Roe (© 624/143-0048). It's open Monday through Friday from 9am to 1pm and 3 to 6pm, and Saturday from 9am to noon.

BEACHES & OUTDOOR ACTIVITIES

Although superb sportfishing put Cabo San Lucas on the map, there's more to do here than drop your line and wait for the Big One. For most cruises and excursions, try to make fishing reservations at least a day in advance; keep in mind that some trips require a minimum number of people. A travel agency can arrange most sports and outings; fishing can also be arranged directly at one of the fishing-fleet offices at the far south end of the marina.

Besides fishing, there's kayaking and boat trips to Los Arcos (the Arches) rock formation or uninhabited beaches. Expect to pay $60 for a sunset kayak around Los Arcos, $40 for morning kayak trips. A variety of boats, including a replica of a pirate ship, provide all-inclusive daytime or sunset cruises. Many of these trips include snorkeling; serious divers have great underwater venues to explore. Horseback riding to Los Arcos and to the Pacific (very popular at sunset) costs $50 for 2 hours.

Whale-watching, between January and March, has become one of the most popular local activities. Guided ATV (all-terrain vehicle) tours take you down dirt roads and through a desert landscape to the old Cabo lighthouse or an ancient Indian village. And then, of course, there's the challenge of world-class golf, a major attraction of Los Cabos.

For a complete rundown of what's available, contact **Xplora Adventours** (© **624/142-9000,** ext. 8316; www.xploraloscabos. com). It offers all tours from all local companies, rather than working with only a select few. Xplora has tour desks in the Westin Regina hotel and at the Huichol store on Lázaro Cárdenas.

ATV TRIPS   Expeditions on ATVs to visit Cabo Falso, an 1890 lighthouse, and La Candelaria, an Indian pueblo in the mountains, are available through travel agencies. A 440-pound weight limit per two-person vehicle applies to both tours. The 3-hour tour to Cabo Falso includes a stop at the beach, a look at some sea-turtle nests (without disturbing them) and the remains of a 1912 shipwreck, a ride over 500-foot sand dunes, and a visit to the lighthouse. Guided tours cost around $45 per person on a single vehicle, or $60 for two riding on one ATV. The vehicles are also available for rent ($35 for 3 hours).

La Candelaria is an isolated Indian village in the mountains 40km (25 miles) north of Cabo San Lucas. Described in *National Geographic,* the old pueblo is known for the practice of white and black witchcraft. Lush with palms, mango trees, and bamboo, the settlement gets its water from an underground river that emerges at

---

Moments Festivals & Events in Cabo San Lucas

An annual dive festival takes place in August. October 12 is the festival of the patron saint of Todos Santos, a town about 105km (65 miles) north. October 18 is the feast of the patron saint of Cabo San Lucas, celebrated with a fair, feasting, music, dancing, and other special events.

the pueblo. The return trip of the tour travels down a steep canyon, along a beach (giving you time to swim), and past giant-sea-turtle nesting grounds. Departing at 9am, the 5-hour La Candelaria tour costs around $80 per person or $100 for two on the same ATV.

BEACHES

All along the curving sweep of sand known as **Playa El Medano (Medano Beach),** on the northeast side of the bay, you can rent snorkeling gear, boats, WaveRunners ($70 per hr.), kayaks, pedal boats, and windsurf boards. You can also take windsurfing lessons. This is the town's main beach; it's a great place for safe swimming as well as for people-watching from one of the many outdoor restaurants along its shore.

Beach aficionados may want to rent a car (see "Getting Around," above) and explore the five more remote beaches and coves between the two Cabos: **playas Palmilla, Chileno, Santa María, Barco Varado,** and **Vista del Arco.** Palmilla, Chileno, and Santa María are generally safe for swimming—but always be careful. The other beaches are not considered safe. Experienced snorkelers may wish to check them out, but other visitors should go for the view only. Always check at a hotel or travel agency for directions and swimming conditions. Although a few travel agencies run snorkeling tours to some of these beaches, there's no public transportation. Your only option for beach exploring is to rent a car.

CRUISES

Glass-bottom boats leave from the town marina every 45 minutes daily between 9am and 4pm. Prices start at $10 for an hour's tour past sea lions and pelicans to see the famous El Arco (Rock Arch), part of Los Arcos rock formation, at Land's End, where the Pacific and the Sea of Cortez meet. Most boats make a brief stop at Playa del Amor or drop you off there if you ask; you can use your ticket to catch a later boat back (be sure to check what time the last boat departs).

A number of daylong and sunset cruises use a variety of boats and catamarans. They cost $30 to $45, depending on the boat, duration of cruise, and amenities. A sunset cruise on the 13m (42-ft.) catamaran *Pez Gato* (© **624/143-3797** or 624/143-5297; pezgato@ 1cabonet.com.mx) departs from the Plaza las Glorias Hotel dock at 5pm. The 2-hour cruise costs $35, which includes margaritas, beer, and sodas. Similar boats leave from the marina and the Plaza las Glorias Hotel. Check with travel agencies or hotel tour desks.

LAND SPORTS

GOLF   Los Cabos has become Mexico's golf mecca, and though most courses are along the Corridor, people look to Cabo San Lucas for information. The Los Cabos golf master plan calls for a future total of 207 holes of golf. Fees listed below are for 18 holes, including golf cart, water, club service, and tax. Summer rates are about 25% lower, and many hotels offer special golf packages. (For specifics on various courses, see "The Lowdown on Golfing in Cabo," below.)

Several specialty tour operators offer golf packages to Los Cabos, which include accommodations, greens fees, and other amenities. These include **Best Golf** (© 888/817-GOLF from the U.S.) and **Sportours** (© 888/GOLF-MEX from the U.S.; www.golfin mexico.com).

The 27-hole course at the **Palmilla Golf Club,** part of the Palmilla resort (© 800/386-2465 in the U.S., or 624/144-5250; open daily 7am to 7pm), was the first Jack Nicklaus Signature layout in Mexico, built in 1992 on 365 hectares (900 acres) of dramatic oceanfront and desert. It's open while the resort is closed for renovations. The course offers your choice of two back-nine options, with high-season greens fees of $215 (lower after 1pm). Low-season fees run $120 to $210.

Another Jack Nicklaus Signature course, the 18-hole Ocean Course at **Cabo del Sol,** is 17km (11 miles) away at the Cabo del Sol resort development in the Corridor (© 800/386-2465 in the U.S., or 624/145-8200). The 7,100-yard course is known for its challenging three finishing holes. Greens fees are $240 to $262. Tom Weiskopf designed the newer 18-hole Desert Course, where greens fees are $218.

Robert Trent Jones Jr. designed the 18-hole, 6,945-yard course at **Cabo Real,** by the Melia Cabo Real Hotel in the Corridor (© 624/144-0232; caborealgolf@1cabonet.com.mx; open daily 6:30am to 6pm), which features holes that sit high on mesas overlooking the Sea of Cortez. Fees run $220 for 18 holes.

El Dorado Golf Course (© 624/144-5451; www.caboreal.com) is a Jack Nicklaus Signature course at Cabo Real that lies next to the Westin Regina hotel. The course is open daily from 7am until dusk. Greens fees are $246 (after 2pm, $168). Carts are included; caddies are $50.

An 18-hole course designed by Roy Dye is at the **Raven Club** in Cabo San Lucas (© 800/854-2314 in the U.S., or 624/143-4653;

The Lowdown on Golfing in Cabo

Los Cabos, one of the world's finest golf destinations, offers an ample and intriguing variety of courses to challenge golfers of all levels.

So many choose to play here not just for the selection, quality, and beauty of the courses, but because of the very reliable weather. The courses highlighted below compare to the great ones in Palm Springs and Scottsdale, with the added beauty of ocean views and a wider variety of desert cacti and flowering plants.

Greens fees are high in Cabo—generally over $200 per round. But these are world-class courses, worth the world-class price. Courses generally offer 50% off rates if you play after 2 or 2:30pm. This is a great time to play—the temperature is cooler, and play is generally faster.

Palmilla Golf Club   The original Cabo course is now a 27-hole layout. The original 18 holes are the Arroyo (Canyon); the new holes are the Ocean 9. That's a bit of a misnomer—although the newer holes lie closer to the water, only one has a true ocean view, with a spectacular play directly down to the beach. You must play the Arroyo for your first nine holes, then choose Mountain and Ocean for your back nine. If you play this course only once, choose the Mountain, which offers better ocean views. The signature hole is the Mountain 5; you hit over a canyon, then down to the greens below over a forced carry. This is target golf, on a semiprivate Jack Nicklaus course constructed with strategy in mind. A mountaintop clubhouse provides spectacular views.

Cabo del Sol   The Ocean Course was the second Jack Nicklaus Signature course constructed in Los Cabos. Its dramatic finishing oceanside holes make it "the Pebble Beach of Baja." It is much more difficult than the Palmilla course, with less room for error.

Don't be fooled by the wide, welcoming first hole. This is challenging target golf, with numerous forced carries—even from the red tees. Seven holes are along the water. The signature hole is 17, which runs by the water, with a forced carry. The newer Desert Course weaves through lush desert landscape and has sweeping views of the Sea of Cortez from almost every hole.

Cabo Real This Robert Trent Jones Jr. design is known for its holes along the Sea of Cortez, which sit high on mesas overlooking the sea; exceptional among these is the frequently photographed 12th. Jones designed the course to test low handicappers, but multiple tees make it enjoyable for average players as well. The par-72 layout is 6,945 yards long and was designed with professional tournament play in mind. The most famous hole is the 15th, right on the beach near the Melia Cabo Real Hotel.

The Raven Club The front and back nines are the work of members of the Dye family, so the course plays like two different courses. Characteristic of Dye design courses, it has deep waste bunkers, subtle terracing up hillsides, and holes built into the natural desert terrain. The most challenging hole is the par-5 7th, around a lake; at 607 yards, it's the longest hole in Mexico. The course is designed to offer a variety of options, from a short course played on front tees to a super-long course with numerous bunkers and hazards. The Dye family redid the whole course in 2002. Although the layout is essentially the same, the course is now considered even better.

El Dorado Golf Course A Jack Nicklaus Signature course at Cabo Real, El Dorado is a links-style course in the Scottish tradition. The layout is challenging—7 holes border the Sea of Cortez and 12 are carved out of two pristine canyons. The oceanview holes are not the only water: manmade lakes are also a part of the scenery. El Dorado bills itself as the "Pebble Beach of Baja"—but then again, so does Cabo del Sol. You decide.

The private course at **Querencia** (© **624/145-6670;** www.loscabosquerencia.com) is a stunning Tom Fazio design. Originally a private club, it now accepts guests of both Las Ventanas and Casa del Mar. Greens fees are $275.

fax 624/143-5809). The entire course overlooks the juncture of the Pacific Ocean and Sea of Cortez, including the famous Land's End rocks. The 607-yard, par-five 7th hole is the longest hole in Mexico. Greens fees are $159 for 18 holes, $119 after 1pm. The course was redone after a 2001 hurricane added substantial water features. It is still a Dye-design course, with a slightly changed layout, and regular players say it's a much-improved experience.

The most economical greens fees in the area are at the public 9-hole **Club Campo de Golf San José** (© **624/142-0900** or 624/ 142-0905), in San José del Cabo. For details, see "Golf," under "San José del Cabo," earlier in this chapter.

OTHER SPORTS   Bicycles, **boogie boards, snorkels, surfboards,** and **golf clubs** are available for rent at **Cabo Sports Center** in the Plaza Náutica on Marina Boulevard (© **624/143-4272**). The center is open Monday through Saturday from 9am to 9pm, Sunday from 9am to 5pm.

You can rent horses at the **Hacienda Hotel** (© **624/143-0123**) or at the **Hotel Melia Cabo San Lucas,** through **Rancho Colín** (© **624/143-3652**), for $20 to $30 per hour. Offerings include guided beach rides and sunset tours to El Faro Viejo (the Old Lighthouse) for $30 to $45 per person and to the Pacific for sunset riding on the beach. Both concessions are open daily 8am to 6pm.

Also recommendable is **Cuadra San Francisco Equestrian Center,** Km. 19.5 along the Corridor (© **624/144-0160,** www.los caboshorses.com), which offers rides with your choice of English or Western saddles. A 2-hour canyon ride in and around Arroyo San Carlos or Venado Blanco costs $65; a 1-hour ride to the beach or desert is $35.

WATERSPORTS

SNORKELING/DIVING   Several companies offer snorkeling; a 2-hour cruise to sites around El Arco costs $30, and a 4-hour trip to Santa María costs $55, including gear rental. Among the beaches visited on different trips are Playa del Amor, Santa María, Chileno, and Barco Varado. Snorkeling gear rents for $10 to $15. Contact **Xplora Adventours** (© **624/142-9135;** www.xploraloscabos.com). For scuba diving, contact **Amigos del Mar** (© **800/344-3349,** fax 310/454-1686 in the U.S.; 624/143-0505, fax 624/143-0887 in Mexico; www.amigosdelmar.com; open daily 8am–4:30pm). Dives are along the wall of a canyon in San Lucas Bay, where you can see "sandfalls" that even Jacques Cousteau couldn't figure out—no one knows their source or cause. There are also scuba trips to Santa María Beach and places farther away, including the Gordo Banks and Cabo Pulmo. Prices start at $40 for a one-tank dive, $70 for two tanks; trips to the coral outcropping at Cabo Pulmo start at $155. Two hours from Cabo San Lucas, Cabo Pulmo is rated for beginners and up. Gordo Banks, for advanced divers, is an underwater mountain about 8km (5 miles) offshore with a black-coral bottom and schools of game fish and manta rays. Resort courses cost $100 per person, and open-water certification costs around $450. Late August through November is the best time to dive, although diving is busiest from October to mid-January—it's important to make reservations in advance if you're planning to dive then. You'll need a wet suit for winter dives.

SPORTFISHING Go to the town marina on the south side of the harbor, where you'll find several fleet operators with offices near the docks. The **panga fleets** offer the best deals; 5 hours of fishing for two or three people costs $200 to $450. To choose one, stroll around the marina and talk with the captains—you may make a better deal. Try **ABY Charters** (© **624/143-0831** or 624/143-0874; abcabo@prodigy.net.mx), or the **Picante/Blue Water Sportfishing Fleet** (© **624/143-2474**; open daily 6:30am–8pm). Both have booths at the sportfishing dock at the far south end of the marina. The going rate for a day on a fully equipped cruiser with captain, guide, and bathroom starts at around $700 for up to four people. For deluxe trips with everything included aboard a 12m (40-ft.) boat, budget $1,250. (See also "The Active Traveler," in chapter 1, for companies that can arrange fishing in advance.) Many larger hotels, like the Solmar Suites, have their own fleets. If you've traveled in your own vessel, you'll need a fishing permit. Depending on the size of the boat, it will cost $15 to $45 per month. Daily permits ($4–$10) and annual permits are also available.

The fishing lives up to its reputation: Bringing in a 100-pound marlin is routine. Angling is good all year, though the catch varies with the season: Sailfish and wahoo are best from June through November; yellowfin tuna, May through December; yellowtail, January through April; black and blue marlin, July through December. Striped marlin are prevalent year-round.

SURFING Good surfing can be found from March through November all along the beaches west of town, and there's a famous right break at Chileno Beach, near the Cabo San Lucas Hotel east of

---

Tips Don't Sweat the One that Got Away

"Catch and release" is strongly encouraged in Los Cabos. Anglers reel in their fish, which are then tagged and released unharmed. The angler gets a certificate and the knowledge that there will still be billfish in the sea when he or she returns.

---

town. (Also see "Surfing" in "San José del Cabo," earlier in this chapter, for details on Playa Costa Azul and Zipper's.) Other good surfing beaches along the corridor are Acapulquito, El Tule, and La Bocana.

The Pacific Coast has yet to face the onslaught of development that's so rapidly changed the east cape. An hour-long drive up the coast to the little towns of Pescadero and Todos Santos can be a great surf journey. They have a couple of good point breaks.

Playa San Pedrito is off the dirt road that begins 7.4 kilometers (4.5 miles) south of the Todos Santos town limits. Follow the signs for SAN PEDRITO CAMPGROUND. The point is very rocky and sharp, but it's a wonderful wave on the right swell direction and tide (northwest swell, rising tide). Another stretch down the road will lead you to Playa los Cerritos (13km/8 miles south of Todos Santos), a lovely beach with a surfable point break off a big headland.

Other beach breaks are rideable at various times, but a vicious shorebreak and strong undertow characterize much of the beach around Todos Santos. While the unruliness of the ocean has helped keep industrial tourism at bay, it also means you have to hunt a little harder to find playful waves.

WHALE-WATCHING   Whale-watching cruises are not to be missed. For information about the excursions, which operate between January and March, see "Whale-Watching" under "San José del Cabo," earlier in this chapter, and "Whale-Watching in Baja: A Primer," in chapter 4.

EXPLORING CABO SAN LUCAS
HISTORIC CABO SAN LUCAS

Sports and partying are Cabo's main attractions, but there are also a few cultural and historical points of interest. The Spanish missionary Nicolás Tamaral established the stone Iglesia de San Lucas (Church of San Lucas) on Calle Cabo San Lucas near the main plaza in 1730; a large bell in a stone archway commemorates the completion of the church in 1746. The Pericúe Indians, who reportedly resisted

Tamaral's demands that they practice monogamy, eventually killed him. Buildings on the streets facing the main plaza are gradually being renovated to house restaurants and shops, and the picturesque neighborhood promises to have the strongest Mexican ambience in town.

NEARBY DAY TRIPS

Travel agencies can book day trips to the city of La Paz for around $55, including beverages and a tour of the countryside along the way. Usually there's a stop at the weaving shop of Fortunato Silva, who spins his own cotton and weaves it into wonderfully textured rugs and textiles. Day trips are also available to Todos Santos ($60), with a guided walking tour of the Cathedral Mission, museum, Hotel California, and various artists' homes. For more information, see chapter 3, "La Paz: Peaceful Port Town." For more on Todos Santos, see "Todos Santos: A Creative Oasis," later in this chapter.

SHOPPING

A popular tourist shopping stop is the open-air market on Plaza Papagayo, on Marina Boulevard opposite the entrance to the Pueblo Bonito resort. However, it mainly has trinkets and traditional souvenirs—little in the way of real craftwork. Be sure to bargain. Most shops are on or within a block or two of Marina Boulevard and the plaza.

The **Puerto Paraíso Entertainment Plaza,** which opened in 2002, is the focal point of the area's shopping, dining, and entertainment. It is located marina-side between Plaza Bonita Mall and Marina Fiesta Resort in the heart of Cabo San Lucas. Shops spread over 50,000 sq. m (54,500 sq. yd.) of air-conditioned space on three levels, with waterfalls, restaurants, and open areas. The marina level holds trendy boutiques and branches of leading chains such as **Guess, Quicksilver, Mossimo,** and **Dolce & Gabbana.** Among the dining options are **Ruth's Chris Steak House** (adjacent to the marina), **Johnny Rocket's, Houlihans, 100% Natural,** and **CinaMomo Cocina and Lounge** (see "Cabo San Lucas After Dark," below). The upper levels have 10 cinemas, a 12-lane bowling alley, a youth-oriented video arcade, and a fast-food court.

Casa Maya Unusual decorative items for the home—Tin lamps, colored glass, and rustic wood furnishings—at excellent prices. Open Monday through Saturday from 9am to 7pm. Calle Morelos between Revolución and 20 de Noviembre. ©/fax **624/143-3197.**

Cuca's Blanket Factory This open-air stand sells the usual Mexican cotton and wool blankets, with an added attraction—you can design your own and have it ready the next day. It's open daily from 9am to 9pm. No credit cards. Lázaro Cárdenas at Matamoros. No phone.

El Callejon   The most eclectic shop in Los Cabos features antiques, unique gifts, paintings, and home furnishings. Local artists make most of the one-of-a-kind items. It's open Monday through Saturday from 10am to 8pm. Vicente Guerrero s/n, between Lázaro Cárdenas and Madero. ⓒ 624/143-1139. Fax 624/143-3188.

Golden Cactus Studio-Gallery   The area's longest-standing art gallery shows original art by regional artists, including Chris Mac-clure, as well as reproductions and posters of popular Mexican works. Open Monday to Saturday 10am to 2pm and 4 to 7pm. Corner of Guerrero and Madero, upstairs. ⓒ 624/143-6399. www.goldencactusgallery.com.

Rostros de México   Walls of wooden masks and carved religious statues are the draw at this gallery, whose name means "Faces of Mexico." Open Monday through Saturday from 10am to 7pm, Sunday from 10am to 2pm. No credit cards. Lázaro Cárdenas at Matamoros. ⓒ 624/143-0558.

WHERE TO STAY

Unless otherwise indicated, all hotel rates listed here are for the high season, which runs from November through Easter; summer rates are about 20% less. Several Cabo San Lucas hotels offer package deals that significantly lower the nightly rate; ask your travel agent for information.

Budget accommodations are scarce in Cabo San Lucas, but the number of small inns and B&Bs is growing. Several notable ones have opened in the past few years. Most larger hotels are well maintained, with packages available through travel agents; these listings focus on smaller, unique accommodations.

VERY EXPENSIVE

Solmar Suites 🎣🎣   Set against sandstone cliffs at the very tip of the Baja Peninsula, the Solmar is beloved by those seeking seclusion, comfort, and easy access to Cabo's diversions. The suites are in two-story white stucco buildings along the edge of a broad beach. They have either a king or two double beds, satellite TV, separate seating areas, and private balconies or patios on the sand. Guests gather by the pool and on the beach at sunset and all day long during the winter whale migration. Advance reservations are necessary almost year-round. A small timeshare complex adjoins the Solmar; some units are available for nightly stays. Rates below include the hotel's mandatory 10% service charge.

Av. Solmar 1, 23410 Cabo San Lucas, B.C.S. ℭ **624/143-3535.** Fax 624/143-0410. www.solmar.com. (Reservations: Box 383, Pacific Palisades, CA 90272; ℭ **800/ 344-3349** or 310/459-9861; fax 310/454-1686.) 194 units. High season $219–$402 double; low season $201–$366 double. AE, MC, V. **Amenities:** Restaurant, with Mexican fiesta Sat night; 3 pools (1 with swim-up bar); excellent sportfishing fleet for long-range diving, fishing, and whale-watching; concierge, tour desk, car-rental desk; salon; room service; laundry and dry cleaning. *In room:* A/C, TV, dataport, minibar, coffeemaker, hair dryer, safe-deposit box.

MODERATE

The Bungalows 🏵🏵 This is one of the most special places to stay in Los Cabos. Each unit (suite or bungalow) is a charming retreat decorated with authentic Mexican furnishings. Terra-cotta tiles, hand-painted sinks, wood chests, blown glass, and other creative touches make you feel as if you're a guest at a friend's home. Each room has a mini kitchenette, purified water, VCR, and designer bedding. The varied rooms surround a lovely heated pool. A brick-paved breakfast nook serves a complete gourmet breakfast, with fresh-ground coffee and fresh juice. Under owner Steve's warm and welcoming management, this is Cabo's most spacious, comfortable, full-service inn, with service that is exceptionally helpful. A 100% smoke-free environment, it is 5 blocks from downtown Cabo.

Miguel A. Herrera s/n, in front of Lienzo Charro, 23410 Cabo San Lucas, B.C.S. ℭ/fax **624/143-5035,** or 624/143-0585. www.cabobungalows.com. 16 units. $90 double; $110–$128 suite. Extra person $20. Rates include breakfast. Ask for summer promotions. AE. Street parking available. **Amenities:** Breakfast room; pool; concierge; tour desk. *In room:* A/C, TV/VCR, dataport, minifridge, coffeemaker.

Los Milagros 🏵 The elegant white two-level buildings that contain the 11 suites and rooms of Los Milagros (the Miracles) border a grassy garden area or small pool. Rooms are individually decorated, with contemporary iron beds, straw headboards, buff-colored tile floors, and artistic details. Some units have kitchenettes, and the master suite has a sunken tub. There's coffee service in the morning on the patio. Evenings are romantic—candles light the garden, and classical music plays. Request a room in one of the back buildings, where conversational noise is less intrusive. Los Milagros is 1½ blocks from the Giggling Marlin and the Cabo Wabo Cantina.

Matamoros 116, 23410 Cabo San Lucas, B.C.S. ℭ/fax **624/143-4566.** www.los milagroshotel.com. 11 units. $84 double. Ask for summer discounts, group rates, and long-term discounts. No credit cards. Limited street parking. **Amenities:** Small pool; e-mail, fax, and telephone service available through the office. *In room:* A/C.

INEXPENSIVE

Cabo Inn 🐸🐸 *Finds*   This three-story hotel on a quiet street is a real find, and it keeps getting better. It's a rare combination of low rates, extra-friendly management, and great, funky style—not to mention extra clean. Rooms are basic and very small; although this was a bordello in a prior incarnation, everything is updated, from the mattresses to the mini refrigerators in the lower-level rooms. Muted desert colors add a spark of personality. Rooms come with either two twins or one queen bed; most have kitchenettes. The rooms surround a courtyard where you can enjoy satellite TV, a barbecue grill, and free coffee. The third floor has a rooftop terrace with a palapa and a small swimming pool. Also on this floor is Juan's Love Palace, aka the honeymoon suite. It's a colorful, palapa-topped, open-air room with hanging *tapetes* (woven palm mats) for privacy. A large fish freezer is available. The hotel's just 2 blocks from downtown and the marina. A lively restaurant next door will even deliver pitchers of margaritas and dinner to your room.

20 de Noviembre and Leona Vicario, 23410 Cabo San Lucas, B.C.S. ©/fax **624/ 143-0819.** www.mexonline.com/caboinn.htm. 20 units. $58 double year-round; $330 double weekly, low season only. No credit cards. Street parking available. **Amenities:** Communal TV and barbecue; small rooftop pool. *In room:* A/C.

Chile Pepper Inn 🐸 *Value*   This bright-yellow stucco building contains simple but very tasteful rooms surrounding a common courtyard. One of the best values in town, Chile Pepper is for those who only need a room for sleeping, but want that room to be clean, stylish, and well appointed. Light wood furnishings are of the hand-carved, rustic variety so popular in Mexico. Palm mats line the floors, and muslin curtains cover the windows that open onto the courtyard. The beds have top-quality orthopedic mattresses and colorful cotton designer bedding; the bathrooms, though small, are decorated in painted tiles with Talavera sinks. Individual air-conditioning units are new and quiet, the in-room phones offer free local calls, and the TV has a large variety of U.S. channels. The one suite has two queen beds in an L-shaped room. It's located 4 blocks from the Hard Rock Cafe on a quiet street, but still close to Cabo's nightlife action.

16 de Septiembre and Abasolo, 23410 Cabo San Lucas, B.C.S. ©/fax **877/708-1918** from the U.S. and Canada, 624/143-0510, or 624/143-8611. www.chilepepper inn.com. 9 units. $75 double; $107 suite. Ask for seasonal promotions. AE, MC, V. Street parking available. *In room:* A/C, TV.

Siesta Suites   Reservations are a must at this immaculate small inn, which opened in early 1994. The rooms have white tile floors and white walls, refrigerators, and sinks. Fifteen have kitchenettes with seating areas. The mattresses are firm, and the bathrooms are large and sparkling clean. Rooms on the fourth floor have two queen beds each. The accommodating proprietors offer free movies and VCRs, a barbecue pit and outdoor patio table on the second floor, and a comfortable lobby with TV. They can also arrange fishing trips. The hotel is 1½ blocks from the marina, where parking is available.

Zapata at Hidalgo, 23410 Cabo San Lucas, B.C.S. ℭ/fax 624/143-2773. www.cabosiestasuites.com. 20 suites. $56 double. No credit cards. Ask for weekly and monthly discounts. **Amenities:** Tour desk; VCR and movie library. *In room:* A/C, TV.

WHERE TO DINE

It's not uncommon to pay a lot for mediocre food in Cabo, so try to get a couple of unbiased recommendations before settling in for a meal. If people are only drinking and not dining, take that as a clue—many seemingly popular places are long on party atmosphere but short on food. Prices decrease the farther you walk inland from the waterfront. Streets to explore for other good restaurants include Hidalgo and Lázaro Cárdenas, plus the marina at the Plaza Bonita Mall. The expected U.S. franchise chains proliferate downtown. Note that many restaurants automatically add the tip to the bill.

VERY EXPENSIVE

Casa Rafael's ℛ INTERNATIONAL   Looking for a little romance? Casa Rafael's, though overpriced, is among the most romantic places in Cabo. Dine in one of the large house's candlelit rooms and alcoves (which are air-conditioned), or outside beside the small swimming pool. Piano music plays in the background while you enjoy a leisurely meal. To start, try sublime smoked dorado paté, or perhaps hearts of palm with raspberry vinaigrette. House specialties—a tasty combination of selections from the meat, seafood, and pasta menus—include Cornish game hen in champagne sauce. Black Angus steaks are imported from the United States; the lamb comes from New Zealand.

Calle Medano and Camino el Pescador. ℭ 624/143-0739. www.allaboutcabo.com. Reservations recommended. Main courses $20–$58. AE, MC, V. Daily 6–10pm. Follow the Hacienda Road toward the ocean; when you top the hill, turn left and drive to the rosy-pink château with an arched front and a patio with caged birds and fountain.

EXPENSIVE

Nick-San ℛℛℛ JAPANESE/SUSHI   Exceptional Japanese cuisine and sushi are the specialties at this air-conditioned restaurant with minimalist decor. A rosewood sushi bar with royal blue tile accents allows diners to watch the master sushi chef at work. An exhibition kitchen behind him demonstrates why this place has been honored with a special award for cleanliness. It's a personal favorite of mine—as well as of many local residents.

Blv. Marina, Plaza de la Danza, Local no. 2. © 624/143-4484. Reservations recommended. Main courses $15–$30; sushi from $3.50. MC, V. Tues–Sun 11:30am–10:30pm.

Peacocks ⋒⋒ INTERNATIONAL   One of Cabo's most exclusive patio-dining establishments, Peacocks emphasizes fresh seafood, creatively prepared. Start with the house paté or a salad of feta cheese with cucumber, tomato, and onion. For a main course, try one of the pastas—linguini with grilled chicken and sun-dried tomatoes is a good choice. More filling entrees include steaks, shrimp, and lamb, all prepared several ways.

Paseo del Pescador s/n, near Hotel Melia Cabo San Lucas. © **624/143-1858.** Reservations recommended. Main courses $15–$35. AE, MC, V. Daily 6–10:30pm.

MODERATE

La Dolce ⋒⋒ ITALIAN   This restaurant is the offspring of Puerto Vallarta's La Dolce Vita, with authentic Italian thin-crust, brick-oven pizzas and other specialties. It seems about 80% of the business is from local customers, underscoring the attention to detail and reasonable prices. The simple menu also features sumptuous pastas and calzones, plus great salads. This is the best late-night dining option.

M. Hidalgo y Zapata s/n. © 624/143-4122. Main courses $8–$18. No credit cards. Mon–Sat 6pm–midnight. Closed Sept.

Mi Casa ⋒ MEXICAN/NOUVELLE MEXICAN   The building's vivid cobalt-blue facade is your first clue that this place celebrates Mexico; the menu confirms that impression. This is one of Cabo's most renowned gourmet Mexican restaurants. Traditional specialties such as *manchamanteles* (literally, "tablecloth stainers"), *cochinita pibil,* and *chiles en nogada* are menu staples. Fresh fish is prepared with delicious seasonings and recipes from throughout Mexico. Especially pleasant at night, the restaurant's tables, scattered around a large patio, are set with colorful cloths, traditional pottery, and glassware.

Calle Cabo San Lucas at Madero, across from the main plaza. © 624/143-1933. Reservations recommended. Main courses $11–$23. AE, MC, V. Daily noon–3pm and 5:30–10:30pm.

INEXPENSIVE

Cafe Canela ⋒⋒ COFFEE/PASTRY/LIGHT MEALS   This cozy cafe and bistro is a welcome addition to the Cabo Marina boardwalk, known for its reasonable prices and friendly service. Espresso drinks, fruit smoothies, and muffins are good eye-openers for early risers. Enjoy a light meal or a tropical drink inside or on the bustling waterfront terrace. The appealing menu also offers breakfast egg wraps, salads (curried chicken salad with fresh fruit), sandwiches (blue-cheese quesadillas with smoked tuna and mango), and pastas. There's full bar service, too.

On the Marina boardwalk, below Plaza Las Glorias Hotel. Local 32 y 33. (© **624/ 143-3435.** Main courses $4–$9; coffee $1.75–$3.50. AE, MC, V. Daily 7am–4:30pm.

Felix's ✿ MEXICAN   This colorful, friendly family-run place has grown up since opening in 1958, going from just serving tacos to offering a full array of tasty Mexican and seafood dishes. Everything's fresh and homemade, including corn tortillas and the numerous and varied salsas—more than 30! Fish tacos made with fresh dorado are superb, as are the shrimp dishes—the coconut mango version, served with homemade mango chutney, is especially tasty. Don't leave without sampling the original Mexican bouillabaisse, a rich stew of shrimp, crab, sea bass, scallops, Italian sausage, and savory seasonings. Mexican specialties include *carne asada* (grilled marinated beef) with chile verde sauce, and chimichangas. There is full bar service; the specialties are fresh fruit margaritas and daiquiris. At breakfast time, this is Mama's Royale Café (see below).

Hidalgo and Zapata s/n. (© **624/143-4290.** Main courses $8–$15. MC, V. Mon–Sat 3–10pm.

Mama's Royale Café ✿✿ BREAKFAST   What a great place to start the day! The shady patio decked with cloth-covered tables and the bright, inviting dining room are both comfortable places to settle in. And the food's just as appetizing. Effrain and Pedro preside over this dining hotspot with well-prepared breakfast selections that include grilled sausage; French toast stuffed with cream cheese and topped with pecans, strawberries, and orange liqueur; several variations of eggs Benedict; home fries; fruit crepes, and, of course, traditional breakfasts, plus free coffee refills. The orange juice is fresh squeezed, and there usually is live marimba or mariachi music to get your morning off to a lively start.

Hidalgo at Zapata. (© **624/143-4290.** Breakfast special $2.50; breakfast a la carte $2.50–$10. MC, V. Daily 7:30am–1pm.

Mocambo's ✿✿ SEAFOOD   The location of this longstanding Cabo favorite is not inspiring—it's basically a large cement building—but the food is. The place is always packed, generally with local diners tired of high prices and small portions. Ocean-fresh seafood is the order of the day, and the specialty platter can easily serve four. The restaurant is 1½ blocks inland from Lázaro Cárdenas.

Leona Vicario and 20 de Noviembre. © 624/143-6070. Main courses $5–$23. No credit cards. Daily 1:30am–10pm.

CABO SAN LUCAS AFTER DARK

Cabo San Lucas is the nightlife capital of Baja. After-dark fun centers on the casual bars and restaurants on Marina Boulevard or facing the marina, rather than a flashy disco scene. You can easily find a happy hour with live music and a place to dance, or a Mexican fiesta with mariachis.

MEXICAN FIESTAS & THEME NIGHTS   Some larger hotels have weekly Fiesta Nights, Italian Nights, and other buffet-plus-entertainment theme nights that can be fun as well as a good buy. Check travel agencies and the following hotels: the **Solmar Suites** (© 624/143-3535), the **Finisterra** (© 624/143-0000), and the **Hotel Melia Cabo San Lucas** (© 624/143-0420). Prices range from $22 (not including drinks, tax, and tips) to $35 (which covers everything, including an open bar with national drinks).

SUNSET WATCHING   At twilight, check out Land's End, where the two seas meet. **Whale Watcher's Bar,** in the Hotel Finisterra (© 624/143-3333), is Los Cabos' premier place for sunset watching. Its location at Land's End—where the two seas meet—offers a world-class view of the sun sinking into the Pacific. The high terrace offers vistas of both sea and beach, as well as magical glimpses of whales from January to March. Mariachis play on Friday from 6:30 to 9pm. The bar is open daily from 10am to 11pm. "Whale margaritas" cost $4; beer, $3. There are two-for-one drinks during happy hour from 4 to 6pm.

HAPPY HOURS & HANGOUTS   If you shop around, you can usually find an *hora alegre* (happy hour) somewhere in town between noon and 7pm. On our last visit, the most popular places to drink and carouse until all hours were the Giggling Marlin, El Squid Roe, and the Cabo Wabo Cantina.

Two places to enjoy live music in a more adult setting are the **Sancho Panza Wine Bar and Bistro** (© 624/143-3212; see description below), and the **El Bistro** restaurant and live jazz bar, on Zaragoza at the corner of Niños Héroes (© 624/143-8999). Both offer classic jazz in an atmosphere that accommodates conversation.

Lounge-style bars are the new thing in Cabo. **CinaMomo Cocina and Lounge,** on the third level of the trendy new Puerto Paraíso mall (local 375; © **624/144-4848**), is the best of the bunch, with an eclectic menu to complement the chic bar. It's open daily from 8am to 2am.

El Squid Roe   El Squid Roe is one of the late Carlos Anderson's inspirations, and it still attracts wild, fun-loving crowds of all ages with its two stories of nostalgic decor and eclectic food that's far better than you'd expect from such a party place. As fashionable as blue jeans, this is a place to see and see what can be seen—women's tops are discarded with regularity, as the dancing on tables moves into high gear. There's also a patio out back for dancing when the tables, chairs, and bar spots are taken. Open daily from noon to 2am. Marina Blv., opposite Plaza Bonita Mall. © **624/143-0655.**

Giggling Marlin   Live music alternates with recorded tunes to get the happy patrons dancing—and occasionally jumping up to dance on the tables and bar. A contraption of winches, ropes, and pulleys above a mattress provides entertainment as couples literally string each other up by the heels—just like a captured marlin. The food is only fair; stick with nachos and drinks. There is live music Wednesday through Sunday from 9pm to midnight during high season. The Giggling Marlin is open daily from 8am to 2am. Beer is $1.75 to $2.50; schooner margaritas cost $4 to $6. Drinks are half-price during happy hour, from 2 to 6pm. Lázaro Cárdenas at Zaragoza, across from the marina. © **624/143-0606.** www.gigglingmarlin.com.

Latitude 22+   This raffish restaurant-bar never closes. License plates, signs, sports caps, and a 959-pound blue marlin are the backdrop for U.S. sports events on six TVs scattered among pool tables, dart boards, and assorted games. Dishes such as hamburgers and chicken-fried steak are available, or you can have breakfast anytime. Happy hour runs from 4 to 6pm. Lázaro Cárdenas s/n, 1 block north of the town's only traffic light. © **624/143-1516.**

Sancho Panza Wine Bar and Bistro   Finally, an alternative to beer bars. Sancho Panza combines a gourmet food market with a wine bar that features live jazz plus an intriguing menu of Nuevo Latino cuisine (Mediterranean food with Latin flair). The place has a cozy neighborhood feel, with tourists and locals taking advantage of the selection of more than 150 wines, plus espresso drinks. During high season, make reservations. Open Monday through Saturday 3pm to midnight. Plaza las Glorias boardwalk, next to the Lighthouse. © **624/143-3212.** www.sanchopanza.com.

DANCING

Cabo Wabo Cantina   Owned by Sammy Hagar (formerly of Van Halen) and his Mexican and American partners, this "cantina" packs in youthful crowds, especially when rumors fly that a surprise appearance by a vacationing musician is imminent. Live rock bands from the United States, Mexico, Europe, and Australia perform frequently. At other times, a disco-type sound system plays mostly rock, plus some alternative and techno. This place is especially popular during the summer, because it's one of the few clubs in Cabo with air-conditioning. For snacks, the Taco-Wabo, just outside the club's entrance, stays up late, too. Beer goes for $3, margaritas for $5. The cantina is open from 11am to 4am. Vicente Guerrero at Lázaro Cárdenas. (*C* 624/143-1188.

Coyote Ugly   Part of the popular chain inspired by the movie by the same name, this is Baja's newest rowdy bar and dance club. The terrace bar opens at 6pm daily, and features TV sports, people-watching, and light snacks. The doors to the spacious, air-conditioned club open at 10pm, but things don't get rolling until about midnight, when the Coyote Girls (bartenders) put on their show. Music is dance, trance, and Latin rock. A beer costs $3, a margarita $7. The boutique opens at 10am, the restaurant at 2pm. The place usually closes around 4am. Marina Blv. s/n, at the entrance to the Puerto Paraíso mall. (*C* **624/143-6969** or 624/143-6966. www.coyoteugly.com.mx. No cover for the terrace. Club cover varies; usually $10.

Kokomo   Lively and tropical in theme and spirit, Kokomo is a happening dance club. It serves lunch and dinner, but the drinks are better than the food. Happy hour features two-for-one drinks daily from 4 to 6pm. Grab a table along the oversized windows looking out over Marina Boulevard for people-watching. Open daily from 7am to 3am. Marina Blv. s/n. (*C* 624/143-0600. kokomo@cabonet.net.mx.

MEN'S CLUBS   Or should they be called "ladies' clubs," since that's who's doing the dancing? In any event, Cabo has a selection of places that offer so-called exotic dancing. **Mermaids,** Lázaro Cárdenas and Vicente Guerrero ((*C* **624/143-3827**), seems to be the most popular. It's open daily from 8:30pm to 3am; the cover charge is $5. **Twenty/20** ((*C* **624/143-5380**), at the corner of Lázaro Cárdenas and Francisco Villa, calls itself a world-class cabaret. It also offers pool tables, satellite TVs, and private dancers. It's open from 8:30pm to 3am, has a cover charge of $7, and accepts major credit cards. It's across the street from McDonald's.

4 North from Los Cabos

The coastline of the Sea of Cortez north of San José has long been a favored destination of die-hard anglers, who fly their private planes to airstrips at out-of-the-way lodges. The coastline has experienced considerable development in the past few years, and hotels have expanded their services to please even those who never plan to set foot on a boat. Housing developments are appearing along the main road, but there's still plenty of space for adventurous campers to find secluded beaches.

The rough dirt Coastal Road runs along the east cape from San José to La Ribera; completing the 89km (55-mile) drive can take up to 4 hours. Along this route you pass by Cabo Pulmo, where Baja's only coral reef lies just offshore. There are no major hotels, restaurants, or dive shops here, and most divers reach the reefs on dive boats from Los Cabos. The more efficient approach to the east cape is to drive paved Highway 1 from San José north to the dirt roads leading off the highway to resorts and communities at Punta Colorado, Buena Vista, Los Barriles, and Punta Pescadero. Public buses from San José stop at major intersections, where you'll need to catch a cab to the hotels. Most guests who stay at the more secluded hotels take a cab from the airport and remain at the hotel.

WHERE TO STAY & DINE

Rancho Buena Vista   A fishing resort with no pretensions, Rancho Buena Vista has several one-story bungalows spread about the grounds. The simple rooms have red-tiled floors, good showers, double beds, and small patios. Hammocks hang under palms and by the swimming pool, and the bar-restaurant is the center of the action. The hotel has an excellent deep-sea fishing fleet with its own dock, and a private airstrip. Note that the info on the website is outdated.

Hwy. 1 at Buena Vista, 56km (35 miles) north of San José del Cabo. ℭ **624/141-0177.** Fax 624/141-0055. (Reservations: P.O. Box 1408, Santa Maria, CA 93456; ℭ 800/258-8200 outside CA, or 805/928-1719; fax 805/925-2990.) www.rancho buenavista.com. 55 units. $185 double. Rates include 3 meals daily. MC, V. **Amenities:** Restaurant/bar; pool; fishing charters; tour desk. *In room:* A/C.

5 Todos Santos: A Creative Oasis ★★★

68km (42 miles) N of Cabo San Lucas

A few years back, Todos Santos became known as "Bohemian Baja." It found its way onto the itineraries of those looking for the latest, the trendiest, and the hippest of artists' outposts—and of those simply weary of the L.A.-ization of Cabo San Lucas.

The art and artistry created here—from the kitchen to the canvas—seems to care less about commercial appeal than about quality, which makes it even more of a draw. Not to be overlooked are the attendant arts of agriculture, masonry, and weavings practiced by some of the town's original residents. From the superb meals at **Café Santa Fe** to an afternoon spent browsing at **El Tecolote Libros,** the best bookstore I've come across in Mexico, Todos Santos is intriguing to its core.

The town is not only a cultural oasis in Baja but an oasis in the true sense of the word—in this desert landscape, Todos Santos enjoys an almost continuous water supply from the peaks of the Sierra de la Laguna mountains. It's just over an hour's drive up the Pacific coast from Cabo San Lucas; you'll know you've arrived when verdant groves of palms, mangos, avocados, and papayas suddenly interrupt the arid coastal scenery.

During the Mission period, the reliable water supply made this valley the only area south and west of La Paz deemed worth settling. In 1723, an outpost mission was established, followed by the full-fledged Misión Santa Rosa de Las Palmas, endowed by one of Spain's leading families, in 1733. The town was then known as Santa Rosa de Todos Santos, eventually shortened to its current name, which translates as "All Saints."

Over the next 200 years, the town alternated between prosperity and difficulty. Its most recent boom lasted from the mid–19th century until the 1950s, when the town prospered as a sugarcane production center and began to develop a strong cultural core. Many of the buildings now being restored and converted into galleries, studios, shops, and restaurants were built during this era.

Demand for older colonial-style structures by artists, entrepreneurs, and foreign residents has resulted in a real estate boom. New shops, galleries, and cafes crop up continuously. The coastal strip south of Todos Santos is in the process of being developed, with its first luxury hotel and spa slated to open sometime in the next 2 years. For the casual visitor, Todos Santos can easily be explored in a day, but a few tranquil inns welcome charmed guests who want to stay a little longer. For additional information and current events, visit www.todossantos-baja.com.

WHAT TO DO IN TODOS SANTOS

During the **Festival Fundador** (Oct 10–14), which celebrates the founding of the town in 1723, streets around the main plaza fill with food, games, and wandering troubadours. Many of the shops and the Café Santa Fe close from the end of September through the festival. A new Arts Festival, held in February, seems to be gaining importance, with film festivals, dance and music performances, and more.

Todos Santos is a good stopover for those traveling between Cabo and La Paz; a day's visit can be arranged through tour companies in Los Cabos or done on your own with a rental car. There are at least half a dozen galleries in town, including the noted **Galería de Todos Santos,** corner of Topete and Legaspi (© 612/145-0040), which features a changing collection of works by regional artists. It's open daily 11am to 4pm (closed Sun May–Nov) and doesn't accept credit cards. The **Galería Santa Fe,** Centenario, across from the plaza (© 612/ 145-0340), holds an eclectic collection of original, creative Mexican folk art and *artesanía* treasures that include Frida-adorned frames and "shrines"—kid-sized chairs decorated in bottle caps, Virgin of Guadalupe images, *milagros,* and more. It's open Wednesday through Monday from 10am to 5pm and accepts Visa and MasterCard.

El Tecolote Libros *(AAA* (© 612/145-0295), though tiny, gets our vote for the best bookstore in Mexico. It carries an exceptional selection of Latin American literature, poetry, children's books, and reference books centering on Mexico. Both English and Spanish editions, new and used, are in stock, along with maps, magazines, cards, and art supplies. Information on upcoming writing workshops and local reading groups is also posted here. The shop is at the corner of Hidalgo and Juárez. It's open Monday through Saturday from 9am to 5pm, and Sunday from 10am to 3pm.

WHERE TO STAY

Consider the elegant **Todos Santos Inn** *AAA,* Calle Legaspi 33, between Topete and Obregón (© 612/145-0040). An impeccable place to stay, it is in a historic house that has served as a general store, cantina, school, and private residence. Details include luxurious white bed linens, netting draped romantically over the beds, Talavera-tile bathrooms, antique furniture, and high, wood-beamed ceilings. Two rooms and two suites border a courtyard terrace and garden, and owner Robert Whiting plans to add a few more. Double rates run from $95 to $135 per night. The suites are air-conditioned, but neither television nor telephone interrupts your relaxed stay. Currently no credit cards are accepted, but that could soon change. Seasonal discounts are available; the inn closes in September.

Fun Fact **You Can Check Out Any Time You Like . . .**

In Todos Santos, the most renowned accommodation is the **Hotel California** (© 612/145-0522), reputed namesake of the famous Eagles song. The hotel was originally constructed in 1928, in part from planks salvaged from a shipwrecked Norwegian vessel. Although the hotel is closed for a complete renovation, it's still worth walking past—you'll find it on Calle Juárez Colonia Centro between Morelos and Marquez de León. Open now are a new restaurant, **La Coronela,** and the **Hotel California Bar.** Both are at the street entry for the hotel, and are open daily from 8am to midnight. The guest rooms were scheduled to open in late 2003.

WHERE TO DINE

For myself—and, I suspect, for many others—a meal at the **Café Santa Fe** 🐾🐾🐾, Calle Centenario 4 (© 612/145-0340), is reason enough to visit Todos Santos. A meal here is likely to be one of the best you will have anywhere, at any price. Much of the attention the town has received in recent years can be directly attributed to this outstanding cafe, and it continues to live up to its lofty reputation. Owners Ezio and Paula Colombo refurbished a large stucco house across from the plaza, creating an exhibition kitchen, several dining rooms, and a lovely courtyard adjacent to a garden of hibiscus, bougainvillea, papaya trees, and herbs.

My favorite room is the one in homage to Frida Kahlo, with reproductions of her work on grand canvases that flatter her more than her originals. The excellent Northern Italian cuisine emphasizes local produce and seafood. Try homemade ravioli stuffed with spinach and ricotta in Gorgonzola sauce, or ravioli with lobster and shrimp, accompanied by an organic salad. In high season the wait for a table at lunch can be long. Everything is prepared fresh when ordered, and reservations are recommended. Main courses run $10 to $15; the cafe accepts MasterCard and Visa. It's open Wednesday through Monday from noon to 9pm, and closed in September and October.

A more casual option, and a magical place to start the day, is the garden setting of the **Caffé Todos Santos,** Calle Centenario 33, across from the Todos Santos Inn (℡ **612/145-0300**). Among the espresso drinks is a bowl-sized caffe latte, accompanied by a freshly baked croissant or a signature cinnamon bun. Lunch or a light meal may include a frittata, or fish filet wrapped in banana leaves with coconut milk. Main courses average $3 to $6. The cafe is open Tuesday through Sunday from 7am to 9pm, Monday from 7am to 2pm. No credit cards.

3

La Paz: Peaceful Port Town

La Paz means "peace," and the feeling seems to float on the ocean breezes of this provincial town. Despite being an important port with almost 200,000 inhabitants and the capital of the state of Baja California Sur, La Paz remains slow-paced and relaxed. It's an easy-going yet sophisticated city, the guardian of "old Baja" atmosphere, with beautiful deserted beaches just minutes away that complement the lively beach and palm-fringed *malecón* (sea wall) that fronts the town center.

The presence of the University of South Baja California has added a unique cultural element that includes museums, a theater, and an arts center. The surrounding tropical desert diversity and uncommon wildlife are also compelling reasons to visit. They lend themselves to countless options for adventurous travelers, including hiking, rock climbing, diving, fishing, and sea kayaking. Islands and islets sit just offshore; once the hiding place for looting pirates, they now attract kayakers and beachcombers. At Espírito Santo and Los Islotes, it's possible to swim with sea lions.

Despite its name, La Paz has historically been a place of conflict between explorers and indigenous populations, traders, and pirates. Beginning in 1535, Spanish conquistadors and Jesuit missionaries arrived, leaving their influence on the architecture and traditions of La Paz. From its founding—when conquistadors saw local Indians wearing pearl ornaments—through the late 1930s, when an unknown disease killed off the oysters in the Bay of La Paz, this was the center of world pearl harvesting. Writer John Steinbeck immortalized a local legend in his novella *The Pearl*.

La Paz is ideal for anyone nostalgic for Los Cabos the way it used to be, before development and burgeoning crowds. From accommodations to taxis, it's also one of Mexico's most outstanding beach-vacation values and a great place for family travelers.

La Paz Area

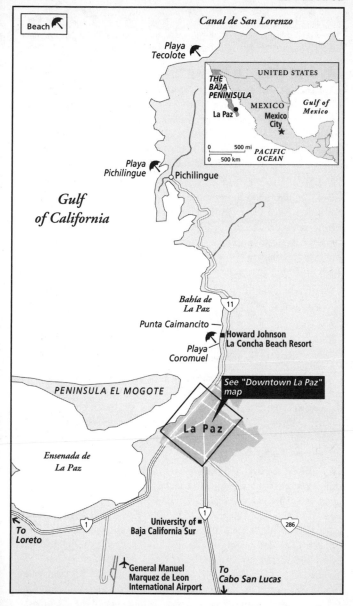

Beach ⛱

Canal de San Lorenzo

Playa
Tecolote

UNITED STATES

THE
BAJA
PENINSULA

MEXICO
La Paz

Gulf of
Mexico

Mexico
City

PACIFIC
OCEAN

0   500 mi
0   500 km

Playa
Pichilingue

Pichilingue

Gulf
of California

Bahía de
La Paz

11

Punta Caimancito

Howard Johnson
La Concha Beach Resort

Playa
Coromuel

See "Downtown La Paz"
map

PENINSULA EL MOGOTE

La Paz

Ensenada de
La Paz

1

To
Loreto

1

University of
Baja California Sur

286

General Manuel
Marquez de Leon
International Airport

To
Cabo San Lucas

1 Essentials

177km (110 miles) N of Cabo San Lucas; 196km (122 miles) NW of San José del Cabo; 1,578km (980 miles) SE of Tijuana

GETTING THERE & DEPARTING

BY PLANE **AeroCalifornia** (© **800/237-6225** in the U.S., or 612/125-1023) has flights to La Paz from Los Angeles, Tijuana, and Mexico City. Aeromexico (© **800/237-6639** in the U.S., 612/ 122-0091, 612/122-0093, or 612612/122-1636) connects through Tucson and Los Angeles in the United States, and flies from Mexico City, Guadalajara, Tijuana, and other points within Mexico.

BY CAR From San José del Cabo, Highway 1 north is the longer, more scenic route; a flatter, faster route is Highway 1 east to Cabo San Lucas, then Highway 19 north through Todos Santos. A little before San Pedro, Highway 19 rejoins Highway 1 north into La Paz; the trip takes 2 to 3 hours. From the north, Highway 1 south is the only choice; the trip from Loreto takes 4 to 5 hours.

BY BUS The Central Camionera (main bus station) is at Jalisco and Héroes de la Independencia, about 25 blocks southwest of the center of town; it's open daily from 6am to 10pm. Bus service operates from the south (Los Cabos, 2½–3½ hr.) and north (as far as Tijuana). It's best to buy your ticket in person the day before, though reservations can be made over the phone. Taxis are available in front of the station.

All routes north and south, as well as buses to Pichilingue ($1.50), the ferry pier, and close to outlying beaches, are available through the Transportes Aguila station, sometimes called the beach bus terminal, on the *malecón* at Alvaro Obregón and Cinco de Mayo (© **612/ 122-7898**). The station is open daily from 6am to 10pm. Buses to Pichilingue depart every hour.

BY FERRY Two SEMATUR car ferries serve La Paz from Topolobampo (the port for Los Mochis) Monday through Saturday at 10pm (10 hr.), and from Mazatlán Sunday through Friday at 3pm (18 hr.). In La Paz, the SEMATUR office, Cinco de Mayo 502 (© **612/125-8899** ext. 109, or 612/122-5005), sells tickets. The office is open daily 8am to 6pm. For information, call © **01-800/ 696-9600** toll-free within Mexico.

The SEMATUR car ferry departs for Topolobampo Monday and Wednesday through Saturday at 11am, and for Mazatlán Sunday through Friday at 3pm. The dock is at Pichilingue, 18km (11 miles)

> ## *Tips* Taking Your Car to the Mainland
>
> Those planning to take their cars on the ferry to the Mexican mainland must meet all the requirements listed in "Getting There" in in chapter 1. Every traveler going to the mainland needs a Mexican Tourist Permit (FMT).
>
> Tourism officials in La Paz say that Tourist Cards are available only in Mexicali, Tecate, Tijuana, Ensenada, and Guerrero Negro, and not in La Paz, although car permits to cross over into the mainland can be issued there. If you do happen to make it as far as La Paz, or anywhere outside the frontier zone, and are found not to have a Tourist Permit (FMT), you are subject to a $40 fine.

north of La Paz. Passengers pay one fee for themselves and another for their vehicles, with prices for cars varying by size. A car less than 5.5m (18 ft) long costs $155. Least expensive is *salon* class, with about 440 bus-type seats ($63 to Mazatlán) in one or more large rooms on the lower deck; these rooms can become very crowded. *Turista* class ($83 to Mazatlán) is next, providing a tiny room with four bunks, a chair, sink, and window, and individual bathrooms/showers down the hall. *Cabina* class ($100 to Mazatlán) is the best, with a small room holding one bunk, chair, table, window, and private bathroom. ***Note:*** Not all classes are available all the time, and ferry schedules change.

SEMATUR ferries are usually, but not always, equipped with a cafeteria and bar. Reserve as early as possible and confirm your reservation 24 hours before departure; you can pick up tickets at the port terminal ticket office as late as the morning of the day you are leaving. **Agencia de Viajes Aome,** Cinco de Mayo 502 at Guillermo Prieto (© **612/125-2346,** ext. 1), is the only agency in La Paz authorized to sell ferry tickets. The office is open daily from 8am to 6pm. For information only, call © **612/125-6588.** Several tour agencies in town book reservations on the ferry, but it is best to buy your ticket in person at the ferry office. For information, you can also call © **01-800/696-9600,** toll-free within Mexico.

Buses to Pichilingue depart from the beach bus terminal of **Transportes Aguila** (© **612/122-7898**) on the *malecón* at Independencia on the hour, from 7am to 6pm, and cost $1.50 each way.

ORIENTATION
ARRIVING
BY PLANE   The airport is 18km (11 miles) northwest of town along the highway to Ciudad Constitución and Tijuana. Airport *colectivos* (minivans) run only from the airport to town ($11), not vice versa. Taxi service is available as well. Most major car-rental agencies have booths inside the airport. Two local numbers are **Budget** (© 612/124-6433), and **Local Car Rental,** Alvaro Obregón 582 (© 612/123-3622).

BY BUS   Buses arrive at the Central Camionera, about 25 blocks southwest of downtown, or at the beach station along the *malecón.* Taxis line up in front of both.

BY FERRY   Buses line up in front of the ferry dock at Pichilingue to meet every arriving ferry. They stop at the beach bus station on the *malecón* at Independencia; it's within walking distance of many downtown hotels if you're not encumbered with luggage. Taxis meet each ferry and cost about $8 to downtown La Paz.

VISITOR INFORMATION
The most accessible visitor information office is on Alvaro Obregón, across from the intersection with Calle 16 de Septiembre (© 612/122-5939; turismo@lapaz.cromwell.com.mx). It's open daily from 9am to 8pm. The extremely helpful staff speaks English and can supply information on La Paz, Los Cabos, and the rest of the region. This doubles as the office for the La Paz Tourist Police, who assist with directions or problems that visitors may encounter.

CITY LAYOUT
Although La Paz sprawls well inland from the *malecón* (the seaside boulevard, Alvaro Obregón), you'll probably spend most of your

---

Moments Festivals & Events in La Paz

February features the biggest and best Carnaval, or Mardi Gras, in Baja, as well as a month-long Festival of the Gray Whale (starting in Feb or Mar). On May 3, La Fiesta de La Paz (Celebration of Peace) celebrates the city's founding by Cortés in 1535, and features *artesanía* exhibitions from throughout southern Baja. The annual marlin-fishing tournament is in August, with other fishing tournaments in September and November. And on November 1 and 2, the Days of the Dead, altars are on display at the Anthropology Museum.

time in the older, more congenial downtown section within a few blocks of the waterfront. The main plaza, Plaza Pública (or Jardín Velasco), is bounded by Madero, Independencia, Revolución, and Cinco de Mayo. The plaza centers on an iron kiosk where public concerts frequently take place in the evening.

GETTING AROUND

Because most of what you'll need in town is on the *malecón* between the tourist information office and the Hotel Los Arcos, or a few blocks inland from the waterfront, it's easy to get around La Paz on foot. Public buses go to some of the beaches north of town (see "Beaches & Outdoor Activities," below), but to explore the many beaches within 81km (50 miles) of La Paz, your best bet is to rent a car or hire a taxi. Several car-rental agencies have offices on the *malecón*.

 FAST FACTS: La Paz

Area Code The telephone area code is **612**.

Banks Banks generally exchange currency during normal business hours: Monday through Friday from 9am to 6pm and Saturday from 10am to 2pm. ATMs are readily available and offer bank exchange rates on withdrawals.

Emergencies Dial ✆ **060**.

Hospitals **Hospital Especialidades Médicas,** in the Fidepaz building (✆ **612/124-0400**), and **Hospital Juan María de Salvatierra,** Nicolas Bravo 1010, Col. Centro (✆ **612/122-1496**).

Internet Access **BajaNet,** Madero 430 (✆ **612/125-9380**) charges 1 peso (10¢) per minute, with a $1 (10-min.) minimum charge. It's open Monday through Saturday 8am to 10pm, Sunday 9am to 9pm.

Marinas La Paz has two marinas: **Marina de La Paz,** at the west end of the *malecón* at Legaspi (✆ **612/125-2112;** marina lapaz@bajavillas.com), and **Club de Yates Palmira,** south of town at Km 2.5 on the Pichilingue Highway Edificio la Plaza (✆ **612/121-6297;** mpalmira@prodigy.net.mx).

Municipal Market The public market is 3 blocks inland, at Degollado and Revolución, and sells mainly produce, meats, and utilitarian wares. Hours are Monday through Saturday 6am to 6pm and Sunday 6am to 1pm.

Parking In high season, street parking may be hard to find in the downtown area, but there are several guarded lots, and side streets are less crowded.

Pharmacy One of the largest pharmacies is **Farmacia Baja California,** Independencia and Madero (© **612/122-0240** or 612/123-4408).

Post Office The *correo* is 3 blocks inland, at Constitución and Revolución (© **612/122-0388**); it's open Monday through Friday 8am to 2pm, Saturday 9am to 1pm.

Tourism Office Located at Km 5.5 Carretera al Norte, Edificio Fidepaz (© **612/124-0199**), it's open daily from 10am to 2pm and 4 to 8pm.

2 Beaches & Outdoor Activities

La Paz combines the unselfconscious bustle of a small capital port city with beautiful isolated beaches not far from town. Well on its way to becoming the undisputed adventure-tourism capital of Baja, it's the starting point for whale-watching, diving, sea kayaking, climbing, and hiking tours throughout the peninsula. Those interested in day adventures can usually arrange everything mentioned above, plus beach tours, sunset cruises, and visits to the sea lion colony, through travel agencies in major hotels or along the *malecón*. You can also arrange activities through agencies in the United States that specialize in Baja's natural history. (See "The Active Traveler," in chapter 1.)

BEACHES

Within a 10- to 45-minute drive from La Paz lie some of the loveliest beaches in Baja. Many rival those of the Caribbean with their clear, turquoise water.

The beaches that line the ***malecón*** are the most convenient in town. Although the sand is soft and white, and the water appears crystal clear and gentle, locals don't generally swim there. Because La Paz is a commercial port, the water is not considered as clean as that in the very accessible outlying beaches. With its colorful playgrounds dotting the central beachfront, as well as numerous open-air restaurants that front the water, the *malecón* is best for a casual afternoon of post-sightseeing lunch and playtime.

The best beach in town is immediately north of town at **La Concha Beach Resort;** nonguests may use the hotel restaurant-bar and rent equipment for snorkeling, diving, skiing, and sailing. It's 10km (6 miles) north of town on the Pichilingue Highway, at Km 5.5. The other beaches are farther north of town, but midweek you may have these far distant beaches to yourself.

At least 10 public buses from the beach bus station at Independencia on the *malecón* depart from 8am to 5:30pm for beaches to the north. The buses stop at the small **Playa Camancito** (5km/3 miles), **Playa Coromuel** (8km/5 miles), **Playa Tesoro** (14km/9 miles), and **Pichilingue** (17km/10½ miles); from the ferry stop, walk north on the highway to the beach. Ask when the last bus will make the return trip. Pichilingue, Coromuel, and Tesoro beaches have palapa-shaded bars or restaurants, which may not be open midweek. You can pack a lunch and just rent a shade umbrella for $1 per group, with tables and chairs available for a minimum consumption charge.

The most beautiful of these outlying beaches is **Playa Tecolote** 🎯🎯, approximately 29km (18 miles) from La Paz at the end of a paved road. The water is a heavenly cerulean blue. There are several restaurants. To get to Playa Tecolote on your own, take a bus as far as Pichilingue; from there, take a taxi the remaining 13km (8 miles). When the taxi drops you off, make arrangements for it to return. The road is paved as far as Playa Tecolote and Playa Balandra (29km/18 miles), and turnoffs to these and other beaches are well marked.

For more information about beaches and maps, check at the tourist information office on the *malecón.* If you want to take a general tour of all the beaches before deciding where to spend your precious vacation days, **Viajes Lybs** (✆ **612/122-4680**) offers a 4-hour beach tour for $22 per person, with stops at Pichilingue, Balandra, and El Tecolote beaches.

CRUISES

A popular and very worthwhile cruise is to **Isla Espíritu Santo** and **Los Islotes** to visit the largest sea lion colony in Baja, stunning rock formations, and remote beaches, with stops for snorkeling, swimming, and lunch. If conditions permit, you may even be able to snorkel beside the sea lions. Both boat and bus tours are available to **Puerto Balandra,** where bold rock formations rising up like humpback whales frame pristine coves of crystal-blue water and ivory sand. **Viajes Palmira,** on the *malecón* across from Hotel Los Arcos (✆ **612/122-4030**), and other travel agencies can arrange these all-day trips, weather permitting, for $67 per person.

WATERSPORTS

SCUBA DIVING Scuba-diving trips are best from June through September. You can arrange them through Fernando Aguilar's **Baja Diving and Services,** Obregón 1665-2 (℃ **612/122-1826;** fax 612/122-8644; bajadiving@lapaz.cromwell.com.mx). Diving sites include the sea lion colony at Los Islotes, distant Cerralvo Island, the sunken ship *Salvatierra,* a 18m (60-ft wall dive, and several sea mounts (underwater mountains) and reefs. Also available is a trip to see hammerhead sharks and manta rays. Rates start at $70 per person for an all-day outing and two-tank dive. Baja Diving recently added a 40-unit sports lodge and beach resort, **Club Hotel Cantamar** (℃ **612/122-7010**). Rates for a double room run $65.

Baja Expeditions, Sonora 586 (℃ **612/125-3828;** fax 612/125-3829; bajaex@balandra.uabcs.mx; open daily 8am–6pm), runs liveaboard and single-day dive trips to the above-mentioned locations and other areas in the Sea of Cortez. Cost is $100 for a two-tank dive. See "The Active Traveler," in chapter 1, for contact information in the U.S. and Canada

SEA KAYAKING Kayaking in the many bays and coves near La Paz has become extremely popular. Many enthusiasts bring their own equipment. Several companies from the United States can arrange kayaking trips in advance (see "The Active Traveler," in chapter 1, for more information). Locally, **Mar y Aventuras,** Topete 564, between 5 de Febrero and Navarro (℃ **612/122-7039** or 612/125-4794; www.kayakbaja.com), also arranges kayaking trips.

SPORTFISHING La Paz, justly famous for its sportfishing, attracts anglers from all over the world. Its waters are home to more than 850 species of fish. The most economical approach is to rent a *panga* (skiff) with guide and equipment for $125 for 3 hours—but you don't go very far out. Super pangas, which have a shade cover and comfortable seats, start at around $180 for two people. Larger cruisers with bathrooms start at $240.

You can arrange sportfishing trips locally through hotels and tour agencies. David Jones of **The Fishermen's Fleet** (℃ **612/122-1313;** www.fishermensfleet.com) uses the locally popular panga-style fishing boat. David is super-professional, speaks English, and truly understands area fishing. Average price is $225 for the boat, but double-check what the price includes—you may need to bring your own food and drinks.

WHALE-WATCHING Between January and March (and sometimes as early as December), 3,000 to 5,000 gray whales migrate from the Bering Strait to the Pacific coast of Baja. The main whale-watching spots are Laguna San Ignacio (on the Pacific, near San Ignacio), Bahía Magdalena (on the Pacific, near Puerto López Mateos—about a 2-hr. drive from La Paz), and Scammon's Lagoon (near Guerrero Negro).

Although it is across the peninsula on the Sea of Cortez, La Paz has the only major international airport in the area and thus has become a center of Baja's whale-watching excursions. Most tours originating in La Paz go to Bahía Magdalena, where the whales give birth in calm waters. Several companies arrange whale-watching tours originating in La Paz or other Baja towns or in the United States; 12-hour tours from La Paz start at around $106 per person, including breakfast, lunch, transportation, and an English-speaking guide. Make reservations at **Viajes Lybs,** 16 de Septiembre 408, between Revolución and Serdán (© **612/122-4680;** fax 612/125-9600).

Most tours from the United States offer birding, sea kayaking, and other close-to-nature experiences during the same trip. See "The Active Traveler," in chapter 1, for details.

You can go whale-watching without joining a tour by taking a bus from La Paz to Puerto López Mateos or Puerto San Carlos at Magdalena Bay (a 3-hr. ride) and hiring a boat there. It's a long trip to do in a day, but there are a few modest hotels in San Carlos. Check at the La Paz tourist office for information.

For a more in-depth discussion, see "Whale-Watching in Baja: A Primer," in chapter 4.

3 A Break from the Beaches: Exploring La Paz

Most tour agencies offer city tours of all the major sights. Tours last 2 to 3 hours, include time for shopping, and cost around $15 per person.

HISTORIC LA PAZ

When Cortés landed here on May 3, 1535, he named it Bahía Santa Cruz. The name didn't stick. In April 1683, Eusebio Kino, a Spanish Jesuit priest, arrived and dubbed the place Nuestra Señora de la Paz (Our Lady of Peace). It wasn't until November 1, 1720, however, that Jaime Bravo, another Jesuit priest, set up a permanent mission. He used the same name as his immediate predecessor, calling it the Misión de Nuestra Señora de la Paz. The mission church stands on La Paz's main square on Revolución between Cinco de Mayo and Independencia, and today the city is called simply La Paz.

The Anthropology Museum ✈ The museum features large, though faded, color photos of Baja's prehistoric cave paintings. There are also exhibits on various topics, including the geological history of the peninsula, fossils, missions, colonial history, and daily life. All information is in Spanish.

Altamirano and Cinco de Mayo. © 612/122-0162. Free admission (donations encouraged). Mon–Fri 8am–6pm; Sat 9am–2pm.

Biblioteca de las Californias The small collection of historical documents and books at the Library of the Californias is the most comprehensive in Baja. The library sometimes shows free international films in the evening.

In the Casa de Gobierno, across the plaza from the mission church on Madero, between Cinco de Mayo and Independencia. For information, call the tourism office (© 612/124-0199). Free admission. Mon–Fri 8am–8pm.

El Teatro de la Ciudad The city theater is La Paz's cultural center, with performances by visiting and local artists. There's no extended calendar available, but bookings include small ballet companies, experimental and popular theater, popular music, and an occasional classical concert or symphony. Contact the box office for details and ticket prices.

Av. Navarro 700. © 612/125-0486.

4 Shopping

La Paz has little in the way of folk art or other treasures from mainland Mexico. The dense cluster of streets behind the Hotel Perla between 16 de Septiembre and Degollado abounds with small shops, some tacky, others quite upscale. This area also holds a very small but authentic Chinatown, dating to the time when Chinese laborers were brought to settle in Baja. Serdán from Degollado south offers dozens of sellers of dried spices, piñatas, and candy. Stores selling crafts, folk art, clothing, and handmade furniture and accessories lie mostly along the *malecón* (Alvaro Obregón), or a block or two in. The municipal market, at Revolución and Degollado, has little of interest to visitors. Something you're sure to notice if you explore around the central plaza is the abundance of stores selling electronic equipment, including stereos, cameras, and televisions. This is because La Paz is a principal port for electronic imports to Mexico from the Far East, and therefore offers some of the best prices in Baja and mainland Mexico.

Antigua California This shop manages to stay in business as others come and go. It carries a good selection of folk art from

throughout Mexico. It's open Monday to Saturday from 9:30am to 8:30pm, Sunday from 10am to 5pm. Paseo Alvaro Obregón 220, at Arreola. ℂ 612/125-5230.

Artesanías Cuauhtémoc (The Weaver) If you like beautiful hand-woven tablecloths, place mats, rugs, and other textiles, it's worth the long walk or taxi ride to this unique shop. Fortunato Silva, an elderly gentleman, weaves wonderfully textured cotton textiles from yarn he spins and dyes himself. He charges far less than what you'd pay for equivalent artistry in the United States. Open Monday through Saturday from 10am to 3pm and 5 to 8pm, and Sunday from 10am to 1pm. Abasolo 3315, between Jalisco and Nayarit. ℂ 612/122-4575.

Dorian's If you've forgotten essentials or want to stock up on duty-free perfume or cosmetics, head for Dorian's, La Paz's major department store. La Paz is a duty-free port city, so prices are excellent. Dorian's carries a wide selection of stylish clothing, shoes, lingerie, jewelry, and accessories as well. Open daily from 9am to 9pm. 16 de Septiembre, between Esquerro and 21 de Agosto. ℂ 612/122-8014.

A Day Trip to El Arco

A day trip by car or guided tour to Los Cabos, at the southern tip of Baja California, where the Pacific Ocean meets the Sea of Cortez, will take you past dramatic scenery and many photogenic isolated beaches. A guided tour that includes lunch and a glass-bottom-boat tour to El Arco in Cabo San Lucas costs $45 to $60 per person; book through most travel agencies. Most tours last from 7am to 6pm, and some include breakfast.

Ibarra's Pottery   Here, you not only shop for tableware, hand-painted tiles, and decorative pottery, you can watch it being made. Each piece is individually hand-painted or glazed, then fired. Open Monday to Friday from 8am to 3pm, Saturday from 8am to noon. Guillermo Prieto 625, between Torre Iglesias and República. ℰ **612/122-0404.**

SENI Jewelry   In addition to exceptionally priced, exquisitely stylish jewelry, you'll find a good selection of Cuban and Veracruz cigars stored in a humidor. It's open Monday to Saturday from 11am to 2pm and 4 to 8pm. No credit cards. Parque Cuauhtémoc, at Paseo Alvaro Obregón. ℰ **612/122-2604.**

5 Where to Stay

EXPENSIVE

Howard Johnson La Concha Beach Resort 𝒜𝒜   This resort's setting, 10km (6 miles) north of downtown La Paz, is perfect: on a curved beach ideal for swimming and watersports. All rooms face the water and have double beds, balconies or patios, and small tables and chairs. Studio and three-bedroom condos with full kitchens are available on a nightly basis in the high-rise complex next door, and are worth the extra price for a family vacation. The hotel offers scuba, fishing, and whale-watching packages.

Km 5 Carretera Pichilingue, 23000 La Paz, B.C.S. ℰ **800/999-2252,** 612/121-6161, or 612/121-6344. Fax 612/122-8644. www.laconcha.com. 113 units. $95 double; $120 jr. suite; $137–$259 condo. AE, DC, MC, V. Free guarded parking. **Amenities:** Restaurant; 2 bars; beachside pool; complete aquatic-sports center with WaveRunners, kayaks, and paddleboats; beach club with scuba program available; tour desk; free twice-daily shuttle to town; room service; laundry service. *In room:* A/C, TV.

MODERATE

Hotel Los Arcos 🕸🕸 *Value*   This three-story neocolonial-style hotel at the west end of the *malecón* is the best place for downtown accommodations, with a touch of tranquillity. Los Arcos is functional in its furnishings and amenities, and the hotel's rambling nooks and crannies are filled with fountains, plants, and even rocking chairs that lend lots of old-fashioned charm. Most of the recently remodeled rooms and suites come with two double beds and a balcony overlooking the pool in the inner courtyard or the waterfront, plus coffeemaker and Jacuzzi tub. I prefer the South Pacific–style bungalows with thatched roofs and fireplaces located in the back part of the property, in an appealing jungle garden shaded by large trees. Satellite TVs carry U.S. channels.

Alvaro Obregón 498, between Rosales and Allende (Apdo. Postal 112), 23000 La Paz, B.C.S. ℂ **800/347-2252** or 714/450-9000 in the U.S., or 612/122-2744. Fax 612/ 125-4313. www.losarcos.com or www.bajahotels.com. 130 units. $85–$90 double; $95 suite; $85 cabana. AE, MC, V. Free guarded parking. **Amenities:** Restaurant, cafeteria, bar with live music; 2 pools (1 heated); sauna; Ping-Pong tables; travel agency; desk for fishing information; room service; laundry. *In room:* A/C, TV, minibar.

Posada de las Flores 🕸🕸 *Finds*   New owner Giussepe Marceletti has continued the tradition of hospitality in this elegant B&B (formerly known as Posada Santa Fe), the best bet for travelers looking for a more refined place to stay in La Paz. Each room is individually decorated with high-quality Mexican furniture and antiques, hand-loomed fabrics, and exquisite artisan details. Bathrooms are especially welcoming, with marble tubs and thick towels. Breakfast is served from 8 to 11am daily, and rates include wake-up service with in-room coffee. It's at the northern end of the *malecón*.

Alvaro Obregón 440, 23000 La Paz, B.C.S. ℂ **612/125-5871**. www.posadadelas flores.com. 5 units, including 1 house. $140 double; $199 suite; $450 master suite. Rates include American breakfast. V, MC. No children allowed. **Amenities:** Small pool; telephone; fax; Internet service available through the office. *In room:* A/C, TV.

INEXPENSIVE

Hotel Mediterrane 🕸🕸   Simple yet stylish, this unique inn mixes Mediterranean with Mexican, making a cozy place for couples or friends to share. All rooms face an interior courtyard and have white tile floors and equipal furniture, with colorful Mexican serapes draped over the beds. Some rooms have minifridges. The location is great—just a block from the *malecón*. The adjacent Trattoria La Pazta restaurant (see "Where to Dine," below) is one of La Paz's best, and there's an Internet cafe next door.

Allende 36, 23000 La Paz, B.C.S. ©/fax **612/125-1195**. www.hotelmed.com. 8 units. Low season $55–$60 double; high season $60–$65 double. Rates include use of kayaks, bicycles, and 1 hr. of Internet service per day. Weekly discounts available. AE, MC, V. *In room:* A/C, TV/VCR.

6 Where to Dine

Although La Paz is not known for culinary achievements, it has a growing assortment of small, pleasant restaurants that are good and reasonably priced. In addition to the usual seafood and Mexican dishes, you can find Italian, French, Spanish, Chinese, and even vegetarian offerings. Restaurants along the seaside *malecón* tend to be more expensive than those a few blocks inland. Generally, restaurant reservations are unnecessary, except perhaps during Easter and Christmas weeks.

MODERATE

Bismark II *⊛* SEAFOOD/MEXICAN   Bismark excels at seafood; you can order fish tacos, chiles rellenos stuffed with lobster salad, marlin "meatballs" and paella, breaded oysters, or a sundae glass filled with ceviche or shrimp. The kitchen prepares extremely fresh dorado, halibut, snapper, or whatever else is in season in a number of ways. Chips and creamy dip are served while you wait. It's a good place to linger over a late lunch. The decor of pine walls and dark wood chairs is reminiscent of a country cafe. The owners will call a cab for you if you wish.

Degollado and Altamirano. © **612/122-4854**. Breakfast $2–$5; main courses $4–$17. MC, V. Daily 10am–10pm. Walk 7 blocks inland on Degollado to Altamirano.

Trattoria La Pazta *⊛⊛* ITALIAN/SWISS   The trendiest restaurant in town, La Pazta gleams with black lacquered tables and white tile; the aromas of garlic and espresso float in the air. The menu features local fresh seafood such as pasta with squid in wine and cream sauce, and crispy fried calamari. Lasagna is homemade, baked in a wood-fired oven. An extensive wine list complements the menu. La Pazta is also appealing for breakfast, or you can simply opt for an espresso and croissant. The restaurant is in front of the Hotel Mediterrane.

Allende 36, 1 block inland from the *malecón*. © **612/125-1195**. Main courses $8–$11; breakfast $2–$4. AE, MC, V. Wed–Mon 7am–11pm.

INEXPENSIVE

Caffé Gourmet FRENCH/CAFE   You'll feel you've suddenly been transported across the Atlantic and onto the Continent in this incongruous but welcome addition to La Paz. Indulge in any number of espresso coffee drinks, plus French and Austrian pastries, while sitting at marble-topped bistro tables. Jazz music plays in the background.

Av. Esquerro and 16 de Septiembre. No phone. Coffees and pastries $1–$3. No credit cards. Mon–Sat 7am–8pm; Sun 9am–3pm.

El Quinto Sol *(Finds* VEGETARIAN   Not only is this La Paz's principle health food market, it's a cheerful, excellent cafe for fresh-fruit *liquados* (shakes), tortas, and vegetarian dishes. Tables sit beside oversized wood-framed windows, with flowering planters in the sills. Sandwiches are served on whole-grain bread—also available for sale—and the potato tacos are an excellent way for vegetarians to indulge in a Mexican staple.

Av. Independencia and B. Domínguez. (C) 612/122-1692. Main courses $1.50–$6.50. No credit cards. Mon–Sat 7am–9:30pm.

7 La Paz After Dark

A night in La Paz logically begins in a cafe along the *malecón* as the sun sinks into the sea—have your camera ready.

A favorite ringside seat at dusk is a table at **La Terraza,** next to the Hotel Perla ((C) 612/122-0777). La Terraza makes good, schooner-sized margaritas. **Pelicanos Bar,** on the second story of the Hotel Los Arcos ((C) 612/122-2744), has a good view of the waterfront and a clubby, cozy feel. **Carlos 'n' Charlie's La Paz-Lapa** ((C) 612/122-9290) has live music on the weekends. **La Cabaña** ((C) 612/122-0777) nightclub in the Hotel Perla features Latin rhythms. It opens at 9:30pm, and there's a $5 minimum.

For dancing, a few of the hottest clubs are: **Video Disco Okey Lasser Club** ((C) 612/122-3133), Alvaro Obregón and Degollado, which plays dance music from the '70s to '90s. **Las Varitas** ((C) 612/125-2025), Independencia and Dominguez, playing Latin rock, ranchero, and salsa. Both are open from 9pm to 3 or 4am, with cover charges around $3 (the charge may be waived or increased, depending on the crowd).

The poolside bar overlooking the beach at **La Concha Beach Resort** ((C) 612/121-6161, or 612/121-6344), Km 5.5 Pichilingue Hwy., is the setting for the ubiquitous Mexican fiesta Friday at 7pm. Price is $18, including tax and tips.

4

Mid-Baja: Loreto,
Mulegé & Santa Rosalía

Halfway between the resort sophistication of Los Cabos and the frontier exuberance of Tijuana lies Baja's midsection, an area rich in history and culture. UNESCO has named the indigenous cave paintings a World Heritage Site, and the area was home to numerous Jesuit missions in the 1700s. These days, travelers come to experience the quiet side of Baja and its remote, wild natural beauty; the area is known for its excellent sea kayaking, sportfishing, and hiking.

Overlooked by many travelers—except avid, informed sportfishers—Loreto is a rare gem that sparkles under the desert sky. Here, the purple hues of the Sierra de la Giganta mountains meet the indigo waters of the Sea of Cortez, providing a spectacular backdrop of natural contrasts for the town's historical past. Mulegé is, quite literally, an oasis in the Baja desert. The only fresh water river (Río Mulegé) in the peninsula flows through town; it's a lush, green place, with towering date palms, olive groves, citrus trees, and flowering gardens. And the port town of Santa Rosalía, while slightly past its prime, makes a worthy detour, with its pastel clapboard houses and unusual steel-and-stained-glass church, designed by Gustave Eiffel (of Eiffel Tower fame).

The region is also a popular jumping-off point for many whale-watching tours; to find out when, where, and how to view these gentle giants, consult the whale-watching primer at the end of this chapter.

1 Loreto & the Offshore Islands ★★

391km (243 miles) NW of La Paz; 536km (333 miles) N of Cabo San Lucas; 1,132km (703 miles) SE of Tijuana

The unpretentious feel of the town of Loreto belies its historical importance. Loreto was the center of the Spanish mission effort during colonial times, the first capital of the Californias, and the first European settlement in the peninsula. Founded on October 25,

The Lower Baja Peninsula

Bahía de Sebastián Vizcaíno
Playa San Rafael
B. San Rafael

Bahía Tortugas
Guerrero Negro
Pto. Nuevo
Scammon's Lagoon

Bahía Asuncion
B. La Asunción
Guadalupe
DESIERTO DE
San Ignacio
VIZCAINO

B. San Carlos
La Trinidad

B. Santa Ana
Gulf of California

Bahía San Hipólito

Santa Rosalía

Laguna de San Ignacio

SE. COYOTE

Mulegé

Bahía Concepción

La Purisima
San Isidro
B. San Basílio

PACIFIC OCEAN

Loreto
Isla Del Carmen

Boca La Soledad
Va. Ignacio Zaragoza

Puerto Adolfo López Mateos
Ciudad Insurgentes

Sea of Cortez

Puerto San Carlos
Ciudad Constitución
B. Santa María
El Ciruelo
Bahía Magdalena
Isla San José

San Ignacio
B. Coyote
Isla La Partida
Isla Espíritu Santo

Pichilingue
Las Cruces
Isla Cerralvo

La Paz
San Pedro
La Ventana
B. de los Muertos

Todos Santos
SIERRA DE LA LAGUNA
Buena Vista
B. de Palmas

Los Barriles
La Rivera

Santiago
Miraflores
Cabo Pulmo

Cabo San Lucas
San José del Cabo

Airport
Beach

0   50 mi
0   50 km

UNITED STATES

Area of Detail
MEXICO
Mexico City
Gulf of Mexico

0   500 mi
0   500 km
PACIFIC OCEAN

1697, it was Father Juan María Salvatierra's choice as the site of the first mission in the Californias. (California, at the time, extended from Cabo San Lucas in the south to the Oregon border in the north.) He held Mass beneath a figure of the Virgin of Loreto, brought from a town in Italy bearing the same name. For 132 years Loreto served as the state capital, until an 1829 hurricane destroyed most of the town. The state capital moved to La Paz the following year.

The Mexican government saw in Loreto the possibility for another megadevelopment along the lines of Cancún, Ixtapa, or Huatulco. It invested in a golf course and championship tennis facility, modernized the infrastructure, and built an international airport and full marina facilities at Puerto Loreto, 26km (16 miles) south of town. The economics, however, didn't make sense, and few hotel investors and even fewer tourists came. In the past 2 years, however, this effort has been revitalized, and the area is seeing a welcome influx of flights, as well as the addition of its first new hotel in years, a stunning new Camino Real. Loreto is a place to keep your eye on, expecting a growing awareness and popularity among travelers looking for the next "new" place to go.

But for now, Loreto remains the wonderfully funky fishing village and well-kept secret it's been for decades. The recent celebration of the town's 300th anniversary had the added benefit of updating the streets, plaza, and mission. Old Town Loreto is now a quaint showplace.

The main reasons to come to Loreto center on the Sea of Cortez and the five islands just offshore: kayaking, sailing, diving, and fishing are all exceptional. Isla del Carmen and Isla Danzante are wonderful overnight sailing destinations. And kayakers launch here for trips to the offshore islands or down the remote coast of the Sierra de la Giganta to La Paz. An abandoned salt-mining town lies on the northwestern tip of Isla del Carmen, and rumors peg it as the site of a new hotel, complete with landing strip. For the present, though, simply enjoy the island as it is—a remote sanctuary for desert wildlife.

ESSENTIALS
GETTING THERE & DEPARTING
BY PLANE The **Loreto International Airport** (airport code: LTO; ℂ **613/135-0499**) is 6km (4 miles) southwest of Loreto. It is serviced by **AeroCalifornia** (ℂ **800/237-6225** in the U.S., 613/135-0500, or 613/135-0555; fax 613/135-0566), which has direct

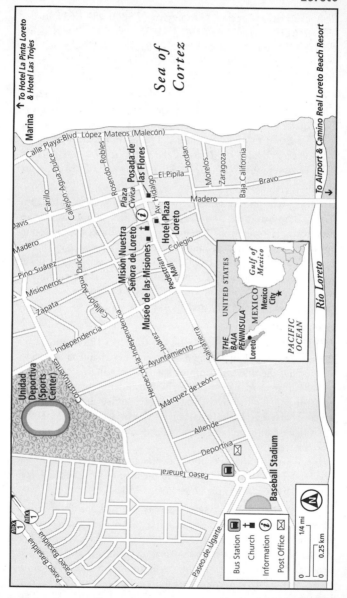

Sea of Cortez

To Hotel La Pinta Loreto & Hotel Las Trojes

Marina

To Airport & Camino Real Loreto Beach Resort

Calle Playa–Blvd. López Mateos (Malecón)

Calle Agua Dulce

Carillo

Rosendo Robles

Posada de las Flores

Jordan

El Pipila

Morelos

Zaragoza

Baja California

Bravo

Plaza Cívica

Davis

Callejón Agua Dulce

Av. Hidalgo

Madero

Madero

Pino Suárez

Misioneros

Zapata

Calle Agua Dulce

Misión Nuestra Señora de Loreto

Hotel Plaza Loreto

Colegio

Pedestrian Mall

Museo de las Misiones

Independencia

Calle Independencia

Heroes de la Independencia

Ayuntamiento

Juárez

Salvatierra

Rio Loreto

Unidad Deportiva (Sports Center)

Constituyentes

Márquez de León

Allende

Deportiva

Paseo Tamaral

Baseball Stadium

Paseo de Ugarte

MEX 1

Paseo Basiliaca

THE BAJA PENINSULA

UNITED STATES

Gulf of Mexico

MEXICO

Mexico City

Loreto

PACIFIC OCEAN

Bus Station

Church

Information

Post Office

1/4 mi

0.25 km

N

flights from Los Angeles; **Aeromexico** (© **800/237-6639** in the U.S., or 613/135-1837; fax 613/135-1838), which has direct flights from San Diego; and **Aerolitoral** (© **613/135-0999**), which has flights from Ciudad Obregón with connections to Tucson and to other cities in Mexico.

BY CAR   From La Paz (4½–5 hr.), take Highway 1 northwest to Ciudad Constitución; from there, continue northeast on Highway 1 to Loreto. This route takes you twice over the mountain range that stretches down the Baja Peninsula, through mountain and desert landscapes, and into the heart of the old mission country. From Tijuana, travel south on Highway 1. The drive takes 17 to 20 hours straight into Loreto.

BY BUS   The bus station, or Terminal de Autobuses (© **613/135-0767**), is on Salvatierra and Paseo Tamaral, a 10-minute walk from downtown. It's open from 7am until midnight. Buses stop in Loreto en route to Santa Rosalía, Tijuana, Mexicali, Guerrero Negro, and La Paz. The trip to La Paz takes 5 hours. You can usually get a ticket for any bus, except during Easter, summer, and Christmas holidays, when buses tend to be more crowded. The bus terminal is a simple building and the staff very friendly and helpful.

ORIENTATION

ARRIVING   At the airport, taxis (© **613/135-1255**) line up on the street to receive incoming passengers. They charge about $5 to Loreto, and the ride takes approximately 10 minutes.

If you plan to rent a car, Budget has a counter at the airport that's open during flight arrivals, and a branch office in town. It's on Hidalgo between Pípila and López Mateos (© **613/135-1090**; open daily 8am–1pm and 3–6pm). Advance reservations are not always necessary.

If you arrive at the bus station, it's about a 10-minute walk to the downtown area and a little farther to the hotels by the water. A taxi from the bus station to the hotels costs $2 to $5.

VISITOR INFORMATION   The city tourist-information office (© **613/135-0411**) is in the southeast corner of the Palacio de Gobierno building, across from the town square. It offers maps, local free publications, and other basic information about the area. It's open Monday through Friday from 9am to 5pm. Information is also available at www.gotoloreto.com, www.tourloreto.com, www.loreto.com, and www.loreto.com.mx.

CITY LAYOUT   Salvatierra is the main street that runs northeast, merging into Avenida Hidalgo, toward the beach. Calle Playa (Bulevar López Mateos, the *malecón*, or boardwalk) runs parallel to the water, and it is along this road where you'll find many of the hotels, seafood restaurants, fishing charters, and the marina. There's an old section of town along Salvatierra, between Madera and Playa, with mahogany and teak homes that date back to the 1800s. Most of the town's social life revolves around the central square and the old mission.

GETTING AROUND   Most addresses don't have a street number; the references are usually the perpendicular streets, or the main square and the mission. There is no local bus service around town. Taxis or walking are the way to go. The town is quite small and manageable for walking. Taxis are inexpensive, with average fares in town ranging from $1.50 to $2.50. The main taxi stand is on Salvatierra, in front of the El Pescador supermarket.

 FAST FACTS: Loreto

Area Code   The telephone area code is **613**.

Banks   There is only one bank in Loreto, where you can exchange currency. **Bancomer** is on Francisco I. Madero, across the street from the Palacio Municipal (City Hall). Bank hours are Monday through Friday from 9am to 3pm. There is also a *casa de cambio* (money-exchange house) on Salvatierra, near the main square.

Beach Safety   The beaches are generally safe for swimming, with the main beach along the *malecón* (sea wall).

General Store   **Super El Pescador,** on Salvatierra and Independencia (✆ **613/135-0060**), is the best place to get toiletries, film, bottled water, and other basic staples, as well as newspapers and telephone calling cards.

Internet Access   **Cafe Internet,** Francisco I. Madero between Hidalgo and Salvatierra (✆ **613/135-0084**), offers Internet access. It is open Monday through Friday from 9am to 2pm and 4 to 7pm, Saturday from 10am to 2pm.

Marinas   Loreto's marina for *pangas* (small fishing boats) is along the *malecón*. Cruise ships and other large boats anchor at Puerto Loreto, also known as Puerto Escondido, 26km (16 miles) south of Loreto. For details about the marina and docking fees, contact the Capitanía de Puerto in Loreto (✆ **613/135-0465**).

Medical Care Medical services are offered at the **Centro de Salud** (© 613/135-0039), Salvatierra 68, near the corner with Allende.

Parking Street parking is generally easy to find in the downtown area.

Pharmacy The **Farmacia del Rosario** (© 613/135-0670) is on Juárez, between Independencia and Zapata, and is open daily from 8am to 10pm.

Post Office The *correo* (© 613/135-0647) is at Deportiva between Salvatierra and Benito Juárez, and is open Monday through Friday from 8am to 3pm.

BEACHES & CRUISES

BEACHES   Beautiful beaches front Loreto and the hotels that surround it. The beaches are safe for swimming, with the main beach along the *malecón,* near El Chile Willie restaurant. It's a popular place for locals, especially on Sunday. Most visitors go to Loreto for the excellent sportfishing and other outdoor activities, so relaxing at the beach is one of the optional pleasures offered by this naturalist's paradise. For those seeking more pristine, secluded beaches, the options are unlimited in the several islands offshore. Isla del Carmen offers several particularly attractive beaches, with the best anchorage on the western shores of the island. You can either take one of the cruises mentioned below or hire a *lancha* (small wooden fishing boats available along the *malecón*) to take you there; the price depends on what you want and how sharp your bargaining skills are (the *lancheros,* or captains, take cash only).

CRUISES   More than cruises, Loreto offers island exploration tours that take in one, or a combination, of the five islands located just offshore. They usually offer the opportunity to visit sea lion colonies and do some snorkeling and beachcombing, for around $35. Arrange cruises through a travel agency, your hotel, or call **Las Parras Tours** (© 613/135-1010; www.lasparrastours.com). Las Parras offers the widest selection of outdoor activities and tours. Each island is unique and offers a spectrum of activities that include sea kayaking, snorkeling, diving, hiking, or simply exploring the local desert flora and fauna (see "A Visit to Isla del Carmen," below).

Moments **Festivals in Loreto**

The feast of the patron saint of Loreto is celebrated September 5 to September 8, with a fair, music, dancing, and other cultural events, closing with the procession of the miraculous figure of the Virgin of Loreto. During October, Loreto celebrates the anniversary of its founding with a series of cultural events that include music and dance. There is also a reenactment of the landing of the Spanish missionaries that is part of a popular festival held from October 19 to October 25.

LAND SPORTS

GOLF The 18-hole **Campo de Golf Loreto,** Bulevar Misión San Ignacio, Fraccionamiento Nopoló (© **613/133-0554,** or 613/133-0788), is quite spectacular, and is probably the least crowded coastal golf course in the area. The back nine holes are more challenging than the front nine, and the 14th hole is reputed to be particularly tough. Reservations are recommended. Prices are $44 for 18 holes and $28 for 9 holes, with an additional $30 for cart, $30 for caddy, and $22 for gear.

HIKING There are virtually no formal trails in the Sierra de la Giganta, but the locals know the way to many magical spots in these towering mountains. Ask at **Deportes Blazer,** Hidalgo 18 (© **613/135-0911**), or call **Las Parras Tours** (© **613/135-1010;** www.lasparrastours.com) for help finding a guide or for current trail information.

HORSEBACK RIDING More practical for this terrain are the mule-riding excursions that visit the San Javier mission. These can be arranged through **Las Parras Tours** (© **613/135-1010;** www.lasparrastours.com). Other horseback riding tours are available through this company, which offers the most options and the friendliest service. It offers mule-trail tours during which you camp and sleep in different ranches in the surrounding area. These tours last 3 to 5 nights, with prices varying according to length, location, and amenities.

SPORTING TOURS Trekking, hiking, mountain biking, and mule- and horseback riding tours are available through **Las Parras Tours** (© **613/135-1010;** www.lasparrastours.com), where José Salas will be happy to explain the many options in detail. Local travel agencies also offer the tours, but most likely will hire them from Las Parras Tours, the best-organized tour operator in Loreto.

Finds A Visit to Isla del Carmen

The largest of Loreto's offshore islands is Isla del Carmen. It is mostly inaccessible and privately owned, so you'll need permission to go ashore. Access to Isla del Carmen is available through one of a number of tour companies in Loreto. Chose your company based on your preferred activity and mode of exploration (usually kayaking, sometimes hiking).

The island was once the site of an impressive salt-mining operation, but increased competition—not to mention the opportunity to earn a dollar from granting landing permissions to tourism purveyors—encouraged the company to shut down and refocus its economic endeavors. You can see the remains of the salt-mining town, completely abandoned in 1983, at the northeastern tip of the island.

Volcanic in origin, Isla del Carmen also has deposits of *coquina*, a limestone-like rock of cemented shell material that was quarried by the Jesuit missionaries for use in constructing the church and other buildings in Loreto. One favorite cove on Isla del Carmen is Puerto Balandra, where bold rock formations rising up like humpback whales frame crystal-blue water and ivory sand.

The craggy desert terrain offers a cornucopia of plant life, including elephant trees with their fragrant leaves and berries, desert asparagus (pickleweed), mesquite trees, jojoba, agave, cardón cacti, and passion flower vines. Be careful of the choya cacti, whose spines enter your skin in a crisscross pattern. To remove them, cut the spines from the plant, then remove them one at a time. The topography alternates between salt-crusted ground, spongy surfaces—a sure sign that snakes, iguanas, and burrowing animals are nearby—and the rocky remains of former riverbeds. There is a variety of fauna as well, including a population of goats that were introduced to the island to provide a meat supply for its inhabitants. Feral cats, black-tailed hares, and birds that include osprey and heila woodpeckers are among the wildlife you'll regularly spot.

TENNIS   You can play tennis at the Nopolo Sports Center's **Centro Tenístico Loreto** (© **613/133-0129**), also known as the John McEnroe Tennis Center, after its designer. There are eight courts, a pool, sundeck, stadium, racquetball court, and pro shop. Court fees are $8 per hour. The fee also gives you access to the pool. If you want to use the pool only, the access fee is $4 for the day. The center is open daily from 7am to 6pm.

WATERSPORTS & ACTIVITIES

SEA KAYAKING   Kayaking season is October through April. **Las Parras Tours** (© 613/135-1010; www.lasparrastours.com) offers sit-on-top kayak tours for beginners ($25–$100). The more expensive tour visits three islands; the guide does all the hard work, while you learn how to paddle close to shore and get to enjoy all the sights. The company also offers kayaking expeditions of 6 to 8 days, with camping on small islands and kayaking between them. They are fully guided with all gear provided, but you should take your own sleeping bag. The kayaking expeditions are approximately $100 per day per person. Puerto Loreto (also known as Puerto Escondido) is also an ideal starting point for experienced kayakers who want to reach Isla Monserrate; call Las Parras Tours for details.

SNORKELING/DIVING   Several companies offer snorkeling; most island exploration trips include snorkeling, and trips to Isla del Carmen, Islas Coronados, Isla Monserrate, and Isla Catalina all include snorkeling opportunities. Some fishing trips carry snorkeling gear on board to give anglers a chance to check out the underwater world. For scuba diving, contact **Las Parras Tours** (© 613/135-1010; www.lasparrastours.com); it offers several diving sites where you can admire the underwater bounty of the Sea of Cortez. Trips cost $70 to $80 per diver, and an SSI-certified dive con instructor guides all tours. Snacks, tanks, and weights are included. The tour company recommends wearing a wet suit from November to May and a skin for the rest of the year. Las Parras also offers a 4-day resort course in diving ($300).

SPORTFISHING   The fishing near Loreto is exceptional, with a different sportfish for every season. Winter months are great for yellowtail, and spring is the time for roosterfish. During the summer, tie into big marlin, sailfish, tuna, dorado, and grouper. For something unusual, take advantage of the run of large Humboldt squid that pass inshore to spawn between Isla del Carmen and Isla Danzante during the fall. These 10-pound, ink-squirting creatures are hard fighting but good eating. The best fishing is said to be in the waters east of Isla del Carmen.

There are several different sportfishing operations in town. The least expensive way to enjoy deep-sea fishing is to pair up with another angler and charter a panga from the **Loreto Sportfishing Cooperative** at the main pier in Loreto, known as Barcena del Malecón (no phone). Prices range from $125 to $250 per boat, depending on the size and availability of shade. You can also arrange your trip in advance through most tour operators or contact the fleets directly. At **Arturo's Fleet,** Calle Juárez (✆ **613/135-0766,** 613/135-0132, or 613/135-0165), trips cost $170 to $340, with rod rentals $10 each, and an extra charge for bait, drinks, and snacks. MasterCard and Visa are accepted, with a 5% surcharge. People with their own boats can launch at the ramp just north of the *malecón* in town or at Puerto Loreto, 26km (16 miles) south of town. If you plan on running out to Isla del Carmen, it's better to launch from Puerto Loreto, which cuts 10km (6 miles) off the crossing. For tackle, head to Deportes Blazer, Hidalgo 18, the catchall sporting goods store in town.

WHALE-WATCHING 𝓡𝓡𝓡   Loreto is the nearest major airport and city to Bahía Magdalena (Magdalena Bay), the southernmost of the major gray-whale-calving lagoons on the Pacific coast of Baja. For more information on popular whale-watching spots and tour operators, see "Whale-Watching in Baja: A Primer," later in this chapter. **Las Parras Tours** (✆ **613/135-1010;** www.lasparrastours.com) conducts whale-watching trips to Magdalena Bay on the Pacific Coast to see gray whales ($119).

HISTORICAL LORETO & OTHER INTERESTING SITES

Misión Nuestra Señora de Loreto was the first mission in the Californias, started in 1699. The catechization of California by Jesuit missionaries was based from this mission, and lasted through the 18th century. The inscription above the entrance reads CABEZA Y MADRE DE LAS MISIONES DE BAJA Y ALTA CALIFORNIA (Head and Mother of the Missions of Lower and Upper California). The current church, a simple building in the shape of a Greek cross, was finished in 1752 and restored in 1976. The original Virgen de Loreto, brought to shore by Padre Kino in 1667, is on display in the church's 18th-century gilded altar. The mission is on Salvatierra, across from the central square.

Adjacent to the mission church is the **Museo de las Misiones,** Salvatierra 16 (✆ **613/135-0441**), of equal or even greater interest. It has a small but complete collection of historical and anthropological exhibits. On display are interesting facts about the indigenous Guaycura, Pericúe, and Cochimí populations, along with accomplishments of the Jesuit missionaries—including their zoological studies, scientific writings, architectural sketches, and details of the role they played in the demise of indigenous cultures. Also on display are several religious paintings and sculptures dating to the 18th century. The museum has a small shop where the INAH (Instituto Nacional de Antropología e Historia) sells books about the history of Mexico and Baja California. The museum is open Tuesday through Sunday from 9am to 1pm and 1:45 to 6pm. Admission is $3.

About 2 hours from Loreto, in a section of the old Camino Real used by Spanish missionaries and explorers, is **Misión San Francisco Javier** 𝒜, one of the best-preserved, most spectacularly set missions in Baja—located high in a mountain valley beneath volcanic walls. Founded in 1699 by the Jesuit priest Francisco María Píccolo, it was the second mission established in California, and completed in 1758. The church was built with blocks of volcanic stone from the Sierra de la Giganta mountains. It is very well preserved, with its original walls, floors, gilded altar, and religious artifacts. Day tours from Loreto, organized by several local tour operators, visit the mission, with stops to view aboriginal cave paintings and an oasis settlement with a small chapel. The trips cost $35 to $50, and some offer mule riding and hiking options. If you are driving a high-clearance four-wheel-drive vehicle and are an experienced off-road driver, you can get there yourself by traveling south on Highway 1 and taking the detour on Km 118. The 25-mile drive takes about 2 hours on a rocky, graded road.

Finds Cave Paintings: A Trip for the Physically Fit

One fascinating excursion that demands good physical condition is a visit to the aboriginal cave paintings of Baja. The tour lasts approximately 12 hours and takes you to the foothills of the Guadalupe mountains, between Loreto and Bahía de los Angeles. The paintings date back an estimated 1,500 years; UNESCO has designated them a part of the historical patrimony of mankind. The murals and petroglyphs are larger and more numerous than those found in Altamira, Spain. The tour takes you on a hike through the desert, where you have to swim in a couple of canyons before you reach the site. Authorized guides must accompany all visitors. Contact **Las Parras Tours** (© **613/135-1010**; www.lasparrastours.com) for more details.

Primer Agua, a palm oasis in a fenced-off section of the Arroyo de San Javier, serves as a prime picnic spot, complete with natural spring and swimming pool. You have to stop by the Nopoló FONATUR offices (© **613/133-0245** or 613/133-0301) to make sure the oasis will be open to visitors on the day you plan your visit and to pay the entrance fee. It is recommended that you do this 2 days prior to your visit to make sure that the gate is open. Access is $5 per person, and it's open from 9am until 6pm. The oasis is closed on Tuesday for pool cleaning. The road to Primer Agua is unpaved and graded, affording fairly easy access during the dry season. The entrance is 6km (4 miles) off Highway 1 on the Km 114 detour.

SHOPPING

Quite frankly, you won't be coming to Loreto to shop, and if you do, you're going to be disappointed. Loreto has little in the way of shopping, either for basics or for folk art and other collectibles from mainland Mexico. There are a handful of the requisite shops selling souvenirs and some *artesanía,* all within a block of the mission. Some, such as the following, are better than others:

El Alacrán This shop carries a fine selection of arts and crafts from throughout Mexico, interesting books about Baja, fine silver jewelry, and handmade and cotton clothing. Open Monday through Saturday from 9:30am to 1pm and 3 to 7pm. Salvatierra and Misioneros. © 613/135-0029.

La Casa de la Abuela "Grandma's House" offers better-than-average knickknacks, with an emphasis on indigenous crafts. Located in the oldest house in Loreto, it also serves coffee, pastries, and light meals. Open Wednesday through Monday from 9am to 10pm. No credit cards. Salvatierra and Calle Misionero, across from the Mission. No phone.

WHERE TO STAY

In general, accommodations in Loreto are the kind travelers to Mexico used to find regularly: inexpensive and unique, with genuinely friendly owner-operators. You can choose between a secluded resort, more casual beachfront inns, and even greater values in town.

EXPENSIVE

Camino Real Loreto Baja Beach & Golf Resort 🎈🎈🎈 *Kids*
Loreto's newest and most deluxe place to stay, the Camino Real is on its own private cove, on a lovely beach, with calm waters perfect for swimming. The hotel boasts the chain's stunning signature architecture, with bold colors and modern angles. The sleek guest rooms have

stone floors and bright color accents. Master suites and Presidential suites have large terraces and private Jacuzzis. The special services and recreational programs make this a great choice for families. Adjacent to Loreto's golf course, it's also ideal for anyone with a passion for the links. Five onsite dining choices plus 24-hour room service mean you never need to leave the premises, but the tour service, which specializes in area eco-tours, will no doubt tempt you to do so. The upper-level Lobby Bar is a spectacular spot for a sunset cocktail.

Paseo de la Mission s/n, Nopolo 23880, Loreto, B.C.S. (©) **800/873-7484** in the U.S., or 613/133-0010. www.caminoreal.com. 156 units. $140 standard double; $170 jr. suite; $200 master suite. Meal plans available. AE, MC, V. **Amenities:** 5 restaurants; 3 bars; swimming pool; golf course; fitness center; concierge desk with nature tours; car-rental desk; tobacco shop; 24-hr. room service; child care; laundry service; Internet access. *In room:* A/C, fan, satellite TV, minibar, hair dryer, safe-deposit box.

Posada de las Flores ★★★ *(Finds)*   The most exclusive hotel in Loreto conveniently sits adjacent to the main square, in the heart of historic Loreto. Every room is beautifully decorated with fine Mexican arts and crafts, including heavy wood doors, Talavera pottery, painted tiles, candles, and scenic paintings. The colors and decor are nouveau colonial, with rustic wood and tin accents. Large bathrooms have thick white towels and bamboo doors. Every detail has been carefully selected, including the numerous antiques tucked into corners. The Italian-owned and -operated hotel exudes class and refinement, from the general ambience to the wake-up service of coffee and pastries. The sophisticated service has a European style.

Salvatierra and Francisco I. Madero, Centro, 23880, Loreto, B.C.S. (©) **877/245-2860** in the U.S., or 613/135-1162. www.posadadelasflores.com. 15 units. $140 standard; $199 jr. suite. Rates include continental breakfast. 15% service charge in lieu of tips is added to your room, board, and bar bill. MC, V. Children under 16 not accepted. **Amenities:** 2 restaurants; bar; rooftop pool with glass bottom; free shuttle to golf course; exclusive tours for guests; car-rental desk. *In room:* A/C, TV, hair dryer.

MODERATE
Hotel La Pinta Loreto ★★   On the beach and close to downtown, La Pinta offers spacious rooms with stone accents, heavy wood furnishings, and views of the offshore islands from individual terraces and private balconies. Accommodations are in two-story buildings that border a central pool and grassy courtyard. Twenty units have fireplaces.

Francisco I. Madero s/n, Playas de Loreto, 23880, Loreto, B.C.S. (©) **613/135-0026.** 48 units. $112 double with fireplace; $89 hacienda-style double; $99 villa with fireplace. Extra person $15. AE, MC, V. **Amenities:** Restaurant; 2 bars; swimming pool; private fishing fleet; tour desk. *In room:* A/C, TV.

Villas de Loreto 👍   One of the best aspects of this comfortable hotel is the friendly staff that makes you feel right at home. The basic rooms have refrigerators and old-style Baja charm, with stone walls and rustic accents. The swimming pool has views of the five offshore islands. While the hotel welcomes families, it is more a quiet getaway for nature lovers. It's on the beach, past the *arroyo* (small riverbed).

Antonio Mijares y Playa. Col. Zaragoza, 23880, Loreto, B.C.S. ✆ 613/135-0586. www.villasdeloreto.com. 13 units. $79 double; $123 beach room double; $173 beach house double. Rates include continental breakfast. MC, V. **Amenities:** Restaurant/bar; swimming pool; bicycles; tour desk. *In room:* A/C, minifridge, coffeemaker.

INEXPENSIVE

Hotel Las Trojes 👍   This unusual bed-and-breakfast is built from authentic wooden granaries *(trojes)* brought over from the state of Michoacán. The rooms have wood interiors, wood floors, and ocean views. A path leads through a yard to the hotel's small, pebbly beach and beach bar. It's rustic and a little run-down, but the service is friendly and the experience quite nice for the price. Las Trojes is 360m (1,200 ft.) north of the La Pinta hotel.

Calle Davis Norte s/n, 23880, Loreto, B.C.S. ✆ **613/135-0277.** www.lastrojes.com. 8 units. Dec–Mar $66 double; April–Nov $55 double. Rates include continental breakfast. No credit cards. **Amenities:** Bar; tour services. *In room:* A/C.

Plaza Loreto   The location, just 1 block from the mission church, makes the Plaza Loreto easy to find and a perennial favorite. Recently remodeled and well maintained, the two-story motel frames a courtyard with shady seating areas. Each of the basic, clean rooms has one or two double beds, a table and two chairs, and a bathroom with shower. Here, you're a short walk from the mission, the museum, several favorite restaurants, and all the notable nightlife.

Paseo Hidalgo 2. Centro. 23880, Loreto, B.C.S. ✆ **613/135-0280.** Fax 613/135-0555. www.hotelplazaloreto.com. 24 units. $62 double; $73 triple. AE, MC, V. **Amenities:** Restaurant/bar. *In room:* A/C, TV.

WHERE TO DINE

Loreto has a surprising variety of dining options, given the town's small size and simple nature. The dominant menu features some combination of seafood and Mexican cuisine, with the ambience and price being the key variables. Among the exceptions is the exquisite **Vecchia Roma** (✆ **613/135-1162**), in the Posada de las Flores hotel, which serves authentic southern Italian cuisine prepared by chef Alessandro Bargelletti. It's open Tuesday through Sunday from 6 to 11pm, and reservations are required.

MODERATE

Carmen's Restaurant ✺ HAMBURGERS/SEAFOOD/MEXI-CAN   It's a popular meeting place for the gringo community, with TV sports, barbecue, ocean views, and a friendly proprietor. Along with Carmen's Snorkelburger, other popular choices are paella and barbecued tri-tips. Breakfast is served American style, and in ample portions. There's usually blues or jazz playing to accompany your meal. Located across from the *malecón*.

Blv. Costero López Mateos s/n. No phone. Main courses $2.50–$8. No credit cards. Daily 7am–11pm.

El Chile Willie ✺✺ SEAFOOD/MEXICAN   El Chile Willie serves an eclectic menu that emphasizes seafood in an appropriate setting—right at the water's edge. The extensive menu features choco clams (a local type of clam, not as bizarre as it sounds), clams Rockefeller, lobster served many different ways, and succulent fish filet baked in foil with tamarind herb sauce. Also available are chicken breast stuffed with nopal cactus, beef burger in barbecue sauce, and (the menu claims) the world's largest Mexican combo for two. During winter months, a semicircular oceanfront window keeps the cool air out while retaining the view; it opens when the weather warms. The place is lively, and its location on the main beach in town makes it great for people-watching, especially during weekend breakfast or lunch. From 4 to 6pm, El Chile Willie features a two-for-one happy hour with free appetizers.

Blv. Costero López Mateos s/n. ✆ **613/135-0677.** Main courses $3–$10. MC, V. Daily 10am–11pm.

El Nido Steakhouse ✺ STEAK/SEAFOOD   The main link in a Baja chain of steak restaurants, El Nido satisfies hearty appetites. Its specialty is a thick cut of prime, tender beef, served with the obligatory salad and baked potato. Seafood options are also available. It's on the main boulevard as you enter Loreto from Highway 1.

Salvatierra 154. ✆ **613/135-0284.** Main courses $6–$20. No credit cards. Daily 2–10:30pm.

Tio Lupe ✺ MEXICAN/SEAFOOD   Elegant yet casual, this adobe-walled, thatched-roof restaurant offers great food in a comfortable atmosphere, surrounded by the works of modern Mexican artists. Although the construction is modern, the restaurant was built using traditional methods and local natural materials. Even the tables are made from cardón cacti. The menu features fairly standard Mexican dishes and seafood; camarones casa de adobe, a plate of grilled shrimp stuffed with cheese and wrapped in bacon, is delicious.

Paseo Hidalgo y Colegio. No phone. Main courses $3–$14. No credit cards. Daily 11am–9:30pm.

INEXPENSIVE

Café Ole 🦀 LIGHT FARE   Along with specialty coffees, this breezy cafe is a good option for breakfast; try eggs with nopal cactus or hotcakes. A not-so-light lunch of a burger and fries, tacos, and some Mexican standards are also on the menu, as are *liquados* (fresh-fruit shakes).

Francisco I. Madero 14. © 613/135-0496. Breakfast $2–$5. Sandwiches $2–$3.50. No credit cards. Mon–Sat 7am–10pm; Sun 7am–2pm.

LORETO AFTER DARK

Although the selection is limited, Loreto seems to offer a place for almost every nightlife preference—from rowdy beach pubs to an elegant billiard bar. Generally, though, closing time is around midnight.

The most elegant finish to an evening is at **Jarros y Tarros,** on Salvatierra, next to Deportes Blazer (just before crossing Francisco I. Madero; no phone). It has a few elegant pool tables, as well as high round tables where you can sit and sip one of the many fine tequilas. Beers run about $2, mixed drinks $3. Open daily from 6pm to 2am, Jarros y Tarros plays exceptional contemporary Latin music and Mexican rock.

Mike's Bar, 2 blocks from the beach on Paseo Hidalgo (© 613/135-1126), is an intimate, friendly place with "gringo bar" written all over it—it's very popular with North American visitors. It's great for sports and people-watching, and has live music most nights from 11:30 until closing. It's open from 11am to 3am daily. TV sports and beers are also a regular specialty at **Carmen's,** on the *malecón* (see "Where to Dine," above).

And, as is the tradition in Mexico, Loreto's central plaza offers a free concert in the bandstand every Sunday evening.

2 Mulegé: Oasis in the Desert 🟊🟊

995km (618 miles) SE of Tijuana; 137km (85 miles) N of Loreto; 496km (308 miles) NW of La Paz; 710km (441 miles) NW of Cabo San Lucas

Verdant Mulegé offers shady cool in an otherwise scorching part of the world. Founded in 1705, it is home to one of the best-preserved and beautifully situated Jesuit missions in Baja. A visit is a worthwhile side trip, if only to take in the view.

Besides the respite of the landscape, Mulegé (pronounced moo-leh-*hay*), at the mouth of beautiful Bahía Concepción, has great diving, kayaking, and fishing. There are also several well-preserved Indian caves with stunning paintings, which can be reached by guided hikes into the mountains. Accommodations are limited and basic. Good beach camping is also available just south of town along the Bahía Concepción.

ESSENTIALS
GETTING THERE & DEPARTING
BY PLANE   The closest international airport is in Loreto, 137km (85 miles) south. From Loreto, you'll need to rent a car or hire a taxi for the 1½-hour trip; taxis average $75 each way. Three airlines fly into Loreto: **AeroCalifornia** (© **800/237-6225** in the U.S., 613/135-0500, or 613/135-0555; fax 613/135-0566) has direct flights from Los Angeles; **Aeromexico** (© **800/237-6639** in the U.S., or 613/135-1837; fax 613/135-1838), operates direct from San Diego; and **Aerolitoral** (© **613/135-0999**) has flights from Ciudad Obregón, with connections to Tucson and to other cities in Mexico.

Small regional or private charter planes can get you all the way to town: **El Gallito,** a well-maintained, graded, 4,000-foot airstrip, adjoins the Hotel Serenidad, Transpeninsular Hwy., Km 30 (no phone, use radio frequency UNICOM 122.8). *Note:* Fuel is generally not available. For additional information, contact the Comandancia del Aeropuerto in Loreto (© **613/135-0565**), from 7am to 7pm daily.

BY CAR   From Tijuana, take Highway 1 direct to the Mulegé turnoff, 998km (620 miles) south (approximately 16 hr.). From La Paz, take Highway 1 north, a scenic route that winds through foothills and then skirts the eastern coastline. The trip takes about 6 hours; it's roughly 480km (300 miles).

BY BUS   There is no bus station in Mulegé, but buses will pick up and drop off passengers on the main highway at the La Cabaña restaurant, at the "Y" entrance to town. Buses running south to Bahía Concepción, Loreto, and La Paz generally pass by about three times a day; buses traveling north to Santa Rosalía, Ensenada, and Tijuana have twice-daily service. Schedules are highly variable, but buses stay for about 20 minutes while dropping off and picking up passengers. Tickets to Tijuana average $30; the one-way fare to La Paz is about $12.

ORIENTATION

ARRIVING   If you arrive by bus, you will be dropped off at the restaurant at the entrance to town. From there, you can walk the few blocks downhill and east into town, or take a taxi. Taxis also line up around the plaza, and usually charge around $2 to $4 for a trip anywhere in town.

VISITOR INFORMATION   There is no official office, but tourist information is available at the office of the centrally located **Hotel Las Casitas,** Calle Francisco Madero 50 (© 615/153-0019). The local laundry, **Efficient Lavamática Claudia,** at the corner of Zaragoza and Moctezuma (© 615/153-0057; open Mon–Sat 8am–6pm), is another prime source for local information, with a well-used community bulletin board. Use the bulletin board for gathering info rather than calling the laundry's phone number, because the staff can't answer questions—the board is a community service. Several maps that list key attractions, as well as a local biweekly English-language newspaper, the *Mulegé Post,* are available throughout town. Also of interest to serious travelers to Mulegé is Kerry Otterstrom's self-published book *Mulegé: The Complete Tourism, Souvenir, and Historical Guide,* available at shops and hotels in town.

The **State Tourism Office of Baja California Sur** can be reached by calling © 612/124-0199, or you may contact the City of Mulegé (© 615/153-0049).

CITY LAYOUT   Mulegé has an essentially east-west orientation, running from the Transpeninsular Highway in the west to the Sea of Cortez. The Mulegé River (also known as Río Santa Rosalía) borders the town to the south, with a few hotels and RV parks along its southern shore. It's easy to find the principal sights downtown, where two main streets will take you either east or west; both border the town's central plaza. The main church is several blocks east of the plaza, breaking with the traditional layout of most Mexican towns. The Bahía Concepción is 11km (7 miles) south of town.

GETTING AROUND   There is no local bus service in town or to the beach, but you can easily walk or take a taxi. Taxis line up around the central plaza, or you can call the taxi dispatch at © 615/153-0420.

Bicycles are available for rent from **Cortez Explorers,** Moctezuma 75-A (© 615/153-0500). Prices start at $15 for the first day, then drop to $10 per day for the first week, and $8 per day after that. It also rents ATVs by the hour, and has full dive- and snorkel-equipment rentals. Open Monday through Saturday from 10am to 1pm and 4 to 7pm.

 FAST FACTS: Mulegé

Area Code The telephone area code is **615**.

Banks There are no banks in Mulegé.

Beach Safety Beaches in the area are generally tranquil and safe for swimming. The more protected waters of Bahía Concepción are especially calm. Avoid swimming at the mouth of the Mulegé River, which is said to be polluted.

Internet Access The Hotel Hacienda has a small Internet cafe; access is $3 per hour.

Medical Care Emergency medical services are offered by the **Mexican Red Cross** (© **615/153-0110**) and the Health Center ISSSTE (© **615/153-0298**).

Parking Street parking is generally easy to find in the downtown area. Note, however, that Mulegé's streets are very narrow, and difficult for RVs and other large vehicles to navigate.

Pharmacy Farmacia Ruben, Calle Francisco Madero s/n, at the northwest corner of the central plaza (no phone), is a small drugstore with a sampling of basic necessities and medicines. The owner speaks some English. Across the plaza, **Supermercado Alba** (no phone) has a somewhat wider selection of other goods and toiletries. Both are open Monday through Saturday from 9am to 7pm.

Post Office The *correo* is at the intersection of calles Francisco Madero and General Martínez, on the north side of the street, opposite the downtown Pemex station (© **615/153-0205**). It is open Monday through Friday from 8am to 3pm, and Saturday from 8 to 11am.

BEACHES & OUTDOOR ACTIVITIES

Mulegé has long been a favorite destination for adventurous travelers looking for a place to relax and enjoy the diversity of nature. Divers, sportfishermen, kayakers, history buffs, and admirers of beautiful beaches all find reasons to stay in this oasis just a little longer.

BEACHES   To the north and east of Mulegé lies the Sea of Cortez, known for its abundance and variety of species of fish, marine birds, and sea mammals. To the north are the mostly secluded beaches of **Bahía Santa Inez** and **Punta Chivato,** both known for their beauty and tranquillity. Santa Inez is reachable by way of a long dirt road that turns off from Highway 1 at Km 151. Twenty-five kilometers (16 miles) south is the majestic **Bahía Concepción,** a 48km (30-mile) long body of water protected on three sides by more than 80km (50 miles) of beaches, and dotted with islands. The mountainous peninsula borders its crystal-clear turquoise waters to the east. Along with fantastic landscapes, the bay has numerous soft, white-sand beaches such as **Santispác, Concepción, Los Cocos, El Burro, El Coyote, Buenaventura, El Requesón,** and **Armenta.** Swimming, diving, windsurfing, kayaking, and other watersports are easily enjoyed, with equipment rentals locally available. Here's a rundown on some of the area beaches with restaurant service:

Punta Arena is accessible off Highway 1, at Km 119. A very good *palapa* restaurant is there, along with camping facilities and primitive beach palapas.

Playa Santispác, at Km 114, has a nice beachfront, lots of RVs in the winter, and two good restaurants (Ana's is the more popular).

Playa El Coyote is the most popular and crowded of the Bahía Concepción beaches. The restaurant El Coyote is on the west side of Highway 1 at the entrance to this beach, .8km (½ mile) from the water; Restaurant Bertha's serves simple meals on the beachfront.

Playa Buenaventura, at Km 94, is the most developed of the beaches, with a large RV park, motel, convenience store, boat ramp, and public restrooms, along with George's Olé restaurant and bar.

FISHING   All of the hotels in town can arrange guided fishing trips to Punta Chivato, Isla San Marcos, or Punta de Concepción, the outermost tip of Bahía Concepción.

The best fishing in the area is for yellowtail, which run in the winter, and summer catches of dorado, tuna, and billfish like marlin and sailfish. Prices run $120 per day for up to three people in a panga, $180 for four in a small cruiser, or $200 and up for larger boats. **Mulegé Sportfishing** (© 615/153-0244) organizes fishing trips in the area.

HIKING & PAINTED CAVE EXPLORATIONS 𝔤𝔤𝔤   One of the big attractions of this region is the large cave paintings in the Sierra de Guadalupe. UNESCO declared the cave paintings a World

Heritage Site, and the locals take great pride in protecting them. Unlike many cave paintings, these are huge, complex murals. You are legally allowed to visit the caves only with a licensed guide.

The most popular series of caves is in **La Trinidad,** a remote rancho 29km (18 miles) west of Mulegé. The guide drives you there, and then the hiking begins. Count on hiking about 6km (4 miles) and getting wet. To reach the caves, several river crossings are necessary in spots deep enough to swim. Rock walls fringe a tight canyon, and there is no way through except by swimming. This river in Cañon La Trinidad allegedly is the source of the river that flows through Mulegé, although it disappears underground for many miles in between.

Among the representations of the cave murals are large deer silhouettes, and a human figure called the "cardón man" because of his resemblance to a cardón cactus.

Another favorite cave-art site is **San Borjitas.** To get there, you travel down a bad four-wheel-drive road to Rancho Las Tinajas, where your guide will take you on foot or by mule to the caves.

For about $35 per person (6 hr., minimum 5 people, lunch included), you can arrange for a guide in Mulegé to take you to La Trinidad; San Borjitas will cost around $50 per person (7 hours, 2 meals included). Check at Hotel Las Casitas or on the board of the local laundry for guide recommendations. One recommended guide is **Salvador Castro** (© 615/153-0232).

SCUBA DIVING & SNORKELING   Although diving here is very popular, be aware that visibility right in Mulegé is marred by the fresh and not-so-fresh water that seems to flow into the sea from the numerous septic tanks in this area. But as you head south into Bahía Concepción, there is excellent snorkeling at the numerous shallow coves and tiny offshore islands. Work the middle of the sandy coves looking for oysters and scallops. For bigger fish and colorful sea life, you'll have to swim out to deeper waters along the edges of each cove.

Boat diving around Mulegé tends to be around Punta de Concepción or north of town at Punta Chivato and the small offshore islands of Santa Inez and San Marcos. Numerous sites are perfect for both snorkeling and scuba. The marine life here is colorful—you're likely to see green moray eels, angelfish, parrot fish, and a variety of lobster—and dolphins and other sea mammals are common sights. The best diving is between August and November, when the visibility averages 30m (100 ft.) and water temperatures are warmer (mid-80s/20s Celsius).

Bea and Andy Sidler's **Cortez Explorers,** Moctezuma 75-A (ⓒ/fax **615/153-0500;** www.cortez-explorer.com), bought out and took over the operations of the well-known Mulegé Divers, and maintains its reputation as one of the best-run dive operations in the state. If Mulegé has become known as a prime dive site in Baja, credit goes to this shop for its excellent prices and exceptional services. It has a great environmental consciousness, too. Cortez Explorers runs trips from a large, custom dive boat, and uses only well-maintained, current equipment.

Two-tank dive trips generally involve a 45-minute boat ride offshore and cost $40 to $65 per person, depending on the equipment needed. Snorkeling trips go for $25 to $35 (again, based on the need to rent equipment). Wet suits, jackets, and farmer johns are available, and they're necessary during winter months. Resort courses are also available.

SEA KAYAKING   Bahía Concepción is a kayaker's dream—clear, calm water, fascinating shorelines, and lots of tempting coves to pull into, with white sandy beaches. Kayaks are the most popular and practical way to explore the pristine coves that dot this shoreline.

Baja Tropicales, at the Hotel Las Casitas, Calle Francisco Madero 50 (ⓒ **615/153-0409;** fax 615/153-0190), is Mulegé's undisputed kayak expert. It also rents kayaks to experienced paddlers for $25 to $35 per day, depending on the type of kayak—open deck, closed deck, single, or tandem. Longer-term rentals are also available, as is full gear, including car racks and VHF radios. In addition, the company offers fully guided, ecologically oriented kayak tours in Bahía Concepción, and full-day "Paddle, Snorkel, Dive & Dine" excursions that combine a day of sporting fun with a seafood fiesta at the firm's palapa restaurant (the Kayak Kafe) on the beach. The trip, meal, and beverages cost $39, with a four-person minimum. The trip departs from the EcoMundo kayaking and natural history center, an extension of Baja Tropicales at Km 111, just south of Playa Santispác. No previous experience is necessary; complete instruction is given at the start of the tour. Baja Tropicales also offers 4- and 5-day trips around Bahía Concepción, down the coast, and even over in Scammon's Lagoon on Baja's west coast.

WINDSURFING   Bahía Concepción, south of Mulegé, gets quite windy in the afternoon and has numerous coves for beginners to practice in. It has never developed the cachet with the hard-core sailboarding crowd that places like Buenavista and La Ventana have, but it's a worthy place to stop and rig up.

EXPLORING MULEGE

Misión Santa Rosalía de Mulegé, founded in 1706 by father Juan de Ugarte and Juan María Basaldúa, is just upstream from the bridge where Highway 1 crosses the Mulegé River. The original mission building was completed in 1766, to serve a local Indian population of about 2,000. In 1770, a flood destroyed nearly all the common buildings, and the mission was rebuilt on the site it occupies today, on a bluff overlooking the river. Although not the most architecturally interesting of Baja's missions, it remains in excellent condition and still functions as a Catholic church, although mission operations halted in 1828.

It's also a popular tour site. A lookout point 30m (100 ft.) behind the mission provides a spectacular vantage point for taking in the view of a grove of palm trees backed by the Sea of Cortez. To reach the mission from town, take Calle Zaragoza (the longest north-south street in Mulegé) south, then cross the river using the small footbridge beneath the elevated highway bridge. Turn back sharply to the right and follow the dirt road through palm groves and up a graded path to the mission. The towers of the church will be visible.

In 1907, a **state penitentiary** was built on a hill overlooking the town of Mulegé. About 15 years ago, a local historian and citizen's group established the small **Museo Regional de Historía** (Regional Museum of History) inside. The institution was known as the "prison without doors" because it operated on an honor system— inmates were allowed to leave every morning to work in town, on the condition that they return when the afternoon horn sounded. Escape attempts were rare, and when they occurred, the other prisoners pursued the escapees to bring them back. It functioned that way until the mid-1970s.

The museum (no phone) details the prison's operations and houses an eclectic collection of local historical artifacts. Admission is by donation, and hours are supposed to be Monday through Friday from 9am to 1pm, but have been known to vary. The museum is at the end of Calle Cananea.

SHOPPING

The town has a limited selection of shops, unless you're looking for basic groceries or auto parts. There are a few exceptions:

Artesanías Cochimi   This shop sells the highest-quality selection of Mexican arts and decorative items in town, including pottery, silver jewelry, and handcrafted iron furniture. Shipping is available. Hours are Monday through Saturday from 9am to 6pm and Sunday from 10am to 2pm. If you call in advance, the owner will open at special hours. No credit cards. Calle Zaragoza and Moctezuma. © 615/153-0378 or 615/153-0452.

Plantas Medicinales Sarah If you're curious about or committed to natural health, this small but complete shop offers mineral salts, teas, powders, spirit waters, and herbs to care for your every ailment. Open Monday through Saturday from 9am to 1pm. No credit cards. Francisco Madero, across from the church. No phone.

WHERE TO STAY

Accommodations in Mulegé are basic, but generally clean and comfortable. The biggest hotel in town, the Hotel Serenidad, has a recent history of closings due to ownership disputes with the local *ejido* (indigenous) community. It is open now, and claims to have resolved all questions of proprietorship.

MODERATE

Hotel Serenidad 🐾🐾 Serenity, seclusion, and casual comfort are the hallmarks of the Serenidad, just south of town between the airstrip and a long stretch of beach. Low-rise, Mediterranean-style buildings border either Mulegé's largest pool (with palapa bar) or a courtyard. Most rooms have working fireplaces, and all have ceiling fans, plus a large bathroom with a skylight. Decor is stylish for the area, and all rooms have a king-size bed, tile floors, and a small seating area with a glass-topped table and chairs. The larger *casitas,* or bungalows, have two bedrooms and two baths, a small living area, and a terrace, making them ideal for families or friends traveling together.

The locally popular restaurant-bar has satellite TV, and on Saturday the place fills up for the weekly pig roast and fiesta with mariachis, a regional specialty. The Serenidad has an adjacent RV park with 10 available spaces. It's on the south side of the mouth of the river, 4km (2½ miles) south of the town center, off Highway 1. The hotel stays open year-round, but the restaurant closes for the month of September.

Km 30 Transpeninsular Hwy. S., P.O. Box 9, CP 23900 Mulegé, B.C.S. © 615/153-0540. Fax 615/153-0311. www.serenidad.com. 48 units. $65 double; $75 1-bedroom suite; $120 2-bedroom casitas. MC, V. Free parking; private airstrip available. **Amenities:** Restaurant/bar; swimming pool with bar; sand volleyball court; telephone and fax service available through the front desk. *In room:* A/C.

INEXPENSIVE

Hotel Hacienda Mulegé 🐾 A former 18th-century hacienda with double courtyards and a small, shaded swimming pool makes

Tips Camping Bahía Concepción

For many people who travel down Baja in RVs, Mulegé is the chosen destination, along with Bahía Concepción. Powdery white beaches, perfectly clear water, and plunging cliffs frame the big bay south of town. It is a coastline you might invent in a dream. You can still just pull out onto some of the many beaches and camp, but an increasing number have been developed into more formal camping arrangements, and several have turned into motor home colonies. Regardless, it's a stunning place. Camping is much less structured in Mexico than it is in the U.S., Canada, or the U.K.; you can't reserve in advance—sites are available on a first-come, first-served basis.

The first beach camping is at **Playa Punta Arena**, 16km (10 miles) south of Mulegé. The beach isn't visible from the road, but like all the beaches here, it is nice. It's an RV spot, but the rough dirt road keeps it from being overrun. You can rent a palapa right on the sand for around $5 per night. Camping is $3 per night.

A few more miles into the bay will bring you to **Playa Santispác.** It has a restaurant/bar, and many snowbirds pull their trailers onto the beach in the fall and stay through spring. Much better for tent campers is **Playa Los Cocos** (Palm Beach), 24km (15 miles) south of Mulegé. Although it's motor home–accessible, it's also very good for tents. Camping is $4 per night, and there are pit toilets and garbage receptacles. **Playa El Coyote,** 27km (17 miles) south of Mulegé, is also nice for tent camping. Sites are $4 per night.

for a comfortable and value-priced place to stay. You couldn't be more centrally located in Mulegé, and the Hacienda is known for its popular bar, which also has satellite TV featuring sporting events. The bar closes for the night between 10 and 11pm, so it shouldn't keep you awake. The cozy restaurant with stone walls and a fireplace also has a pleasant patio. Rooms surround the courtyard, and have beds with foam mattresses and brightly colored Mexican accents. Bathrooms are simple but large, with showers.

Calle Francisco Madero 3, Mulegé, B.C.S., ½ block east of the central plaza. ℂ **615/153-0021.** Fax 615/153-0481. 24 units. $35 per room. No credit cards. Free parking. **Amenities:** Restaurant/bar; small swimming pool; tourist guide services; currency exchange, book exchange, fax available at front desk; room service; laundry service. *In room:* A/C, TV.

Hotel Las Casitas ⟨R⟩ *Value* This long-standing favorite welcomes many repeat visitors, along with the local literati—it is the birthplace of Mexican poet Alan Gorosave. Rooms are in a courtyard just behind (and adjacent to) the Las Casitas Restaurant, one of Mulegé's most popular. The basic, recently remodeled accommodations have high ceilings, tile bathrooms, and rustic decor. Plants fill a small central patio for guests' use, but the more socially inclined gravitate to the popular restaurant and bar, which is open daily from 7am to 10pm. The place is especially lively on weekends—on Friday evenings there's a Mexican fiesta. The inn and restaurant are on the main east-west street in Mulegé, 1 block from the central plaza.

Calle Francisco Madero 50, Col. Centro 23900 Mulegé, B.C.S. ℂ **615/153-0019.** Fax 615/153-0190. 8 units. $35 double. MC, V. Limited street parking available. **Amenities:** Restaurant/bar; tour desk. *In room:* A/C.

WHERE TO DINE

The must-have meal in Mulegé is the traditional pig roast. It's an event, with the pig roasted Polynesian-style in a palm-lined open pit for hours, generally while guests enjoy a few beers or other beverages. Homemade tortillas, salsas, an assortment of toppings, and the ubiquitous rice and beans accompany the succulent cooked pork. Remember—it's more than a pig, it's a party. The perennially popular pig roasts happen each Saturday night at both the **Las Casitas** restaurant and the **Hotel Serenidad** (see "Where to Stay," above). The meal costs about $10.

Another Mulegé—and Mexican—dining staple is the taco. The best are reportedly found at the taco stand adjoining Las Casitas or at the popular **Taqueria Doney,** at Madero and Romero Rubio, just as you enter town, past the *depósito* (warehouse) on the right.

MODERATE

Las Casitas ⟨RR⟩ SEAFOOD/MEXICAN La Casitas remains a popular mainstay with both locals and visitors to Mulegé. The bar has a steady clientele day and night and often features special sporting events on satellite TV. Dine either in the interior stone-walled dining area or on its adjoining, plant-filled patio. Live music sometimes plays from 6pm on, and Fridays feature a Mexican fiesta and buffet. If you're just dining off the menu, how can you resist fresh lobster for $10? The menu offerings are standard fare with an emphasis on fresh seafood, but the quality is good, and you can see the extra-clean exhibition kitchen as you enter.

Calle Francisco Madero 50. ℂ 615/153-0019. Breakfast $1.50–$4; main courses $3–$11. MC, V. Daily 7am–10pm.

Los Equipales ☆ MEXICAN/SEAFOOD   First off, you won't find any here—*equipales*, that is. (Equipales are rustic palm-and-leather bucket chairs.) In their place, this restaurant has white faux-wicker chairs that are comfy but hardly authentic. This is one of Mulegé's ever-popular hangouts, with homestyle cooking matched by family-friendly service. Its second-story location offers diners the only lofty view in town, and this is the only place in Mulegé that serves complimentary chips and salsa with the meal. The specialties are traditional Mexican fare and Sonoran beef, especially barbecued ribs. Tropical drinks, like mango margaritas, are also popular.

Calle Moctezuma, 2nd floor. ℂ 615/153-0330. Main courses $3–$10. No credit cards. Daily 8am–10pm.

INEXPENSIVE

Eduardo's MEAT/CHINESE   Most of the time, Eduardo's is known for its grilled meats—tender ribs, traditional *carne asada* (grilled marinated beef), and thick steaks. On Sunday, Eduardo serves an extensive buffet of Chinese food. White plastic chairs somewhat diminish the attractiveness of the stone-walled dining area, but the graciously friendly service compensates. Full bar service is also available. Located across the street from the downtown Pemex station.

Gnl. Martinez. ℂ 615/153-0258. Main courses $3–$10. No credit cards. Fri–Sat and Mon–Wed 4–10pm; Sun 1–8pm.

El Candil MEXICAN   Filling platters of traditional Mexican fare at reasonable prices are the specialty of this casual restaurant, which has been run by the same family for more than 3 decades. Tacos are always popular, but the best of the house is the heaping Mexican combination plate.

Zaragoza 8, near the central plaza. No phone. Main courses $2–$8. No credit cards. Mon–Sat 11am–11pm; Sun 1–8pm.

MULEGE AFTER DARK

Los Juncos, on Romero Rubio behind Las Casitas; the bar at the **Hotel Serenidad;** and the bar at the **Hotel Las Casitas** are the current hotspots in Mulegé's relatively lukewarm nightlife scene.

3 A Side Trip from Mulegé: Santa Rosalía

61km (38 miles) N of Mulegé

In an arroyo north of Mulegé is Santa Rosalía, a unique mining town dating to 1855. Founded by the French, the town has a decidedly European architectural ambience, though a distinctly Mexican culture inhabits it. Pastel clapboard houses surrounded by picket fences line the streets, giving the town its nickname, *ciudad de madera* (city of wood). Its large harbor and the rusted ghost of its copper-smelting facility dominate the central part of town bordering the waterfront.

The town served as the center for copper mining in Mexico for years; a French company, Compañía de Boleo (part of the Rothschild family), obtained a 99-year lease in the 1800s. Operations began in 1885 and continued until 1954, when the Mexicans regained the use of the land. During the French operation, more than 644km (400 miles) of tunnels were built underground and in the surrounding hills, primarily by Indian and Chinese laborers. Mexican President Porfirio Díaz originally granted the lease to the German shipping company, Casa Moeller, which sold the mining operation rights to the Rothschild family but retained exclusive rights to transport ore from the mine. Following the reversion of the mining operations to the Mexican government, the facility was plagued with problems, including the alleged leakage of arsenic into the local water supply, so the plant was permanently closed in 1985.

The French influence is apparent everywhere in Santa Rosalía—especially in the colonial-style wooden houses. The French also brought over thousands of Asian workers, who have integrated into the local population (Chinese cuisine is still particularly popular here), along with the German and French residents. The French administrators built their homes on the northern Mesa Francia, the part of town where you'll find the museum and historic buildings, while the Mexican residents settled on the southern Mesa Mexico. The town still has a noticeably segregated feel.

Today Santa Rosalía, with a population of 14,000, is notable for its man-made harbor—the recently constructed Marina Santa Rosalía, complete with concrete piers, floating docks, and full docking accommodations for a dozen ocean cruisers. Santa Rosalía is the main seaport of northern Baja, located directly across from Guaymas. A ferry link established during the mining days still operates between the two ports. Because this is the prime entry point of manufactured goods into Baja, the town abounds with auto-parts and electronic appliance stores, along with shops selling Nikes and sunglasses.

The town has no real beach to speak of, and fewer recreational attractions. The rusted, dilapidated smelting foundry, railroad, and pier all border the docks and give the town an abandoned, neglected atmosphere.

EXPLORING SANTA ROSALIA

The principal attraction in Santa Rosalía is the **Iglesia de Santa Barbara,** a structure of galvanized steel designed by Gustave Eiffel (of Eiffel Tower fame) in 1884. It was originally created for the 1889 Paris World Expo, where it was displayed as a prototype for what Eiffel envisioned as a sort of a prefab mission. The concept never took off, and the structure was left in a warehouse in Brussels, where it was later discovered and destined for Baja by officials of the mining company. Section by section the church was transported, then reassembled in Santa Rosalía in 1897. The somber gray exterior belies the beauty of the intricate stained-glass windows viewed from inside.

Along with the church, the other obligatory site to see is the **ex-Fundación del Pacífico,** or **Museo Histórico Minero de Santa Rosalía.** Located in a landmark wooden building, it houses a permanent display of artifacts from the days of Santa Rosalía's mining operations. There are miniature models of the town and its buildings, old accounting ledgers and office equipment, and samples of the minerals extracted from local mines. It's open Monday through Saturday from 8:30am to 2pm and 5 to 7pm. Admission is $1.50.

Bordering the museum are the most attractive of the clapboard houses, painted in a rainbow of delicious colors—mango, lemon, blueberry, and cherry. The wood used to construct these houses was the return cargo on ships that transported copper to refineries in Oregon and British Columbia during the 1800s.

Other sites of note are the Plaza Benito Juárez, or central *zócalo* (square) that fronts the Palacio Municipal, or City Hall (© **615/ 152-2345** or 615/152-2238), an intriguing structure of French colonial design. The streets of Constitución, Carranza, Plaza, and Altamirano border the square. Just down Constitución is the **Biblioteca Mahatma Gandhi,** more notable for the uniqueness of its name in Mexico than for the library itself, which is the only one in operation between Ensenada and La Paz. The library has a permanent exhibition of historic photos on display.

WHERE TO STAY & DINE

Santa Rosalía claims to have the best bakery in all of Baja—**El Boleo**
(© **615/152-0310**)—which has been baking crusty French
baguettes since the late 1800s. It's on Avenida Obregón at Calle 3,
3 blocks west of the church, and is open daily from 8am to 6pm.

Hotel Francés (☆☆)   Founded in 1886, the Hotel Francés once set
the standard of hospitality in Baja Sur, welcoming European digni-
taries and hosting the French administrators and businessmen of the
mining operations. Today, it has a worn air of elegance, but retains
its position as the most welcoming accommodation in Santa Rosalía. The lobby, restaurant-bar, and colonial-style wraparound
veranda make up the front part of the building. Rooms are in the
back, with wooden porches and balconies that overlook a small
courtyard pool and wooden lounge chairs between the two sections.
Each room has individually controlled air-conditioning, plus windows that open for ventilation. Floors are wood-planked, and the
bathrooms are beautifully tiled, although small. You have a choice
of two double beds or one king-size bed. Security boxes and telephone service are available in the lobby. The popular restaurant is
open daily from 6am to 1pm. It currently serves breakfast only;
check to see whether it has added other meals.

Calle Jean Michel Cousteau s/n, Santa Rosalía B.C.S. ©/fax **615/152-2052**. 17
units. $44 single or double. No credit cards. Free parking. **Amenities:** Restaurant/
bar; small pool. *In room:* A/C, TV.

4 Whale-Watching in Baja: A Primer

Few sights inspire as much reverence as close contact with a whale in
its natural habitat. The thrill of seeing one of these giant inhabitants
of the sea up close is a life-changing event for many people. Few
places in the world can offer as complete an experience as Mexico's
Baja peninsula. The various protected bays and lagoons on the
Pacific coast are the preferred winter waters for migrating gray whales
as they journey south to mate and give birth to their calves.

   While the entire Pacific coast of the Baja peninsula offers opportunities for whale sightings, the experience is particularly rewarding
in the protected areas of the El Vizcaíno Biosphere Reserve, where a
large number of whales can be seen easily. This area encompasses
the famous Laguna Ojo de Liebre—also known as Scammon's
Lagoon—close to Guerrero Negro, Laguna San Ignacio, and Bahía
Magdalena.

Tips **Should I Take a Tour or Hire a Boat?**

You'll often get a better deal if you hire a local panga operator; head down to the local pier to price it. Expect to pay anywhere from $30 to $45 per person for a day trip with a local
guide (plus a tip for good service); an organized tour can run
almost double that price. It's always a good idea to check for
licensed, experienced operators who know how to approach
the whales with calm, caution, and respect for the environment. The most important thing about whale-watching is to
enjoy it while practicing guidelines that ensure both your
safety and the safety of the whales. (We've recommended several tour operators and organizations below.)

Because these protected waters offer ideal conditions for gray
whales during the winter, the neighboring towns have developed the
necessary infrastructure and services to accommodate whale-watchers.
Avid eco- and adventure-lovers seem to follow their own migratory
patterns and arrive at these shores between January and March to gaze
in awe at the gentle cetaceans.

WHAT YOU'LL SEE

Gray whales are the favorite species for whale-watchers because they
tend to swim and feed mostly in coastal shallows, occasionally rest-
ing with their abdomens on the bottom, while their close relatives
prefer to frequent the deeper realms of the ocean. Whale-watching
in one of Baja's lagoons can be truly exciting—at times, gray whales
appear to be on all sides, displaying the full spectrum of typical
whale behavior.

Watchers might be showered with a cloud of water from a whale
spouting (clearing its blowhole) or might witness an enormous male
spyhopping—lifting its head vertically out of the water, just above
eye level, to pivot around before slipping back into the water. Perhaps the most breathtaking spectacle of all is a breach, when a whale
propels itself out of the water and arches through the air to land on
its back with a splash. These gray whales are known to be so friendly
and curious that they frequently come up to the whale-watching
boats and stay close by, sometimes allowing people to pet them.

To be close to these magnificent creatures is a privilege. Above all,
respect their environment and their integrity as inhabitants of the
marine world.

The Bloody History of a Whale-Watching Haven

Located 40km (25 miles) southwest of Guerrero Negro is Laguna Ojo de Liebre, also known as Scammon's Lagoon. It takes its name from an infamous whaler, Charles Melville Scammon, who followed a pod of gray whales into Laguna Ojo de Liebre. Taking advantage of geography—the lagoon has a very narrow mouth—he managed to slaughter the entire lot by using explosive harpoons. Before Scammon's "accomplishment," gray whales had remained safe from whalers because of their aggressive nature when under attack. But after Scammon's massacre, scores of whalers hopped on the bloody bandwagon, killing an estimated 10,000 gray whales in less than 20 years, and bringing the population close to extinction. (In an ironic turn of events, Scammon became a naturalist of some note later in life and wrote an important book about whales and the whaling industry.) The gray whales have made a remarkable comeback in the last 20 years—so much so that they are now off the endangered-species list.

WHICH TOWN? WHICH TOUR?

Regardless of where you decide to stay in Baja, you most likely will easily find tours to the whale-watching areas of Bahía Magdalena and the lagoons of Ojo de Liebre and San Ignacio. (For whale-watching tours that depart from La Paz, see chapter 3.) If you want to center your visit on whale-watching, the best places to visit are Guerrero Negro, San Ignacio, Ciudad Constitución, Puerto San Carlos, and Puerto López Mateos.

While the above-mentioned towns have basic facilities, Loreto may actually be the wisest base to choose; it has a well-developed tourist infrastructure and a number of lovely resort hotels. From here, whale-watching cruises along the Pacific coast are easily accessible. The trips take you by road to Bahía Magdalena, where you board a skiff to get up close to the gentle giants. En route you get a chance to view the spectacular desert landscape; guides offer a wealth of natural and historical information. Locally based **Las Parras**

Tours (© 613/135-1010; www.lasparrastours.com) offers excellent excursions; it's one of many groups that run expeditions to see the whales. Included among them is the U.S.-based **Baja Expeditions,** 2625 Garnet Ave., San Diego, CA 92109 (© **800/843-6967,** or 612/125-3828 in La Paz). Prices for package trips from Loreto run $95 to $125 per person for a daylong trip.

Guerrero Negro sits on the dividing line between southern and northern Baja. It has a modest but well-developed tourism infrastructure in an otherwise industrial town; it's the site of the world's largest evaporative saltworks. Despite the industrial nature of the town, the lagoon where gray whales calve and spend the winter has remained safe and has witnessed a remarkable comeback of this almost-extinct species. This is partly because the salt produced in Guerrero Negro is shipped from an offshore artificial island, built away from the whale area, and also because of the designation of the area as part of the El Vizcaíno Biosphere Reserve in 1988.

San Ignacio is a small town built by the Spaniards in the middle of a palm oasis, and is full of Jesuit history. It is the ideal point of departure for **Laguna San Ignacio** 🐋🐋, 74km (46 miles) southwest of the town. The San Ignacio lagoon is an excellent spot for whale-watching because it is common for whales in this area to approach the small whale-watching boats, occasionally coming close enough to allow you to touch them.

Bahía Magdalena is another spot preferred by wintering gray whales. Two towns on the bay's shore offer whale-watching tours. **Puerto López Mateos,** on the northern shore, is the closest town to the whales' calving areas. Accommodations are limited to a few modest hotels and restaurants, but several boat operators offer tours. For recommendations, contact the **Unión de Lancheros y Servicios Turísticos del Puerto** (© 613/131-5171), an association of fishing-boat operators on Adolfo López Mateos, or the **Sociedad Cooperativa de Servicios Turísticos** (© 613/131-5112 or 613/131-5198).

Puerto San Carlos offers a more developed tourism infrastructure, with well-appointed hotels and restaurants, trailer parks, travel agencies, a bus station, and other services. To arrange a tour, try **Viajes Mar y Arena,** Puerto La Paz s/n (© **613/136-0076;** fax 613/136-0232).

Ciudad Constitución, the largest of the three towns, is 61km (38 miles) inland. It has a well-developed tourism infrastructure, with tour organizers that offer daily whale-watching tours during the season.

GETTING THERE To get to Puerto López Mateos, take the only road going west from Loreto for about 121km (75 miles). When you arrive in the town of Insurgentes, turn right and continue 2.4km (1½ miles) to the PUERTO LOPEZ MATEOS exit. Turn left and continue 34km (21 miles) to Puerto López Mateos. To get to Puerto San Carlos, take the same road west to Insurgentes, then drive south about 24km (15 miles) until you reach Ciudad Constitución. From Ciudad Constitución, take the exit marked PUERTO SAN CARLOS, and continue the remaining 63km (39 miles) to town. Both routes are well paved and maintained.

5

Northern Baja: Tijuana, Rosarito Beach & Ensenada

Northern Baja California is not only Mexico's most infamous border crossing, it's also the land that claims to be the birthplace of the original Caesar salad and the margarita. Who could resist that? As you travel south along the Pacific coastline, the towns of Tijuana, Rosarito Beach, and Ensenada together make one of the most important introductions to Mexico. The trip combines the boisterous, the beachy, and the beautiful of Baja.

Long notorious as a party-hard, 10-block border town, Tijuana has cleaned up its act a bit on its way to becoming a full-scale city. A growing number of sports and cultural attractions now augment the legendary shopping experience and wild nightlife. Rosarito Beach remains a more tranquil resort town, despite recently spending time in Hollywood's spotlight; the decidedly laid-back atmosphere makes it easy to enjoy miles of beachfront. Continue south past stellar surf breaks, golf courses, and fish-taco stands, and Ensenada emerges, a favored port of call and a lovely town with plenty of appeal for active travelers.

EXPLORING NORTHERN BAJA

If you have a car, it's easy to venture into Baja Norte from Southern California for a few days' getaway. Since 1991, American car-rental companies have allowed customers to drive their cars into Baja. Whether you drive your own car or a rented one, you'll need Mexican auto insurance in addition to your own; it's available at the border in San Ysidro or through the car-rental companies (see "Getting Around" in chapter 1).

It takes relatively little time to cross the international border in Tijuana, but be prepared for a delay of an hour or more on your return to the United States through San Diego—with increased

A Suggested Itinerary

Begin your trip in Tijuana with an afternoon or overnight stay that includes watching some fast-paced jai alai (see "Outdoor Activities & Spectator Sports," in section 1, "Tijuana: Bawdy Border Town," for in-depth information), then head down the coast to the seaside town of Rosarito Beach, and then on to Puerto Nuevo and Ensenada.

security measures for entering the U.S., this is an especially diligent point of entry. If you take local buses down the Baja coast (which is possible), the delays come en route rather than at the border.

1 Tijuana: Bawdy Border Town

26km (16 miles) S of San Diego

In northern Baja California, the first point of entry from the West Coast of the U.S. is infamous Tijuana, a town that continues to delude travelers into thinking that a visit there means they've been to Mexico. An important border town, Tijuana is renowned for its hustling, carnival-like atmosphere and easily accessible decadence.

But Tijuana is increasingly an important city in Mexico; the population has swelled to nearly two million, making it the second-largest city on the Pacific coast of North America (after Los Angeles). Despite obvious signs of widespread poverty, the town claims one of the lowest unemployment rates in the country, thanks to the rise in *maquiladoras,* the foreign-owned manufacturing operations that continue to proliferate under NAFTA (North American Free Trade Agreement). High-rise office buildings testify to increased prosperity, as does the rise of a white-collar middle class that shops at modern shopping centers away from the tourist zone. And there's tourism from elsewhere in northern Mexico; the availability of imported goods and the lure of a big-city experience draw visitors.

Tijuana's "sin city" image is gradually morphing into that of a shopper's mecca and a nocturnal playground. Vineyards associated with the growing wine industry are nearby, and an increasing number of cultural offerings are joining the traditional sporting attractions of greyhound racing, jai alai, and bullfights. Tijuana first earned notoriety during the U.S. Prohibition, when scores of visitors found the time and the inclination to come here, to the site of the world's

Tijuana

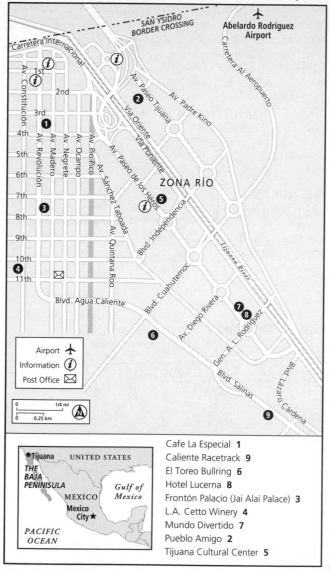

Cafe La Especial **1**
Caliente Racetrack **9**
El Toreo Bullring **6**
Hotel Lucerna **8**
Frontón Palacio (Jai Alai Palace) **3**
L.A. Cetto Winery **4**
Mundo Divertido **7**
Pueblo Amigo **2**
Tijuana Cultural Center **5**

largest saloon bar, The Whale. Around the same time, the Hotel Casino de Aguacaliente—the first resort of its kind in Mexico—attracted Hollywood stars and other celebrities with its casino, greyhound racing, and hot-springs spa.

Like many large cities in developing nations, Tijuana is a mixture of new and old, rich and poor, modern and traditional. You are less likely to find the Mexico you may be expecting—charming town squares and churches, abundant bougainvillea, and women in colorful embroidered skirts and blouses—and more likely to find an urban culture, a profusion of U.S.-inspired goods and services, and relentless hawkers playing to the thousands of tourists who come for a taste of Mexico.

ESSENTIALS
GETTING THERE & DEPARTING

A visit to Tijuana requires little in the way of formalities—no passport or tourist card is required of people who stay less than 72 hours in the border zone. If you plan to stay longer, you must have a tourist card, available free of charge from the border crossing station, or from any immigration office.

BY PLANE **AeroCalifornia** (℡ **800/237-6225** in the U.S., or 664/684-2100) has nonstop or direct flights from Los Angeles; **Aeromexico** (℡ **800/237-6639** in the U.S., 664/683-2700, or 664/638-8444; www.aeromexico.com) has connecting flights from Houston, New York, Culiacán, Hermosillo, Guadalajara, La Paz, and Mexico City. **Mexicana** (℡ **800/531-7921** in the U.S., 664/634-6566, www.mexicana.com) has direct or connecting flights from Guadalajara, Los Angeles, Mexico City, and Cancún.

BY CAR If you plan to visit only Tijuana and are arriving from Southern California, you should consider leaving your car behind, because the traffic can be challenging. One alternative is to walk across the border; you can either park your car in one of the safe, long-term parking lots on the San Diego side for about $8 a day, or take the San Diego Trolley to the border. Once you're in Tijuana, it's easier to get around by taxi than to take on the local drivers. Cab fares from the border to downtown Tijuana run about $5. You can also charter a taxi to Rosarito for about $20 (one-way) or to Ensenada for $100 (one-way).

To reach Tijuana from the U.S., take I-5 south to the Mexican border at San Ysidro. The drive from downtown San Diego takes about half an hour.

Many car-rental companies in San Diego allow customers to drive their cars into Baja California, at least as far as Ensenada. Cars from **Avis** (© **800/331-1212** or 619/688-5000) and **Southwest** (© **619/497-4800**) may be driven as far as the 28th parallel and Guerrero Negro, the dividing line that separates Baja into two states, North and South. **Bob Baker Ford** (© **619/297-5001,** ext. 9) allows its cars to be driven the entire 1,000-mile stretch of the Baja Peninsula.

Keep in mind that if you drive in, you'll need Mexican auto insurance in addition to your own. You can get it in San Ysidro, just north of the border at the San Ysidro exit; from your car-rental agency in San Diego; or from a AAA office if you're a member.

From the south, take Highway 1 (Carretera Transpeninsular) north to Tijuana. It's a long and sometimes difficult drive.

BY TROLLEY   From downtown San Diego, you also have the option of taking the bright-red trolley headed for San Ysidro and getting off at the last stop (it's nicknamed the Tijuana Trolley for good reason). From here, just follow the signs to walk across the border. It's simple, quick, and inexpensive; the one-way trolley fare is $2. The last trolley leaving for San Ysidro departs downtown around midnight; the last returning trolley from San Ysidro is at 1am. On Saturday, the trolley runs 24 hours.

BY BUS   **Five Star Tours,** in San Diego at the intersection of Broadway and Kettner (© **619/232-5049;** fax 619/575-3075), offers specialized trips across the border. For $50 for the first person and $5 per extra person, the company will take you across the border, recommend shops and restaurants, or take you to the Cultural Center, then pick you up to return to San Diego at a pre-established time. You must make reservations 24 hours in advance.

Also from San Diego, **Gray Line Tours** (© **619/238-4777**) offers a tour to Tijuana for $20. It's not a regularly scheduled tour, so call ahead to check departure dates and times. **Contact Tours** (© **619/477-8687**) also offers a tour to Tijuana for $28.

ORIENTATION

ARRIVING   Upon arrival at the airport, buy a ticket inside the building for a taxi, which can be shared by up to five passengers. It costs about $9 to and from anywhere in the city. Public buses to downtown Tijuana, marked CENTRO, are also available and cost 45¢ per passenger. The airport is about 8km (5 miles) east of the city.

The major car-rental agencies all have counters at the airport, open during flight arrivals: **Avis** (✆ **800/331-1212** from the U.S., or 664/683-2310); **Budget** (✆ **800/527-0700** from the U.S., or 664/683-2905); **Hertz** (✆ **800/654-3131** from the U.S., or 664/683-2080); and **National** (✆ **800/328-4567** from the U.S., or 664/683-8115). Advance reservations are not always necessary, but they are recommended. You can usually get a better rate if you make your reservation in the U.S.

If you've come to Tijuana on the San Diego Trolley or if you leave a car on the U.S. side of the border, you will walk through the border crossing. The first structure you'll see on your left is a Visitor Information Center, open daily from 9am to 7pm; ask for a copy of the *Baja Visitor* magazine and the *Baja Times*. From here, you can easily walk into the center of town or take a taxi.

Tijuana taxicabs are easy to find, available at most of the visitor hot spots. It's customary to agree upon the rate before stepping into the cab, whether you're going just a few blocks or hiring a cab for the afternoon. One-way rides within the city cost between $4 and $8, and tipping is optional. Some cabs are "local" taxis, frequently stopping to take on or let off other passengers during your ride; they are less expensive than private cabs.

VISITOR INFORMATION   Prior to your visit, you can write for information, brochures, and maps from the Tijuana Convention & Visitors Bureau, P.O. Box 434523, San Diego, CA 92143-4523. You can also get a preview of events, restaurants, and more online at www.seetijuana.com. Once in Tijuana, pick up visitor information at the **Tijuana Tourism Board,** Paseo de los Héroes 9365, Zona Río (✆ **888/775-2417** toll-free in the U.S., or 664/686-1345; www.seetijuana.com). You can also try the **Mexican Tourism Office** (✆ **664/688-0555;** open Mon–Fri from 8am–5pm, Sat and Sun from 10am–2pm), or the **National Chamber of Commerce** (✆ **664/685-8472;** open Mon–Fri 9am–2pm and 4–7pm). Both have offices at the corner of Avenida Revolución and Calle 1, and are extremely helpful with maps and orientation, local events of interest, and accommodations; in addition, the tourism office provides legal assistance for visitors who encounter problems while in Tijuana.

The following countries have **consulate offices** in Tijuana: the **United States** (✆ **664/622-7400**), **Canada** (✆ **664/684-0461**), and the **United Kingdom** (✆ **664/681-7323** or 664/686-5320).

FAST FACTS: Tijuana

Area Code The local telephone area code is **664**.

Banks Banks exchange currency during business hours, generally Monday through Friday from 8:30am to 6pm and Saturday from 9am to 2pm. Major banks with ATMs and *casas de cambio* (money-exchange houses) are easy to find in all the heavily trafficked areas discussed in this book. The currency of Mexico is the peso, but you can easily visit Tijuana (or Rosarito and Ensenada, for that matter) without changing money because dollars are accepted virtually everywhere.

Climate & Weather Tijuana's climate is similar to Southern California's. Don't expect sweltering heat just because you're south of the border, and remember that the Pacific waters won't be much warmer than off San Diego. The first beaches you'll find are about 24km (15 miles) south of Tijuana.

Pharmacy Sanborn's (© 664/688-1462), the 24-hour megastore with a pharmacy, has several locations in Tijuana; one is at the corner of Avenida Revolución and Calle 8. Numerous discount pharmacies are along Avenida Constitución and Avenida Revolución; one to try is **Farmacias Roma** (© 664/688-0426, home delivery 664/681-8522).

Post Office The main *correo*, at Calle 11 at Avenida Negrete (© 664/627-2699), is open Monday through Friday from 8am to 7pm, and Saturday from 9am to 1pm.

Taxes & Tipping A value-added tax of 10%, called **IVA** *(Impuesto al Valor Agregado)*, is added to most bills, including those in restaurants. This does not represent the tip; the bill will read "IVA incluído," but you should add about 15% for the tip if the service warrants.

EXPLORING TIJUANA

One of the first major tourist attractions below the border is also one of the strangest—the **Museo de Cera** (Wax Museum), Calle 1 no. 8281, at the corner of Madero (© **664/688-2478**). Featured statues include the eclectic mix of Whoopi Goldberg, Laurel and Hardy, and Bill Clinton, arranged in an exhibit otherwise dominated by figures from Mexican history. If you aren't spooked by the not-so-lifelike figures of Aztec warriors, brown-robed friars, Spanish princes, and 20th-century military leaders (all posed in period dioramas), step into the Chamber of Horrors, where wax werewolves and sinister sadists lurk in the shadows. When the museum is mostly empty, which is most of the time, the dramatically lit Chamber of Horrors can be a little creepy. This side-street freak show is open daily from 10am to 8pm, and admission is $1.50.

For many visitors, Tijuana's "main event" is the bustling **Avenida Revolución,** the street whose reputation precedes it. Beginning in the 1920s, American college students, servicemen, and hedonistic tourists discovered this street as a bawdy center for illicit fun. Some of the original attraction has fallen by the wayside: Gambling was outlawed in the 1930s, back-alley cockfights are also illegal, and the same civic improvements that repaved Revolución to provide trees, benches, and wider sidewalks also vanquished the girlie shows whose barkers once accosted passersby. Drinking and shopping are the main order of business these days; while revelers from across the border knock back tequila shooters and dangle precariously at the upstairs railings of glaring bars, bargain hunters peruse the never-ending array of goods (and not-so-goods) for sale. You'll find the action between calles 1 and 9; the information centers (mentioned earlier) are at the north end, and the landmark jai alai palace anchors the southern portion. To help make sense of all those tchotchkes, see "Shopping," below.

Visitors can be easily seduced—then quickly repulsed—by touristtrap areas like Avenida Revolución, but it's important to remember that there's more to Tijuana than American tourism. If you're looking to see a different side of Tijuana, the best place to start is the **Centro Cultural Tijuana,** Paseo de los Héroes at Mina (© **664/ 687-9600;** www.cecut.gob.mx [a Spanish-only website]). You'll easily spot the ultramodern Tijuana Cultural Center complex, designed by irrepressible modern architect Pedro Ramírez Vásquez. Its centerpiece is that gigantic sand-colored dome housing an OMNIMAX theater, which screens different 45-minute films (subjects range from science to space travel). The center houses the **Museum of Mexican Identities'** permanent collection of artifacts from pre-Hispanic times through the modern political era, plus a gallery for visiting exhibits, which have included everything from the works of artist Diego Rivera to a well-curated yet disturbing exhibit chronicling torture and human rights violations through the ages. Music, theater, and dance performances take place in the center's concert hall and courtyard, and there's also a cafe and an excellent museum bookshop. Call to check the concert schedule during your visit. The center also holds the new Museum of the Californias. The center is open daily from 9am to 8:30pm. Admission to the museum's permanent exhibits is free; there's a $2 charge for the special-event gallery, and tickets for OMNIMAX films are $4 for adults and $2.50 for children.

Don't be discouraged if the Cultural Center sounds like a field trip for school children; it's a must-see, if only to drag you away from tourist kitsch and into the more sophisticated Zona Río (river area). While there, stop to admire the wide, European-style Paseo de los Héroes. The boulevard's intersections are gigantic traffic circles *(glorietas)*, at the center of which stand statuesque monuments to leaders ranging from Aztec Emperor Cuauhtémoc to Abraham Lincoln. Navigating the congested glorietas will require your undivided attention, however, so it's best to pull over to admire the monuments.

In the Zona Río you'll find some classier shopping and a colorful local marketplace, plus the ultimate kid destination, **Mundo Divertido,** Paseo de los Héroes at Calle José María Velasco (© **664/634-3213** and 664/634-3214). Literally translated, it means "fun world," and one parent described it as the Mexican equivalent of "a Chuck E. Cheese's restaurant built inside a Malibu Grand Prix." You get the idea—noisy and frenetic, it's the kind of place kids dream about. Let them choose from miniature golf, batting cages, a roller coaster, a kid-sized train, a video game parlor, and go-carts. There's a food court with tacos and hamburgers; if you're in luck, the picnic area will be festooned with streamers and piñatas for some fortunate child's birthday party. The park is open weekdays from noon to 8pm, Saturday and Sunday from 10am until 8:30pm. Admission is free, and several booths inside sell tickets for the various rides.

The fertile valleys of Northern Baja produce most of Mexico's finest wines and export many high-quality vintages to Europe; most are not available in the U.S. For an introduction to Mexican wines, stop into **Cava de Vinos L.A. Cetto** (L.A. Cetto Winery), Av. Cañón Johnson 2108, at Avenida Constitución Sur (© **664/685-3031**). Shaped like a wine barrel, this building's striking facade is made from old oak aging barrels in an inspired bit of recycling. In the entrance stand a couple of wine presses (ca. 1928) that Don Angel Cetto used back in the early days of production. His family still runs the winery, which opened the impressive visitor center in 1993. L.A. Cetto bottles both red and white wines, some of them award winners, including petite sirah, nebbiolo, and cabernet sauvignon. Most bottles cost about $5; the special reserves are a little more than $10. The company also produces tequila, brandy, and olive oil, all for sale here. Admission is $2.50 for a tour and generous tasting (for those 18 and older only; those under 18 are admitted free with an adult but cannot taste the wines), $3 with souvenir wine glass. Open Monday through Friday from 9:30am to 6:30pm, Saturday from 9:30am to 5:30pm. Tours run Monday through Friday 10am to 2pm and 4 to 5:30pm, and Saturday 10am to 2pm.

OUTDOOR ACTIVITIES & SPECTATOR SPORTS

BULLFIGHTING While some insist this spectacle promotes a cruel disregard for animal rights, others esteem it as a richly symbolic drama involving the courage Ernest Hemingway called "grace under pressure." Whatever your opinion, bullfighting has a prominent place in Mexican heritage and is even considered an essential element of the culture. The skill and bravery of matadors is closely linked with cultural ideals regarding machismo, and some of the world's best perform at Tijuana's two stadiums. The season runs from May through September, with events held Sunday at 4:30pm. Ticket prices range from $17 to $40 (the premium seats are on the shaded side of the arena), and can be purchased at the bullring or in advance from San Diego's **Five Star Tours** (© 619/232-5049). **El Toreo** (© 664/686-1510) is 3.2km (2 miles) east of downtown on Bulevar Agua Caliente at Avenida Diego Rivera. **Plaza de Toros Monumental,** or Bullring-by-the-Sea (© 664/680-1808), is 10km (6 miles) west of downtown on Highway 1-D (before the first toll

---

Moments First Crush: The Annual Harvest Festival

If you enjoyed a visit to L.A. Cetto, Tijuana's winery (or Ensenada's Bodegas de Santo Tomás, discussed later in this chapter), then you might want to come back for the Harvest Festival, held each year in late August or early September. Set amongst the endless vineyards of the fertile Guadalupe Valley, the day's events include the traditional blessing of the grapes, wine tastings, live music and dancing, riding exhibitions, and a country-style Mexican meal. L.A. Cetto offers a group excursion from Tijuana (about an hour's drive); San Diego's Baja California Tours (© 619/454-7166) also organizes a day-long trip from San Diego.

station); it perches at the edge of both the ocean and the California border. You can take a taxi easily to El Toreo—fares are negotiable, and around $10 one-way should be fair. You can also negotiate a fare to Bullring-by-the-Sea, but fares are unpredictable.

DOG RACING   There's satellite wagering on U.S. horse races at the majestic **Caliente Racetrack,** off Bulevar Agua Caliente, 4.8km (3 miles) east of downtown, but these days only greyhounds actually kick up dust at the track. Races are held daily at 7:45pm, with Saturday and Sunday matinees at 2pm. General admission is free, but bettors in the know congregate in the comfortable Turf Club; admission there is $10, refundable with a wagering voucher. For more information, call ℰ **664/685-7833,** or 619/231-1910 in San Diego. For other racing information, call ℰ **800-PICK-BAJA.**

GOLF   Once the favorite of golfing celebrities and socialites (and a very young Arnold Palmer) who stayed at the now-defunct Agua Caliente Resort, the **Tijuana Country Club,** Bulevar Agua Caliente at Avenida Gustavo Salinas (ℰ **664/681-7855**), is near the Caliente Racetrack and behind the Grand Hotel Tijuana; it's about a 10-minute drive from downtown. The course is well maintained and frequented mostly by business travelers staying at nearby hotels, many of which offer golf packages (see Grand Hotel Tijuana in "Where to Stay," below). Weekend greens fees are $40 a person, and optional cart rental is $20 per cart; club rental is $20, with caddies an additional $20 plus tip. Ask for seasonal specials. Stop by the pro shop for balls, tees, and a limited number of other accessories; the clubhouse also has two restaurants, complete with cocktail lounges.

JAI ALAI   A lightning-paced ballgame played on a slick indoor court, jai alai (pronounced *high*-ah-lye) is an ancient Basque tradition incorporating elements of tennis, hockey, and basketball. You can't miss the **Frontón Palacio,** Avenida Revolución at Calle 7 (ℰ **664/685-3687,** 664/688-0125, or 619/231-1910 in San Diego); it's a huge, box-like arena in the center of town, painted with giant red letters spelling JAI ALAI. Games are held Monday through Saturday at 8pm, with matinee events Monday and Friday at noon. General admission is $2, and there are betting windows inside the arena.

SHOPPING

Tijuana's biggest attraction is shopping—ask any of the 44 million people who cross the border each year to do it. They come to take advantage of reasonable prices on a variety of merchandise: terra-cotta and colorfully glazed pottery, woven blankets and serapes, embroidered dresses and sequined sombreros, onyx chess sets, beaded necklaces and bracelets, silver jewelry, leather bags and huarache sandals, rain sticks (bamboo branches filled with pebbles that simulate the patter of raindrops), hammered-tin picture frames, thick drinking glasses, novelty swizzle sticks, Cuban cigars, and Mexican liquors like Kahlúa and tequila. You're permitted to bring $800 worth of purchases back across the border (sorry, no Cuban cigars allowed), including 1 liter of alcohol per person.

When most people think of Tijuana, they picture **Avenida Revolución,** which appears to exist solely for the extraction of dollars from American visitors. Dedicated shoppers quickly discover that most of the curios spilling out onto the sidewalk look alike, despite the determined seller's assurances that their wares are the best in town. Browse for comparison's sake, but for the best souvenir shopping, duck into one of the many *pasajes,* or passageway arcades, where you'll find items of a slightly better quality and merchants willing to bargain. Some of the most enjoyable pasajes are on the east side of the street between calles 2 and 5; they also provide a pleasant respite from the quickly irritating tumult of Avenida Revolución.

An alternative is to visit **Sanborn's,** Avenida Revolución between calles 8 and 9 (✆ **664/688-1462**), a branch of the Mexico City department store long favored by American travelers. It sells an array of regional folk art and souvenirs, books about Mexico in both Spanish and English, and candies and fresh sweet treats from the bakery—and you can have breakfast in the sunny cafe.

One of the few places in Tijuana to find better-quality crafts from a variety of Mexican states is **Tolán,** Avenida Revolución between calles 7 and 8 (✆ **664/688-3637**). In addition to the obligatory selection of standard Avenida Revolución souvenirs, you'll find blue glassware from Guadalajara, glazed pottery from Tlaquepaque, crafts from the Oaxaca countryside, and distinctive tilework from Puebla. Prices at Tolán are fixed, so you shouldn't try to bargain the way you can in some of the smaller shops and informal stands. If a marketplace atmosphere and spirited bargaining are what you're looking for, head instead to **Mercado de Artesanías** (crafts market), Calle 2 and Avenida Negrete, where vendors of pottery, clayware, clothing, and other crafts fill an entire city block.

Shopping malls are as common in Tijuana as in any big American city; you shouldn't expect to find typical souvenirs there, but shopping alongside residents and other intrepid visitors is often

---

Tips **Where to Park in Tijuana**

Plaza Río Tijuana has ample free parking and is just across the street from the Cultural Center, where private lots charge $5 to $8 to park.

---

more fun than feeling like a sitting-duck tourist. One of the biggest, and most convenient, is **Plaza Río Tijuana,** Paseo de los Héroes at Avenida Independencia (© **664/684-0402**), an outdoor plaza anchored by several department stores and featuring dozens of specialty shops and casual restaurants. Other shopping malls are listed at www.seetijuana.com/tijuanasite/shopping_centers.htm.

On the other side of Paseo de los Héroes from Plaza Río Tijuana is **Plaza del Zapato,** a two-story indoor mall filled with only shoe *(zapato)* stores. Though most are made with quality leather rather than synthetics, inferior workmanship ensures they'll likely last only a season or two. But with prices as low as $30, why not indulge? For a taste of everyday Mexico, visit **Mercado Hidalgo,** 1 block west at avenidas Sánchez Taboada and Independencia, a busy indoor-outdoor marketplace where vendors display fresh flowers and produce, sacks of dried beans and chiles by the kilo, and a few souvenir crafts (including some excellent piñatas). Morning is the best time to visit the market, and you'll be more comfortable paying with pesos, since most sellers are accustomed to a local crowd.

WHERE TO STAY

When calculating room rates, always remember that hotel rates in Tijuana are subject to a 12% tax.

Grand Hotel Tijuana *&* Popular with business travelers and visiting celebrities, and for society events, the hotel has the best-maintained public and guest rooms in Tijuana, which helps make up for what it lacks in regional warmth. You can see the hotel's 32-story mirrored twin towers from all of the surrounding city. Modern and sleek in design, it opened in 1982—at the height of Tijuana's prosperity—under the name Fiesta Americana, a name locals (and many cab drivers) still use. Rooms have spectacular views of the city from the top floors. The Vegas-like lobby gives way to several ballrooms and an airy atrium that serves elegant international cuisine at dinner and weekend brunch. Next to the atrium is a casual Mexican restaurant, beyond which the Vegas resemblance resumes with an indoor shopping arcade.

The hotel offers a golf package for $82 per person—it includes one night's lodging with a welcome cocktail and a round of 18 holes (including cart) at the adjacent Tijuana Country Club.

Agua Caliente 4500, Tijuana (P.O. Box BC, Chula Vista, CA 92012). ℂ **800/GRANDTJ** in the U.S., or 664/681-7000 in Tijuana. Fax 664/681-7016. www.grandhoteltij. com.mx. 422 units. $151 double; $196–$213 suite. AE, MC, V. Free underground parking. **Amenities:** 2 restaurants; lobby bar; heated pool; sauna; concierge; tour desk; business center; shopping arcade; 24-hr. room service; laundry and dry cleaning. *In room:* A/C, dataport, minibar, iron, safe-deposit boxes.

Hotel Lucerna ℱ Once the most chic hotel in Tijuana, Lucerna now feels slightly worn, but the place still has personality. The flavor is Mexican colonial—wrought-iron railings and chandeliers, rough-hewn heavy wood furniture, brocade wallpaper, and traditional tiles. The hotel is in the Zona Río, away from the noise and congestion of downtown, so a quiet night's sleep is easily attainable. All the rooms in this five-story hotel have balconies or patios but are otherwise unremarkable. Sunday brunch is served outdoors by the swimming pool; there's also a coffee shop that provides room service. The staff is friendly and attentive.

Av. Paseo de los Héroes 10902, Zona Río, Tijuana. ℂ **800/582-3762** in the U.S., or 664/634-2000; www.hotel-lucerna.com.mx. 167 units. $85 double; $88 suite. AE, DC, MC, V. **Amenities:** Restaurant; swimming pool; tour desk; room service; laundry service. *In room:* A/C, TV, Internet access, coffeemaker, hair dryer, iron.

WHERE TO DINE
EXPENSIVE

Cien Años ℱℱℱ MEXICAN An elegant and gracious Zona Río restaurant offering artfully blended Mexican flavors (tamarind, poblano chile, mango) in stylish presentations. Try chile rellenos stuffed with shrimp in lobster sauce, delicate *calabaza* (squash-blossom) soup, or huitlacoche (corn mushroom) tamales. The most adventurous diners can sample garlicky ant eggs or buttery *guisanos* (cactus worms). If you're interested in true haute cuisine, the buzz around Tijuana is all about this place.

Calle José María Velasco 1407. ℂ **664/634-3039** or 664/634-7262. Main courses $12–$30. AE, DC, MC, V. Daily 1pm–midnight.

La Costa ℱ MEXICAN-STYLE SEAFOOD Fish gets top billing here, starting with hearty seafood soup. There are combination platters of half a grilled lobster, stuffed shrimp, and baked shrimp; fish filet stuffed with seafood and cheese; and several abalone dishes.

Calle 7 no. 8131 (just off Av. Revolución), Zona Centro. ℂ **664/685-8494.** Main courses $8–$20. AE, DC, MC, V. Daily 10am–midnight.

MODERATE

Hard Rock Cafe AMERICAN/MEXICAN   Had an overload of Mexican culture? Looking for a place with all the familiar comforts of home? Then head for the Tijuana branch of this ubiquitous watering hole, which promises nothing exotic; it serves the standard Hard Rock chain menu, which admittedly features an outstanding hamburger, in the regulation Hard Rock setting (dark, clubby, walls filled with rock 'n' roll memorabilia). While the restaurant's street presence is more subdued than most Hard Rock locations, you'll still spot the trademark Caddie emerging from above the door. Prices are in line with what you'd see in the U.S.—and therefore no bargain in competitive Tijuana.

520 Av. Revolución (near Calle 1), Zona Centro. ℂ 664/685-0206. Menu items $5–$10. AE, MC, V. Daily 11am–2am.

INEXPENSIVE

Cafe La Especial MEXICAN   Tucked away in a shopping pasaje at the bottom of some stairs (turn in at the taco stand of the same name), this restaurant is a well-known shopper's refuge and purveyor of home-style Mexican cooking at reasonable (though not dirt-cheap) prices. The gruff, efficient waitstaff carry out platter after platter of *carne asada* (grilled marinated beef) served with fresh tortillas, beans, and rice—it's La Especial's most popular item. Traditional dishes like tacos, enchiladas, and burritos round out the menu, augmented by frosty cold Mexican beers.

Av. Revolución 718 (between calles 3 and 4), Zona Centro. ℂ 664/685-6654. Menu items $4–$12. MC, V. Daily 9am–10pm.

Carnitas Uruapán ☆☆ MEXICAN   *Carnitas*—marinated pork roasted on a spit till falling-apart tender, then served in chunks with tortillas, salsa, cilantro, guacamole, and onions—are a beloved dish in Mexico and the main attraction at Carnitas Uruapán. It serves the meat by the kilo (or portion thereof) at long, communal wooden tables to a crowd of mostly locals. A half-kilo of carnitas is plenty for two people and costs around $12, including beans and that impressive array of condiments. It's a casual feast without compare, but vegetarians need not apply. The original is a little hard to find, but this branch is in the fashionable Zona Río. A third location, which specializes in seafood as well, is on Paseo de los Héroes at Avenida Rodríguez (no phone).

Blv. Díaz Ordáz 12650 (across from Plaza Patria), La Mesa. ℂ 664/681-6181. Menu items $2.50–$8. No credit cards. Daily 8am–5am.

La Fonda de Roberto 🐸🐸 MEXICAN   Although its location may seem out-of-the-way on the map, this modest restaurant's regular appearances on San Diego "Best Of" lists attest to its continued appeal. A short drive (or taxi ride) from downtown Tijuana, La Fonda's colorful dining room opens onto the courtyard of a kitschy 1960s motel, complete with retro kidney-shaped swimming pool. The festive atmosphere is perfect for enjoying a variety of regional Mexican dishes, including decent chicken mole and generous portions of *milanesa* (beef, chicken, or pork pounded paper thin, then breaded and fried). A house specialty is *queso fundido,* deep-fried cheese with chiles and mushrooms, served with a basket of freshly made corn tortillas.

In the La Sierra Motel, 2800 Blv. Cuauhtémoc Sur Oeste (Av. 16 de Septiembre, on the old road to Ensenada). ⓒ **664/686-4687.** Most dishes $5–$11. MC, V. Tues–Thurs 10am–10pm.

TIJUANA AFTER DARK

Avenida Revolución is the center of the city's nightlife; many compare it with Bourbon Street in New Orleans during Mardi Gras—except here it's a regular occurrence, not a once-a-year blowout. Tijuana has several lively discos; perhaps the most popular is **Baby Rock,** 1482 Diego Rivera, Zona Río (ⓒ **664/634-2404**), a cousin to Acapulco's lively Baby O, which features everything from Latin rock to rap. It's near the Guadalajara Grill restaurant.

Also popular in Tijuana are sports bars, featuring wagering on events from all over the United States as well as races from Tijuana's Caliente track. The most popular of these bars cluster in the **Pueblo Amigo** and **Vía Oriente** areas and around **Paseo Tijuana** in the Zona Río, a new center designed to resemble a colonial Mexican village. Even if you don't bet on the horses, you can soak up the atmosphere. Two of the town's hottest discos, **Rodeo de Media Noche** (ⓒ **664/ 682-4967**) and **Señor Frogs** (ⓒ **664/682-4962**), are in Pueblo Amigo, as is **La Tablita de Tony** (ⓒ **664/682-8111**), an Argentinian restaurant. Pueblo Amigo is less than 3.2km (2 miles) from the border, a short taxi ride or—during daylight hours—a pleasant walk.

2 Rosarito Beach & Beyond: Baja's First Beach Resorts

55km (34 miles) S of San Diego; 29km (18 miles) S of Tijuana

Just a 20-minute drive south of Tijuana and a complete departure in ambience, Rosarito Beach is a tranquil, friendly beach town. It also

The Upper Baja Peninsula

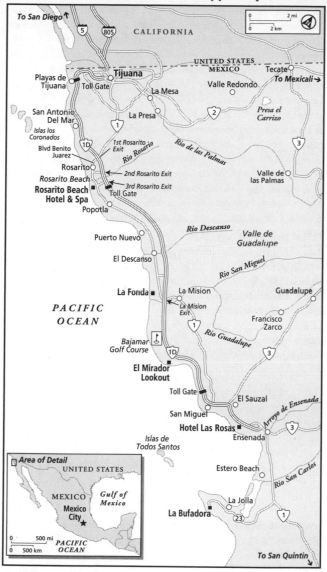

To San Diego↑

CALIFORNIA

UNITED STATES
MEXICO

Tecate
To Mexicali→

Playas de
Tijuana
Tijuana
Toll Gate
La Mesa
Valle Redondo

San Antonio
Del Mar
La Presa
Presa el
Carrizo

Islas los
Coronados

Blvd Benito
Juarez
1st Rosarito
Exit
Rio Rosario
Rio de las Palmas

Valle de
las Palmas

Rosarito
2nd Rosarito Exit

Rosarito Beach
3rd Rosarito Exit

Rosarito Beach
Hotel & Spa
Toll Gate

Popotla

Rio Descanso
Valle de
Guadalupe

Puerto Nuevo

El Descanso
Rio San Miguel

La Fonda
La Mision
Guadalupe

PACIFIC
OCEAN
La Mision
Exit
Francisco
Zarco

Rio Guadalupe

Bajamar
Golf Course

El Mirador
Lookout

Toll Gate
El Sauzal
Arroyo de Ensenada

San Miguel

Hotel Las Rosas
Ensenada

Islas de
Todos Santos

Estero Beach
Rio San Carlos

La Jolla

La Bufadora

To San Quintin↓

Area of Detail

UNITED STATES

MEXICO
Gulf of
Mexico

Mexico
City★

PACIFIC
OCEAN

0   500 mi
0   500 km

gained early renown during the U.S. Prohibition, when the elegant Rosarito Beach Hotel catered to Hollywood stars. This classic structure still welcomes numerous guests, despite the fact that its opulence has lost some luster. Hollywood has likewise played a major part in Rosarito's recent renaissance—it was the location for the soundstage and filming of the Academy Award–winning *Titanic.* The Titanic Museum at **Foxploration** here continues to draw fans of the film (see "En Route from Rosarito to Ensenada," below).

Two roads run between Tijuana and Ensenada (the largest and third-largest cities in Baja)—the scenic, coast-hugging toll road (marked CUOTA, or 1-D), and the free but slower-going public road (marked LIBRE, or 1). We strongly recommend starting out on the toll road, but use the free road along Rosarito Beach if you'd like to easily pull on and off the road to shop or look at the view. The beaches between Tijuana and Rosarito are also known for excellent surf breaks.

VISITOR INFORMATION   The best source of information is **Baja California Tourism Information** (© **800/522-1516** in California, Arizona, or Nevada; 800/225-2786 in the rest of the U.S. and Canada; or 619/298-4105 in San Diego). This office provides advice and makes hotel reservations throughout Baja California. You can also contact the local **Secretaria de Turísmo,** Km 28 Carretera Libre Tijuana–Ensenada Local 13B (© **661/612-0200;** rosarito@ turismobc.gob.mx). The office is open Monday through Friday from 8am to 5pm, and Saturday and Sunday from 10am to 3pm.

EXPLORING ROSARITO BEACH

Once a tiny resort town that remained a secret despite its proximity to Tijuana, Rosarito Beach saw an explosion of development in the prosperous '80s; now it's settled down into its own spirited personality. Why does its popularity persist? Location is one reason—it's the first beach resort town south of the border, and party-minded tourists aren't always too discriminating. This should give you an idea of the crowd to expect on holiday weekends and during school breaks.

Reputation is another draw: For years the **Rosarito Beach Hotel & Spa** (see "Where to Stay," below), built around 1927, was the preferred hideaway of celebrities and other fashionable Angelenos. Movie star Rita Hayworth and her husband Prince Aly Khan vacationed here; Paulette Goddard and Burgess Meredith were married at the resort. Although the hotel's entry still features the gallant inscription POR ESTA PUERTA PASAN LAS MUJERES MAS HERMOSAS DEL MUNDO ("Through this doorway pass the most beautiful women in the world"), today's vacationing starlets are more often found at resorts on Baja's southern tip. While the glimmer (as well as the glamour) has worn off, the Rosarito Beach Hotel is still the most interesting place in town, and nostalgia buffs will want to stop in for a look at some expert tile- and woodwork, as well as the panoramic murals throughout the lobby. Check out the colorful Aztec images in the main dining room, the magnificently tiled restrooms, and the glassed-in bar overlooking the sparkling pool and beach, or peek into the original owner's mansion on the property (now home to a spa and gourmet restaurant).

Rosarito Beach has caught the attention of Hollywood for years; most recently, the megahit *Titanic* was filmed here in a state-of-the-art production facility. *Titanic*'s allure is fading fast, however, and the former set was remodeled into an interactive museum with broader appeal.

If it's not too crowded, Rosarito is a good place to while away a few hours. Swim or horseback ride at the beach, then dine on fish tacos or tamales from any one of a number of family-run stands along Bulevar Benito Juárez, the town's main (and only) drag. You can have a drink at the local branch of Ensenada's enormously popular Papas & Beer (see "Rosarito Beach After Dark," below), or shop for souvenirs along the Old Ensenada Highway just south of town.

SHOPPING

The dozen or so blocks north of the Rosarito Beach Hotel abound with the stores typical in Mexican border towns; curio shops, cigar and *licores* (liquor) stores, and *farmacias* (where drugs like Viagra, Retin-A, Prozac, Rogaine, and many more are available at low cost and without a prescription). Rosarito has also become a center for carved furnishings—plentiful downtown along Bulevar Benito Juárez—and pottery, best purchased at stands along the old highway, south of town. A reliable but more expensive furniture shop is **Casa la Carreta,** Km 29.5 on the old road south of Rosarito (© **661/ 612-0502;** www.casalacarreta.net), where you can see plentiful examples of the best workmanship—chests, tables, chairs, headboards, cabinets, and cradles.

WHERE TO STAY

Rosarito Beach Hotel & Spa *Value*   Although this once-glamorous resort has been holding steady since its heyday, the vestiges of vacationing movie stars, a casino, and 1930s elegance have been all but eclipsed by the glaring nighttime neon and party-mania that currently define the former retreat. Despite the resort's changed personality, unique features of artistic construction and lavish decoration remain, setting it apart from the rest. Located along a wide stretch of a family-friendly beach, the hotel draws a mixed crowd. The stately on-site home of the original owners has been transformed into the full-service Casa Playa Spa, where massages and other treatments are only slightly less costly than in the U.S.

You'll pay more for an ocean view, and more for the newer, air-conditioned rooms in the tower; the older rooms in the poolside building may have only ceiling fans, but they prevail in the character department, with hand-painted trim and original tile.

Blv. Benito Juárez, Zona Centro, Rosarito, B.C. Mexico (P.O. Box 430145, San Diego, CA 92143). ℂ 800/343-8582 or 1-866/ROSARITO U.S., or 661/612-0144. Fax 661/612-1125. www.rosaritohtl.com. 280 units. $59–$129 double Sept–June; $89–$139 double July–Aug and U.S. holidays. 2 children under 12 stay free in parent's room. Packages available. MC, V. Free parking. **Amenities:** 2 restaurants; bar; 2 swimming pools; racquetball and tennis courts; kids' playground; room service. *In room:* TV.

WHERE TO DINE

While in Rosarito, you may want to try Chabert's or the more casual Azteca Restaurant, both in the Rosarito Beach Hotel. Outside the hotel, a branch of **Puerto Nuevo's Ortega's** (ℂ **661/612-0022**) on the main drag is the place for lobster; early risers out for a stroll can enjoy fresh, steaming-hot tamales, a traditional Mexican breakfast treat sold from sidewalk carts for around 50¢ each.

El Nido 𝄪𝄪 MEXICAN/STEAKS   One of the first eateries in Rosarito, El Nido remains popular with visitors unimpressed by the flashier, neon-lit joints that pop up to please the college-age set. The setting is Western frontier, complete with rustic candles and rusting wagon wheels; sit outside in the enclosed patio, or opt for the dark, cozy interior warmed by a large fireplace and open grill. The mesquite fire is constantly stoked to prepare the grilled steaks and seafood that are El Nido's specialty; the menu also includes free-range (and super-fresh) quail and venison from the owner's ranch in the nearby wine country. Meals are reasonably priced and generous, including hearty bean soup, American-style green salad, baked potatoes, and all the fresh tortillas and zesty salsa you can eat.

Blv. Juárez 67. ℂ **661/612-1430**. Main courses $5.50–$20. No credit cards. Daily 8am–midnight.

ROSARITO BEACH AFTER DARK

Because the legal drinking age in Baja is 18, the under-21 crowd from Southern California tends to flock across the border on Friday and Saturday nights. The most popular spot in town is **Papas & Beer** (© 661/612-0444), part of the Rosarito Beach Hotel. It's a relaxed come-as-you-are-type club on the beach, just a block north of the hotel. Even for those young in spirit only, it's great fun, with open-air tables and a bar surrounding a sand volleyball court. Or choose from several other adjacent clubs, each offering booming music, spirited dancing, and all-night-long energy. Cover charges vary depending on the season, the crowd, and the mood of the staff. The **Salon Méxican** (© 661/612-0144), in the Rosarito Beach Hotel, attracts a slightly more mature crowd, with live music on Friday, Saturday, and Sunday nights.

EN ROUTE FROM ROSARITO TO ENSENADA

A few miles south of Rosarito proper lies the seaside production site of the 1997 megablockbuster *Titanic*. A 240m-long (800-ft.) *Titanic* replica was constructed for filming, and many local citizens served as extras in the movie. Although the gargantuan ship was sunk and destroyed during filming, soundstages still contain partial sets (like a first-class hallway) and numerous props, including lifeboats, furnishings, and crates from dockside scenes. Fox Studio's **Foxploration** (© 661/614-0110) interactive museum covers several acres and can hold up to 3,000 visitors, with exhibits that showcase the art of making movies. Hands-on exhibits demonstrate everything from optical illusions to computer generation of special effects. Props and scenery from various Fox Studio movie sets are on view throughout, but the star attraction is the Titanic Expo, with a wealth of memorabilia and props from the movie. The steady flow of curious visitors prompted the opening of Foxploration. It's open Thursday to Monday from 10am to 6pm (daily around holidays and during busy seasons). Admission is $12 for adults, $9 for children 3 to 11.

Leaving Rosarito, drive south on the toll highway or the local-access old road that parallels it. In addition to the curious juxtaposition of ramshackle villages and luxurious vacation homes, you'll pass a variety of restaurants and resorts—this stretch of coastline has now surpassed Rosarito in drawing the discriminating visitor. Many places are so Americanized you feel as though you never left home, so our favorites are the funkier, more colorfully Mexican places, like Calafia restaurant, Puerto Nuevo lobster village, and La Fonda resort (see "Where to Stay" and "Where to Dine," below). After La Fonda, be sure to get back on the toll road, because the old road veers inland and you don't want to miss what's coming next.

Development falls off somewhat for the next 24km (15 miles), but the coastline's natural beauty picks up. You'll see green meadows running down to meet white-sand beaches and wild sand dunes, as you skirt rocky cliffs reminiscent of the coast at Big Sur. The ideal place to take it all in is El Mirador lookout, about 18km (11 miles) south of La Fonda. Feel the drama build as you climb up the stairs and gasp at the breathtaking view, which sweeps from the deep-blue open sea past steep cliffs and down the curved coastline to Salsipuedes Point, around which lies Ensenada. If vertigo doesn't trouble you, look straight down from El Mirador's railing, and you'll see piles of automobiles lying where they were driven off before El Mirador was built. Whether the promontory was a popular suicide spot or merely a junkyard with an enticing twist is best left to urban legend-makers; it nevertheless reinforces your sense of a different culture—nowhere in image-conscious California would that twisted pile of metal be left on the rocks.

A few miles farther south on the toll road, you'll come to a sign for SALSIPUEDES BAY (the name means "leave if you can"). The dramatic scenery along the drive ends here, so you can take the exit if you want to turn around and head north again. If you plan to do some camping, head down the near-mile-long, rutted road to Salsipuedes Campground, set under olive trees on a cliff. Each campsite has a fire ring and costs $5 a day (day use is also $5). There's a natural rock tub with hot-spring water at the campground, and some basic cottages that rent for $30 a day. There is no easy access to the beach, known for its good surfing, from the campground.

Ensenada, with its shops, restaurants, and winery, is another 24km (15 miles) away.

NEARBY GOLF

Bajamar (© **800/225-2418** in the U.S., or 646/155-0152), 32km (20 miles) north of Ensenada, is a self-contained resort with 27 truly spectacular holes of golf. It's the place to go if you want to feel just like you're in the United States. Conceived as a planned community with vacation home/s and a country club, Bajamar suffered when the bottom dropped out of '80s speculation, leaving a lot of unbuilt house pads on cul-de-sacs behind the grandiose guardhouse. The main attraction is now the golf club and sister hotel, which play host to high-level retreats, conventions, and Asian tourists attracted by great golf deals. Featuring oceanfront Scottish-style links reminiscent of the courses on the Monterey Peninsula, Bajamar lets you combine any two of its three nine-hole courses. Public greens fees for 18 holes (including mandatory cart) are $75 Sunday through Thursday, and $85 Friday or Saturday. Hotel guests pay $5 less, but the **Hacienda Bajamar** offers a bevy of golf packages (see "Where to Stay," below). Services include a pro shop, putting and chipping greens, a driving range, and an elegant bar and restaurant.

WHERE TO STAY

Hotel Hacienda Bajamar 🏨🏨   Situated 32km (20 miles) north of Ensenada, Hacienda Bajamar is tucked away in the Bajamar golf resort and community. Popular with business conventions and family gatherings, Bajamar is as Americanized as it gets, and so is this hotel, near the clubhouse. The hotel is built like an early Spanish mission, with an interior outdoor plaza and garden surrounded by long arcades shading guest-room doorways. The 27 holes of golf are the main draw—the long road from the highway is lined with signs for phases of the surrounding vacation-home development that never really got off the ground. Rooms and suites are very spacious and comfortable, with vaguely colonial furnishings and luxurious bathrooms. A variety of golf packages are available, including pricing for couples with only one golfer. For greens fees, see "Nearby Golf," above.

Hwy. 1-D, Km 77.5 (mailing address: 416 W. San Ysidro Blv., Suite #L-732, San Ysidro, CA 92173). © **800/225-2418** U.S., or 646/155-0152; www.golfbajamar.com. 80 units. $84–$112 double; $184–$208 suite. Children under 12 stay free in parent's room. Golf packages available. AE, MC, V. **Amenities:** Restaurant; heated swimming pool; tennis courts; spa; concierge; tour desk; business center; room service; laundry and dry cleaning. *In room:* A/C, TV.

Hotel Las Rocas 🏨🏨   This polished hotel is run by an American, for Americans, and it shows. English is spoken fluently everywhere, and there are only as many signs in Spanish as you'd expect to see in Los Angeles. Built in Mediterranean style, with gleaming white stucco, cobalt-blue accents, and brightly painted tiles everywhere, Las Rocas has a lovely setting perched above the sea. There's no beach below the rocky edge, but the hotel's oceanfront swimming pool and secluded whirlpool lagoons more than make up for it. The thatched-roof *palapa* in the poolside garden serves tropical drinks and snacks, and swaying palms rustle throughout the property. Like most Baja resorts, Las Rocas is oriented toward the sea, so all rooms have an oceanfront private terrace. The rooms and suites are very nicely furnished in Mexican colonial style, and bathrooms are well equipped and beautifully tiled. The restaurant makes outstanding guacamole, which you can order by the bowl for chip-dipping at the indoor or poolside bar. *Tip:* Try to stay in the main building, and don't rule out a suite—even the $115 junior suite is spacious and includes a romantic fireplace and minikitchen.

Km 38.5 Free Road (P.O. Box 189003 HLR, Coronado, CA 92178-9003). ⓒ 888/ **LAS-ROCAS** in the U.S., or 646/612-2140. www.lasrocas.com. 72 units. Low season $83–$117 double, $128–$223 suite; high season $97–$133 double, $150–$313 suite. Senior discounts and packages available. AE, MC, V. Take the second Rosarito exit off the toll road, then drive 10km (6 miles) south, or follow the free road south from Rosarito; Las Rocas will be on the right. **Amenities:** Restaurant; pool with Jacuzzi; tour desk. *In room:* A/C, TV.

La Fonda 🐴 (*Value*) Just as American-style Las Rocas has its staunch devotees, plenty of folks are loyal to La Fonda's rustic rooms, which don't have minibars, state-of-the-art TVs, or phones. What they do have is an adventuresome appeal unlike any other northern Baja coast resort, a place for people who truly want to get away from it all. Relaxation and romance are the key words at this small hotel and restaurant, which opened in the '50s and hasn't changed a whole lot since. Perched cliffside above a wide, sandy beach, all of La Fonda's rooms have wide-open views of the breaking surf below. Although there are some newer motel-style rooms,

---

(*Fun Fact* **The Bartender Who Launched a Thousand Hangovers**

The hotel and restaurant Rancho La Gloria claims to be the birthplace of the margarita. Here's the deal: Carlos "Danny" Herrera says he invented the drink in 1948 for movie starlet Marjorie King, who allegedly fared badly if she drank any type of alcohol other than tequila. But she didn't want to appear unladylike by downing straight tequila—so Danny added fresh lime juice and Cointreau to soften the taste for Margarita, as she was known south of the border. The libation quickly gained popularity with fellow hotel guests and Hollywood friends Phil Harris and Alice Faye. Soon the concoction was being mixed up at La Plaza, a hotel in La Jolla, California, before making its way to Los Angeles and eventual beverage superstardom.

---

the older apartments with fireplaces (some with kitchenettes) have more charm. To reach them, guests use narrow winding staircases, much like the pathway down to the sand. The best rooms are numbers 18 to 22, closest to the sand and isolated from the main building; ask for one of these when you reserve. During particularly cold months, unheated La Fonda can get chilly—an important consideration. At the very least, be sure you're in a room with a fireplace.

Ensenada is a scenic 45-minute drive south, and Puerto Nuevo a mere 13km (8 miles) up the road—if you decide you need to leave this hideaway at all.

Hwy. 1-D, Km 59, La Misión exit. (Mailing address: P.O. Box 430268, San Ysidro, CA 92143.) No phone. 22 units. $55 standard; $75 deluxe (with fireplace and/or full kitchen). No credit cards. Write for reservations; allow 2 weeks for response. **Amenities:** Restaurant/bar (see "Where to Dine," below). *In room:* TV.

WHERE TO DINE

A bit less than 5km (3 miles) south of Rosarito Beach, elaborate stucco portals beckon drivers to **Calafia** (© 661/612-1581), a restaurant and trailer park that isn't visible from the highway. We don't recommend the dismal accommodations, but Calafia's restaurant is worth a stop, if only to admire the impressive setting above the crashing surf. Your meal is served at tables on terraces, balconies, and ledges wedged into the rocks all the way down to the bottom, where an outdoor dance floor and wrecked Spanish galleon sit on the beach. At night, when the outdoor landings are softly lit, and the mariachis' gentle strumming complements the sound of crashing waves, romance is definitely in the air. The menu is standard Mexican fare with the addition of some Americanized dishes like fajitas, but it's all prepared well and served with fresh, warm tortillas and good, strong margaritas. Calafia serves breakfast, lunch, and dinner daily. Another excellent choice for sunset cocktails is the Moroccan-style **Hotel Cafe Americana,** Carretera Libre a Ensenada, Km 51 (© **661/612-0070** or 661/612-0490), a private home turned inn and restaurant with whimsical white minarets. The bar offers a superb selection of premium tequilas, for sipping by the fire or on a dramatic oceanfront terrace.

A trip down the coast just wouldn't be complete without stopping at **Puerto Nuevo,** a tiny fishing town with nearly 30 restaurants—all serving exactly the same thing! Some 40 years ago the fishermen's wives here started serving local lobsters from the kitchens of their simple shacks; many eventually added small dining rooms to their

Tips Surfing, Northern Baja Style

From California and beyond, surfers come to the northern Baja coastline for perpetual right-breaking waves, cheap digs and eats, and *Endless Summer*–type camaraderie.

Undoubtedly, the most famous surf spot in all of Mexico is Killers, at Todos Santos Island. This was the location of the winning wave in the 1997–98 K2 Challenge (a worldwide contest to ride the largest wave each winter—and be photographed doing it). Killers is a very makeable wave for confident, competent surfers. To get there you need a boat. You can get a lift from the local *panga* (skiff) fleet, for about $100 for the day. That's pretty much the going rate, and the tightly knit Ensenada *pangueros* aren't eager to undercut each other. It's about 16km (10 miles) out to the island; there you'll anchor and paddle into the lineup. You must bring everything you'll need—food, drink, sunscreen, and so on.

Other less radical and easier–to-reach spots include Popotla, just south of Rosarito, where you'll walk to the beach through the Popotla trailer park. Calafia, also just a mile or two south of Rosarito, has a reeling right point that can get extremely heavy. San Miguel is the point break just south of the final tollbooth on the highway into Ensenada. It's an excellent wave but generally crowded.

If you're a surfer looking to get your bearings or a spectator wanting to get your feet wet, stop by Inner Reef (Km 34½; no phone). Opened in 1998 by a friendly Southern California ex-pat named Roger, this tiny shack offers all the essentials: wax, leashes, patch kits, surfboard sales and rentals, even expert repairs at bargain prices. Roger is there from noon until sunset every day in summer, and from Wednesday to Sunday in winter.

homes or built proper restaurants. The result is a lobster lover's paradise, where a feast of lobster, beans, rice, salsa, limes, and fresh tortillas costs around $10. Puerto Nuevo is 19km (12 miles) south of Rosarito on the Old Ensenada Highway (parallel to the toll Hwy. 1)—just drive through the arched entryway, park, and stroll the town's three or four blocks for a restaurant that suits your fancy.

Some have names, and some don't; **Ortega's** is one of the originals, and has expanded to five locations within the village. There's also **La Casa de la Langosta** ("House of Lobster"), which even opened a branch in Rosarito Beach. But regulars prefer the smaller, family-run spots, where mismatched dinette sets and chipped plates underscore the earnest service and personally prepared dinners.

About 16km (10 miles) farther south, roughly halfway between Rosarito and Ensenada, is the **La Fonda** hotel and restaurant (no phone; see "Where to Stay," above). Plenty of San Diegans make the drive Sunday mornings for La Fonda's outstanding buffet brunch, an orgy of meats, traditional Mexican stews, *chilaquiles* (a saucy egg-and-tortilla scramble), fresh fruits, and pastries. Breakfast, lunch, and dinner are always accompanied by a basket of Baja's best flour tortillas (try rolling them with some butter and jam at breakfast). The best seating is under thatched umbrellas on La Fonda's tiled terrace overlooking the breaking surf; live music keeps the adjacent bar jumping on Friday and Saturday nights (strolling mariachis entertain the rest of the time). House specialties include banana pancakes, pork chops with salsa verde, succulent glazed ribs, and a variety of seafood; plan to walk off your heavy meal along the sandy beach below, accessible by a stone stairway. Relaxing ambience coupled with exceptionally good food and service make La Fonda a must-see along the coast. Sunday brunch is around $12 a person; main courses otherwise are $4 to $15. Open daily from around 9am to 10pm; Sunday's buffet brunch is from 10am to 3:30pm.

3 Ensenada: Port of Call (★

135km (84 miles) S of San Diego; 110km (68 miles) S of Tijuana

Ensenada is an attractive, classic town on a lovely bay, surrounded by sheltering mountains. About 40 minutes from Rosarito, it's the kind of place that loves a celebration. Almost any time you choose to visit, the city is festive—be it for a bicycle race or a seafood festival.

One of Mexico's principal ports of call, Ensenada welcomes half a million visitors a year, attracted to its beaches, excellent sportfishing, nearby wineries, and surrounding natural attractions.

GETTING THERE   After passing through the final tollbooth, Highway 1-D curves sharply toward downtown Ensenada. Watch out for brutal metal speed bumps slowing traffic into town—they're far less forgiving on the average chassis than those in the U.S.!

VISITOR INFORMATION The **Tourist and Convention Bureau booth** (© 646/178-2411) is at the western entrance to town, where the waterfront-hugging Bulevar Lázaro Cárdenas—also known as Bulevar Costero—curves away to the right. The booth is open daily from 9am till dusk and can provide a downtown map, directions to major nearby sites, and information on special events throughout the city. As in most of the commonly visited areas of Baja, one or more employees speak English fluently. Eight blocks south you'll find the **State Secretary of Tourism,** Blv. Lázaro Cárdenas 1477, Government Building (© **646/172-3022;** fax 646/172-3081), which is open Monday through Friday from 9am to 7pm, Saturday from 10am to 3pm, and Sunday from 10am to 2pm. Both offices have extended hours on U.S. holidays. Taxis park along López Mateos.

EXPLORING ENSENADA

Ensenada is technically a "border town," but part of its appeal is its multilayered vitality, born out of being concerned with much more than tourism. The bustling port consumes the entire waterfront—beach access is north or south of town—and the Pacific fishing trade and agriculture in the fertile valleys surrounding the city dominate the economy. Try not to leave Ensenada without getting a taste of its true personality; for example, stop by the indoor-outdoor fish market at the northernmost corner of the harbor. Each day, from early morning to midday, merchants and housewives gather to assess the day's catch—tuna, marlin, snapper, plus many other varieties of fish and piles of shrimp from the morning's haul.

Outside the market is the perfect place to sample the culinary craze of Baja California, the Baja fish taco. Several stands prepare this local treat; strips of freshly caught fish are battered and deep fried, then wrapped in corn tortillas and topped with shredded cabbage, cilantro, salsa, and various other condiments. They're delicious, cheap, and filling, and it's easy to see why surf bums and collegiate vacationers consider them a Baja staple.

Elsewhere in town, visit the **Bodegas de Santo Tomás Winery,** Av. Miramar 666 at Calle 7 (© **646/178-2509;** www.santotomas. com.mx). While most visitors to Mexico are quite content quaffing endless quantities of cheap *cerveza* (beer), even part-time oenophiles should pay a visit to this historic winery—the oldest in Mexico, and the largest in all of Baja. It uses old-fashioned methods of processing grapes grown in the lush Santo Tomás Valley, first cultivated by Dominican monks in 1791. A 45-minute tour introduces you to low-tech processing machinery, hand-hammered wood casks, and cool, damp stone aging rooms; it culminates in an invitation to sample several Santo Tomás vintages, including an international-medal-winning cabernet and delightfully crisp sparkling blanc de blanc. The wood-paneled, church-like tasting room is adorned with paintings of mischievous altar boys being scolded by stern friars for pilfering wine or ruining precious grapes. Anyone used to the pretentious, assembly-line ambience of trendier wine regions will relish the friendly welcome and informative tour presented here. Tours in English start Monday through Saturday at 10am, 11am, 12pm, 1pm, and 3pm. Admission is $6, including a tasting of three low-priced wines; $10 more gets you a souvenir wineglass and a tasting of 12 high-priced wines. Wines for sale cost $6.50 to $20 a bottle. *Note:* Most of the winery's product is exported for the European market.

Be sure to poke around Santo Tomás a bit after your tour concludes. The little modern machinery installed here freed up a cavernous space now used for monthly jazz concerts, and a former aging room has been transformed into La Embottelladora Vieja ("the old aging room") restaurant (see "Where to Dine," below). Across the street stands La Esquina de Bodegas ("the corner wine cellar"), former aging rooms for Santo Tomás. The industrial-style building now functions as a gallery showcasing local art, with a skylit bookstore on the second level and a small cafe (punctuated by giant copper distillation vats) in the rear.

Ensenada's primary cultural center is the **Centro Cívico, Social y Cultura,** Bulevar Lázaro Cárdenas at Avenida Club Rotario. The impressive Mediterranean building was formerly Riviera del Pacífico, a glamorous 1930s bayfront casino and resort frequented by Hollywood's elite. Tiles in the lobby commemorate "Visitantes Distinguidos 1930–1940," including Marion Davies, William Randolph Hearst, Lana Turner, Myrna Loy, and Jack Dempsey. Now used by the Rotary Club as offices and for cultural and social events, the main building is open to the public. Elegant hallways and ballrooms evoke bygone elegance, and every wall and alcove glows with original murals depicting Mexico's colorful history. Lush formal gardens span the front of the building, and there's a small art gallery on one side. Through the lobby, facing an inner courtyard, is Bar Andaluz, which is open to the public sporadically. It's an intimate, dark-wood place where you can just imagine someone like Papa Hemingway holding cocktail-hour court beneath that colorful toreador mural.

A NEARBY ATTRACTION   South of the city, a 45-minute drive along the rural Punta Banda peninsula, is one of Ensenada's major attractions: **La Bufadora,** a natural sea spout in the rocks. With each incoming wave, water is forced upward through the rock, creating a geyser whose loud grunt gave the phenomenon its name (*la bufadora* means "buffalo snort"). Local fishermen who ply these waters have a much more lyrical explanation for this roaring blowhole. According to local legend, a mother gray whale and her calf were just beginning their migration from the safety of Baja's San Ignacio lagoon to Alaska. As they rounded Punta Banda, the curious calf squeezed into a sea cave, only to be trapped. The groan that this 70-foot high blowhole makes every time it erupts is the sound of the stranded calf still crying for his mother, and the tremendous spray is his spout.

From downtown Ensenada, take Avenida Reforma south (Hwy. 1) to Highway 23 west. It's a long, meandering drive through a semi-swamplike area untouched by development; look for grazing animals, bait shops, and fishermen's shacks along the way. La Bufadora is at the end of the road, and once parked ($1 per car in crude dirt lots), you must walk downhill to the viewing platform, at the end of a 540m (1,800 ft.) pathway lined with souvenir stands. In addition to running a gauntlet of determined vendors featuring the usual wares, visitors can avail themselves of inexpensive snacks at the sole restaurant located there, including tasty fish tacos. Visitation is enormous, but long-standing plans to pave the dirt parking lots and build permanent restaurants and shops have yet to become a reality.

SPORTS & OUTDOOR ACTIVITIES

FISHING   Ensenada, which bills itself as "the yellowtail capital of the world," draws sportfishermen eager to venture out from the beautiful Bahía de Todos Santos (Bay of All Saints) in search of the Pacific's albacore, halibut, marlin, rockfish, and sea bass. A wooden boardwalk parallel to Bulevar Lázaro Cárdenas (Costero) near the northern entrance to town provides access to the sportfishing piers and their many charter-boat operators. Open-party boats leave early, often by 7am, and charge around $35 per person, plus an additional fee (around $5) for the mandatory fishing license. Nonfishing passengers must, by law, also be licensed. Those disinclined to comparison shop the boats can make advance arrangements with San Diego–based **Baja California Tours** (© **619/454-7166**). In addition to daily fishing excursions, it offers 1- to 3-night packages including hotel, fishing, some meals, and transportation from San Diego.

HIKING   Ensenada is the gateway city to the **Parque Nacional Constitución de 1857.** Located on the spine of the Sierra de Juárez, the park was once a heavily used mining area. Most of the mines are now defunct. In contrast to the dry and sometimes desolate surroundings of much of the northern peninsula, the 5,000-hectare (12,350-acre) preserve averages about 1,200m (4,000 ft.) in altitude and is covered in places with pine forests. The most idiosyncratic thing, however, is the sight of a good-sized lake in an alpine setting. The park has no developed trails other than a 10km (6-mile) one that circumnavigates the lake, Laguna Hanson, but there are endless opportunities for blazing your own. To get there, take Mexico Highway 3 south from Ensenada and exit at the graded dirt access road at Km 55. The park entrance road is gravel and generally well maintained, but can be really rough after a rainy year. It's 35km (22 miles) to the park entrance. If the entrance is staffed, you'll be asked for a modest entrance fee.

The **Parque Nacional Sierra San Pedro Mártir** is to Baja California what Yosemite is to Alta California. Almost 81,000 hectares (200,000 acres) of the highest mountains on the peninsula have been preserved. The highest, Picacho del Diablo (Devil's Peak), rises to 3,046m (10,154 ft.). Views from the summit encompass both oceans and an immense stretch of land. Best of all, it's virtually unvisited, something that sets it apart from the normal national park experience in Los Estados Unidos.

Farther south on Highway 1 from Ensenada, you'll come to a signed turnoff for the park at Km 140, soon after you pass the little town of Colonet. The sign also says OBSERVATORIO. Fill up with gas in Colonet—there is no more until you exit this way again—and reset your trip odometer at the turnoff. In between, it's entirely possible to put on a gas-guzzling 242km (150 miles) of rugged driving. It's 76km (47 miles) to the park entrance.

You'll find a high alpine realm of flower-speckled meadows, soaring granite peaks, and year-round creeks. Official trails are few and far between, but anyone who's good with a map and compass or even just good at wandering off and finding his or her way back can have a great time hiking. Cow trails (yes, cows in a national park) are numerous. Four year-round creeks drain the park and make great destinations. Picacho del Diablo is a difficult but rewarding overnight hike and long scramble. Always remember that you're in one of the most rugged and remote places in all of Baja, and it's quite likely that if you get lost or hurt, nobody will come looking for you.

SEA KAYAKING The rocky coastline of Punta la Banda is a favorite first trip for beginning ocean kayakers. There are several secluded beaches, sea caves, and terrific scenery. Many kayakers use La Bufadora as a launching point to head out to the Todos Santos Islands. It's about 11km (7 miles) from La Bufadora to the southern and larger of the two islands. The first 4.8km (3 miles) follow a rocky coast to the tip of Punta la Banda. From here it's time to size up the wind, the waves, and the fog. If the coast is clear, take a compass heading and begin the 6km (4-mile) open-water crossing. Bring water and camping gear to spend a night on the pristine island. **Dale's La Bufadora Dive Shop** (℗ 646/154-2045) has kayak rentals and is open weekends or by prior reservation. **Southwest Sea Kayaks** (℗ 619/222-3616) in San Diego leads weekend trips to the island several times a year.

SCUBA DIVING & SNORKELING La Bufadora is a great dive spot with thick kelp and wonderful sea life. Get underwater and zoom through lovely kelp beds and rugged rock formations covered in strawberry anemones and gypsy shawl nudibranchs. You may also spot spiny lobsters and numerous large fish. It's possible to swim right over to the blowhole, but use extreme caution in this area—you don't want to end up like that mythical whale calf. **Dale's La Bufadora Dive Shop** (℗ 646/154-2045) is on shore at the best entry point. The staff will set you up with fills and advice.

Several dive shops in Ensenada, including **Almar,** 149 Av. Macheros (℗ 646/178-3013), and **Baja Dive Expeditions,** at the Baja Beach and Tennis Club (℗ 646/173-0220), will arrange boat dives to the Todos Santos islands, which sit at the outer edge of Todos Santos Bay. The diving here is similar to the diving at Catalina or the other California Channel Islands—lots of fish, big kelp, urchins, and jagged underwater rock formations. The visibility varies widely, depending on the swell.

SHOPPING

Ensenada's equivalent of Tijuana's Avenida Revolución is crowded Avenida López Mateos, which runs roughly parallel to Bulevar Lázaro Cárdenas (Costero); the highest concentration of shops and restaurants is between avenidas Ruiz and Castillo. Beggars fill the street. Sellers are less likely to bargain than those in Tijuana—they're used to gullible cruise-ship buyers. Compared to Tijuana, there is more authentic Mexican art- and craftwork in Ensenada, pieces imported from rural states and villages where different skills are traditionally practiced. Though from the outside it looks dusty and unlit, **Curiosi-dades La Joya,** Ave. López Mateos 725 (© **646/178-3191**), is a treasure trove of stained-glass lamps, hangings, and other handcrafted curios. Piles of intricately designed glass lampshades lie side-by-side with colorful tiles and wrought-iron birdcages, the shop's other specialty. The shopkeepers here are stubborn about bargaining, perhaps because they know the value of their unusual wares.

You'll see colorfully painted glazed pottery wherever you go in northern Baja. It ranges in quality, from sloppy pieces quickly painted with a limited palette to intricately designed, painstakingly painted works evocative of Tuscan urns and pitchers. The best prices are at the abundant roadside stands lining the old road south of Rosarito, but if you're willing to pay extra for quality, head to **Artesanías Colibrí,** 855 Av. López Mateos (© **646/178-1312**). Here you can learn about the origins of this Talavera style—how invading Moors set up terra-cotta factories in the Spanish city of Talavera, and subsequent migration brought the art to the Mexican state of Puebla.

WHERE TO STAY

Estero Beach Resort ⋒   About 10km (6 miles) south of downtown Ensenada, this sprawling complex of rooms, cottages, and mobile-home hookups is popular with families and active vacationers. The bay and protected lagoon at the edge of the lushly planted property are perfect for swimming and launching sailboards; there's also tennis, horseback riding, volleyball, and a game room with Ping-Pong and billiards. The guest rooms are a little worn, but no one expects fancy at Estero Beach. The beachfront restaurant serves a casual mix of seafood, Mexican fare, hamburgers, fried chicken, and omelets. Some suites and 5 of the 15 cottages have kitchenettes, and some can easily accommodate a whole family.

Estero Beach. (Mailing address: Apdo. Postal 86, Ensenada, BC, Mexico.) © **646/176-6225.** www.hotelesterobeach.com. 94 units. $95–$156 double; cottage $75–$120 double; $448 presidential suite. From Ensenada, take Hwy. 1 south; turn right at ESTERO BEACH sign. MC, V. **Amenities:** Restaurant; tennis court; game room. *In room:* TV.

Hotel Las Rosas ⋒⋒   One of the most modern hotels in the area, Hotel Las Rosas still falls short of most definitions of luxurious, yet the pink oceanfront hotel 3.2km (2 miles) outside Ensenada is the favorite of many Baja aficionados. It offers most of the comforts of an upscale American hotel—which doesn't leave room for much Mexican personality. The atrium lobby is awash in pale pink and seafoam green, a color scheme that pervades throughout—including the guest rooms, sparsely furnished with quasitropical furniture. Some rooms have fireplaces and/or in-room whirlpools, and all have balconies overlooking the pool and ocean. One of the resort's main photo-ops is the swimming pool that overlooks the Pacific and features a vanishing edge that appears to merge with the ocean beyond. If you're looking to maintain the highest comfort level possible, this would be your hotel of choice.

Hwy. 1, 3.2km (2 miles) north of Ensenada. (Mailing address: Apdo. Postal 316, Ensenada, BC, Mexico.) © 646/174-4310. 48 units. $126–$190 double. Children under 12 $16; extra adult $22. MC, V. **Amenities:** Restaurant; cocktail lounge; swimming pool; tennis and racquetball courts; basic workout room; cliff-top hot tub; tour desk; room service; massage; laundry service. *In room:* A/C, TV.

San Nicolás Resort Hotel Most rooms at this modern motor inn face the courtyard or have balconies overlooking the swimming pool—and the place is surprisingly quiet for being right on the main drag. The hotel also has a disco and a branch of Caliente Sports Book, where you can gamble on games and races throughout the U.S.

Av. López Mateos and Guadalupe, Ensenada. (Mailing address: P.O. Box 437060, San Ysidro, CA 92073-7060.) © 646/176-1901. Fax 646/176-4930. www.sannicolas. com.mx. 147 units. $99–$134 double; $146–$291 suite. Extra person $10. AE, MC, V. **Amenities:** Restaurant; cocktail lounge; swimming pool. *In room:* A/C, TV.

Villa Fontana Days Inn This motel is notable for its out-of-place architecture—who'd expect a peak-roofed, gabled, New England–style structure in a land dominated by red-tiled roofs? This bargain-priced motel is otherwise unremarkable; well located and cleanly run by the Days Inn chain, it has a small pool and enclosed parking. Most of the 65 rooms have showers, rather than tubs, in the bathrooms. Ask for a room at the back, away from street noise.

Av. López Mateos 1050, Ensenada. © 800/4-BAJA-04 U.S., or 646/178-3434. www.villafontana.com.mx. 65 units. Summer $60 double; $115 suite. Rates are higher on holidays, lower midweek and in winter. Rates include continental breakfast. Internet discounts available. AE, MC, V. **Amenities:** Pool. *In room:* A/C, TV.

WHERE TO DINE

El Charro MEXICAN You'll recognize El Charro by its front windows: Whole chickens rotate slowly on the rotisserie in one, while a woman makes tortillas in the other. This little place has been here since 1956 and looks it, with charred walls and a ceiling made of split logs. The simple fare consists of such dishes as half a roasted chicken with fries and tortillas, or *carne asada* (grilled marinated beef) with soup, guacamole, and tortillas. Giant piñatas hang from the walls above the concrete floor. Kids are welcome; they'll think they're on a picnic. Wine and beer are served, and beer is cheaper than soda.

Av. López Mateos 475 (between Ruiz and Gastellum). © 646/178-3881. Menu items $5–$12; lobster $20. No credit cards. Daily 11am–2am.

El Rey Sol 🏵️🏵️ FRENCH/MEXICAN   Opened by French expatriates in 1947, the family-run El Rey Sol has long been considered Ensenada's finest eatery. Decked out like the French flag, this red, white, and blue building is a beacon on busy López Mateos. Wrought-iron chandeliers and heavy oak farm tables add to the country French ambience, but the menu's prices and sophistication belie the casual decor. House specialties include seafood puff pastry; baby clams steamed in butter, white wine, and cilantro; chicken in brandy and chipotle chile cream sauce; tender grilled steaks; and homemade French desserts. Portions are generous, however, and always feature fresh vegetables from the nearby family farm. Every table receives a complimentary platter of appetizers at dinnertime; lunch is a hearty three-course meal.

Av. López Mateos 1000 (at Blancarte). © 646/178-1733. Reservations recommended for weekends. Main courses $9–$19. AE, MC, V. Daily 7:30am–10:30pm.

La Embottelladora Vieja 🏵️🏵️🏵️ *Finds* FRENCH/MEXICAN   If you're planning to splurge on one fine meal in Ensenada (or all of northern Baja, for that matter), this is the place. Hidden on an industrial side street and attached to the Bodegas de Santo Tomás winery, it looks more like a chapel than the elegant restaurant it is. Sophisticated diners will feel right at home in the stylish setting, a former winery aging room now resplendent with red oak furniture (constructed from old wine casks), high brick walls, and crystal goblets and candlesticks on linen tablecloths. The wine list is exemplary, featuring bottles from Santo Tomás and other Baja vintners, and the "Baja French" menu features dishes carefully crafted to include or complement wine. Look for appetizers like abalone ceviche or cream of garlic soup, followed by grilled swordfish in cilantro sauce, filet mignon in port wine–Gorgonzola sauce, or quail with tart sauvignon blanc sauce.

Av. Miramar 666 (at Calle 7). © 646/174-0807. Reservations recommended for weekends. Main courses $8–$20. AE, MC, V. Lunch and dinner; call for seasonal hours.

ENSENADA AFTER DARK

No discussion of Ensenada would be complete without mentioning **Hussong's Cantina,** Av. Ruiz 113, near Avenida López Mateos

Valle de Guadalupe: Mexico's Wine Country

Beyond the lure of Tijuana and tequila, an exploration of Mexico's wine country, in the northern Baja peninsula, makes for an offbeat and intriguing side trip to the area.

A 29km (18-mile) drive northeast of Ensenada along Highway 3 will bring you to the Valle de Guadalupe (Guadalupe Valley), the heart of Mexico's small but blossoming wine industry. Although most connoisseurs tend to be dismissive of Mexico's wine efforts, in recent years the production and quality have made quantum leaps, and several Mexican vintages have earned international acclaim.

Spanish missionaries first introduced wine to Baja California in 1701, when a Jesuit priest, Father Juan de Ugarte, planted the peninsula's first grape vines. In 1791, the first vineyards were established in these fertile valleys at Mision Santo Thomas.

The Valle de Guadalupe is in the "world wine strip," a zone of lands with the climate and porous soil that result in ideal conditions for grape growing—similar to those found in northern California, France, Spain, and Italy. Northern Baja's dry, hot summers and cool, humid winters, added to a stream of cool breezes, make the conditions in Guadalupe Valley especially conducive for vineyards, similar to what you would find in the Mediterranean.

(② 646/178-3210); just like the line from *Casablanca*, "everyone goes to Rick's," everyone's been going to Hussong's since the bar opened in 1892. Nothing much has changed in the last century— the place still sports Wild West–style swinging saloon doors, a long bar to slide beers along, and strolling mariachis bellowing to rise above the din of revelers. There's definitely a minimalist appeal to Hussong's, which looks as if it sprang from a south-of-the-border episode of *Gunsmoke.* Beer and tequilas at astonishingly low prices are the main order of business. Be aware that hygiene and privacy are a low priority in the restrooms.

While the crowd (a pleasant mix of tourists and locals) at Hussong's can really whoop it up, they're amateurs compared to those

In 1905, the Mexican government granted political asylum to 100 families from Russia, who arrived in Guadalupe Valley to cultivate grapes. These were the pioneers of grape cultivation in the area, and many of the present-day residents are descendents of those Russian families. The Museo Communitario del Valle de Guadalupe, on Francisco Zarco (no phone), has displays and artifacts from this curious time of cultural conversion.

The best time to visit the Valle de Guadalupe is in late August, during Las Fiestas de la Vendimia (Harvest Festivals). Various vineyards schedule a multitude of activities, including tastings, classical music concerts, and Masses celebrating the harvest. If you plan to dine or spend the night, **Adobe Guadalupe** (© **649/631-3098** in the U.S., or 646/155-2094; www.adobeguadalupe.com), one of the few places to stay in Guadalupe Valley, is both an inn and a boutique winery. The double rate of $125 includes breakfast; the four-course dinner goes for $50 per person ($35 without wine).

Winery tours are available at the **Casa Pedro Domecq, Chateau Camou,** and **Monte Xanic** vineyards, all located in Guadalupe Valley.

who frequent **Papas & Beer,** Avenida Ruiz near Avenida López Mateos (© **646/178-4231**), across the street. A tiny entrance leads to the upstairs bar and disco, where the music is loud and the hip young crowd is definitely here to party. Happy patrons hang out of the second-story windows calling out to their friends, and stopping occasionally to eat *papas* (french fries) accompanied by local beers. Papas & Beer has quite a reputation with the Southern California college crowd, and has opened a branch in Rosarito Beach (see "Rosarito Beach After Dark," earlier in this chapter). You've probably noticed bumper stickers for these two quintessentially Baja watering holes, but they don't just give them away. In fact, each bar has several souvenir shops along Avenida Ruiz.

Index

See also Accommodations and Restaurant indexes below.

FROMMER'S® MEMORABLE WALKS

Chicago
London

New York
Paris

San Francisco

FROMMER'S® WITH KIDS GUIDES

Chicago
Las Vegas
New York City

Ottawa
San Francisco
Toronto

Vancouver
Washington, D.C.

SUZY GERSHMAN'S BORN TO SHOP GUIDES

Born to Shop: France
Born to Shop: Hong Kong,
  Shanghai & Beijing

Born to Shop: Italy
Born to Shop: London

Born to Shop: New York
Born to Shop: Paris

FROMMER'S® IRREVERENT GUIDES

Amsterdam
Boston
Chicago
Las Vegas
London

Los Angeles
Manhattan
New Orleans
Paris
Rome

San Francisco
Seattle & Portland
Vancouver
Walt Disney World®
Washington, D.C.

FROMMER'S® BEST-LOVED DRIVING TOURS

Britain
California
Florida
France

Germany
Ireland
Italy
New England

Northern Italy
Scotland
Spain
Tuscany & Umbria

HANGING OUT™ GUIDES

Hanging Out in England
Hanging Out in Europe

Hanging Out in France
Hanging Out in Ireland

Hanging Out in Italy
Hanging Out in Spain

THE UNOFFICIAL GUIDES®

Bed & Breakfasts and Country
  Inns in:
  California
  Great Lakes States
  Mid-Atlantic
  New England
  Northwest
  Rockies
  Southeast
  Southwest
Best RV & Tent Campgrounds in:
  California & the West
  Florida & the Southeast
  Great Lakes States
  Mid-Atlantic
  Northeast
  Northwest & Central Plains

Southwest & South Central
  Plains
  U.S.A.
Beyond Disney
Branson, Missouri
California with Kids
Central Italy
Chicago
Cruises
Disneyland®
Florida with Kids
Golf Vacations in the Eastern U.S.
Great Smoky & Blue Ridge Region
Inside Disney
Hawaii
Las Vegas
London
Maui

Mexio's Best Beach Resorts
Mid-Atlantic with Kids
Mini Las Vegas
Mini-Mickey
New England & New York with
  Kids
New Orleans
New York City
Paris
San Francisco
Skiing & Snowboarding in the West
Southeast with Kids
Walt Disney World®
Walt Disney World® for
  Grown-ups
Walt Disney World® with Kids
Washington, D.C.
World's Best Diving Vacations

SPECIAL-INTEREST TITLES

Frommer's Adventure Guide to Australia &
  New Zealand
Frommer's Adventure Guide to Central America
Frommer's Adventure Guide to India & Pakistan
Frommer's Adventure Guide to South America
Frommer's Adventure Guide to Southeast Asia
Frommer's Adventure Guide to Southern Africa
Frommer's Britain's Best Bed & Breakfasts and
  Country Inns
Frommer's Caribbean Hideaways
Frommer's Exploring America by RV
Frommer's Fly Safe, Fly Smart

Frommer's France's Best Bed & Breakfasts and
  Country Inns
Frommer's Gay & Lesbian Europe
Frommer's Italy's Best Bed & Breakfasts and
  Country Inns
Frommer's Road Atlas Britain
Frommer's Road Atlas Europe
Frommer's Road Atlas France
The New York Times' Guide to Unforgettable
  Weekends
Places Rated Almanac
Retirement Places Rated
Rome Past & Present

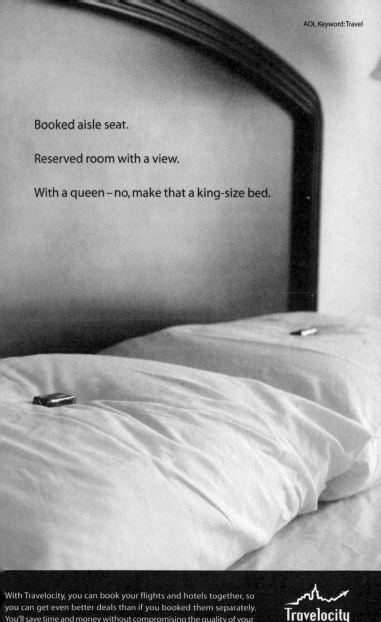

Fly.
Sleep.
Save.

Now you can book your flights and
hotels together, so you can get even better deals
than if you booked them separately.

Travelocity
Visit www.travelocity.com
or call 1-888-TRAVELOCITY